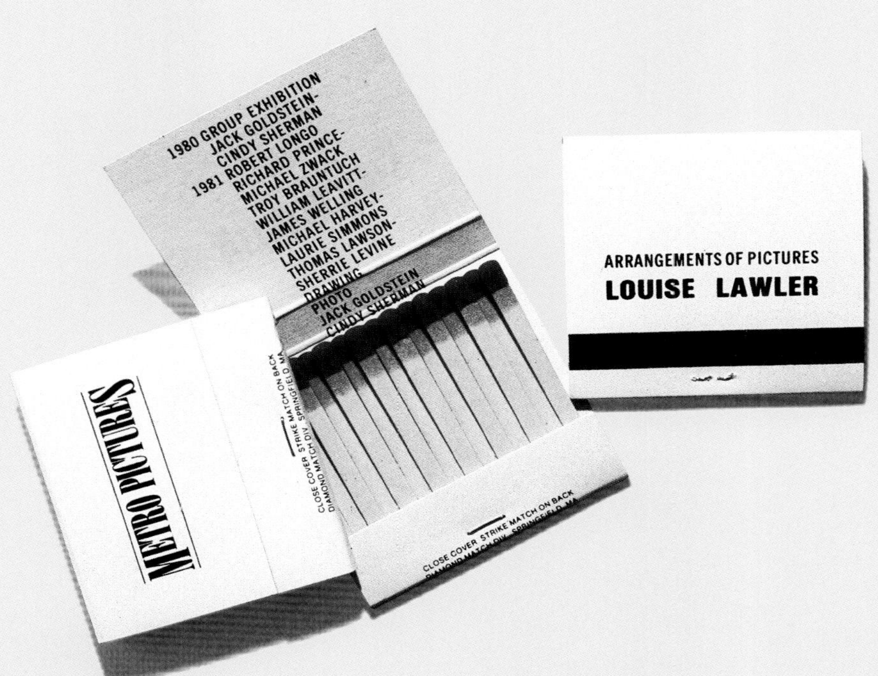
1980 GROUP EXHIBITION
JACK GOLDSTEIN-
CINDY SHERMAN
1981 ROBERT LONGO
RICHARD PRINCE-
MICHAEL ZWACK
TROY BRAUNTUCH
WILLIAM LEAVITT-
JAMES WELLING
MICHAEL HARVEY-
LAURIE SIMMONS
THOMAS LAWSON-
SHERRIE LEVINE
DRAWING
PHOTO
JACK GOLDSTEIN
CINDY SHERMAN
METRO PICTURES
CLOSE COVER STRIKE MATCH ON BACK
ARRANGEMENTS OF PICTURES
LOUISE LAWLER

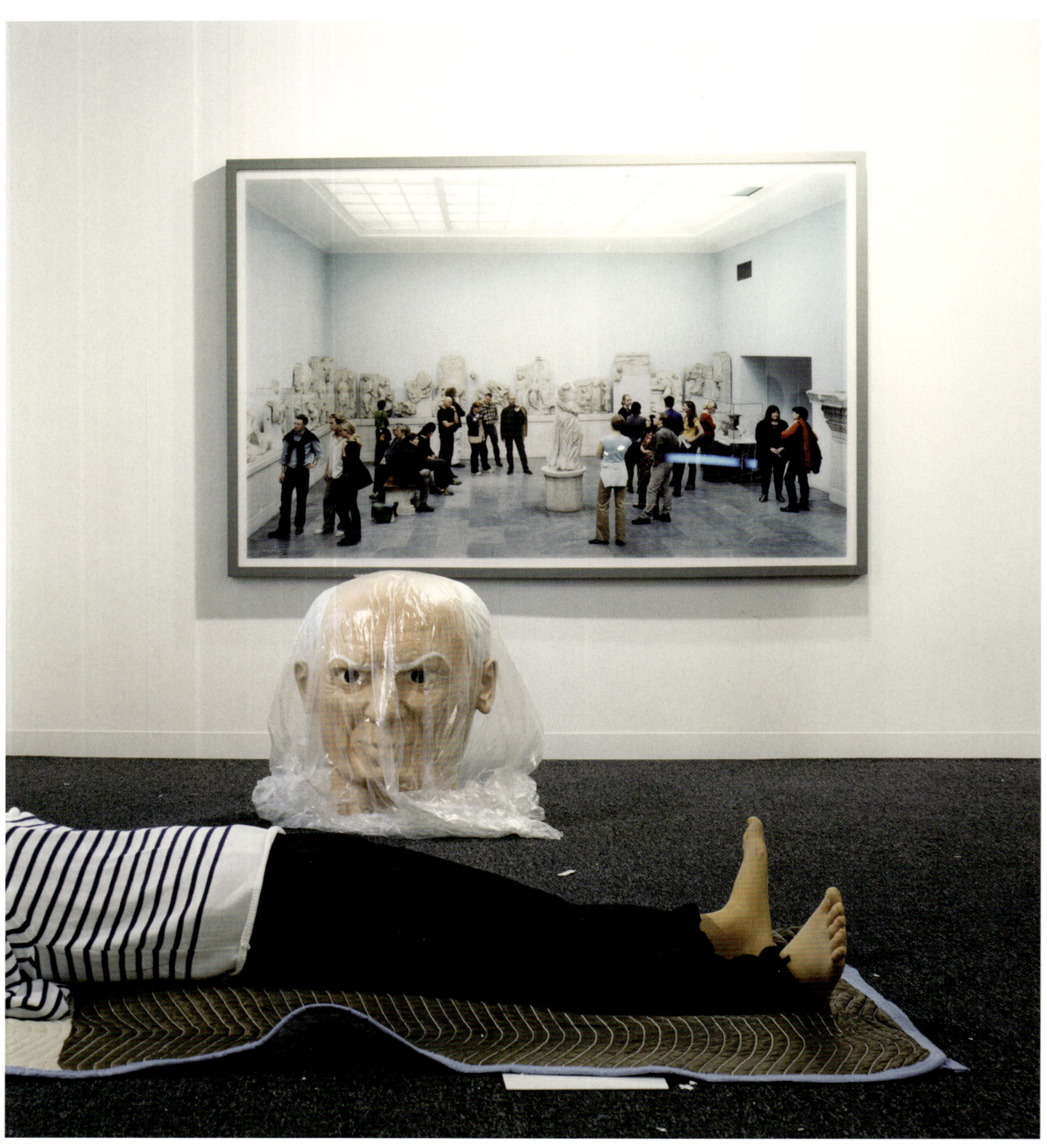

Big, 2002/2003
cibachrome, 52 3/4 x 46 1/2 inches

LOUISE LAWLER AND OTHERS

Contributions by
George Baker
Jack Bankowsky
Andrea Fraser
Isabelle Graw
Philipp Kaiser
Birgit Pelzer

Kunstmuseum Basel, Museum für Gegenwartskunst

Hatje Cantz Publishers

Sponsors

Fonds für künstlerische Aktivitäten im Museum für Gegenwartskunst
der Emanuel Hoffmann-Stiftung und der Christoph Merian Stiftung

Stanley Thomas Johnson Foundation
Migros-Kulturprozent

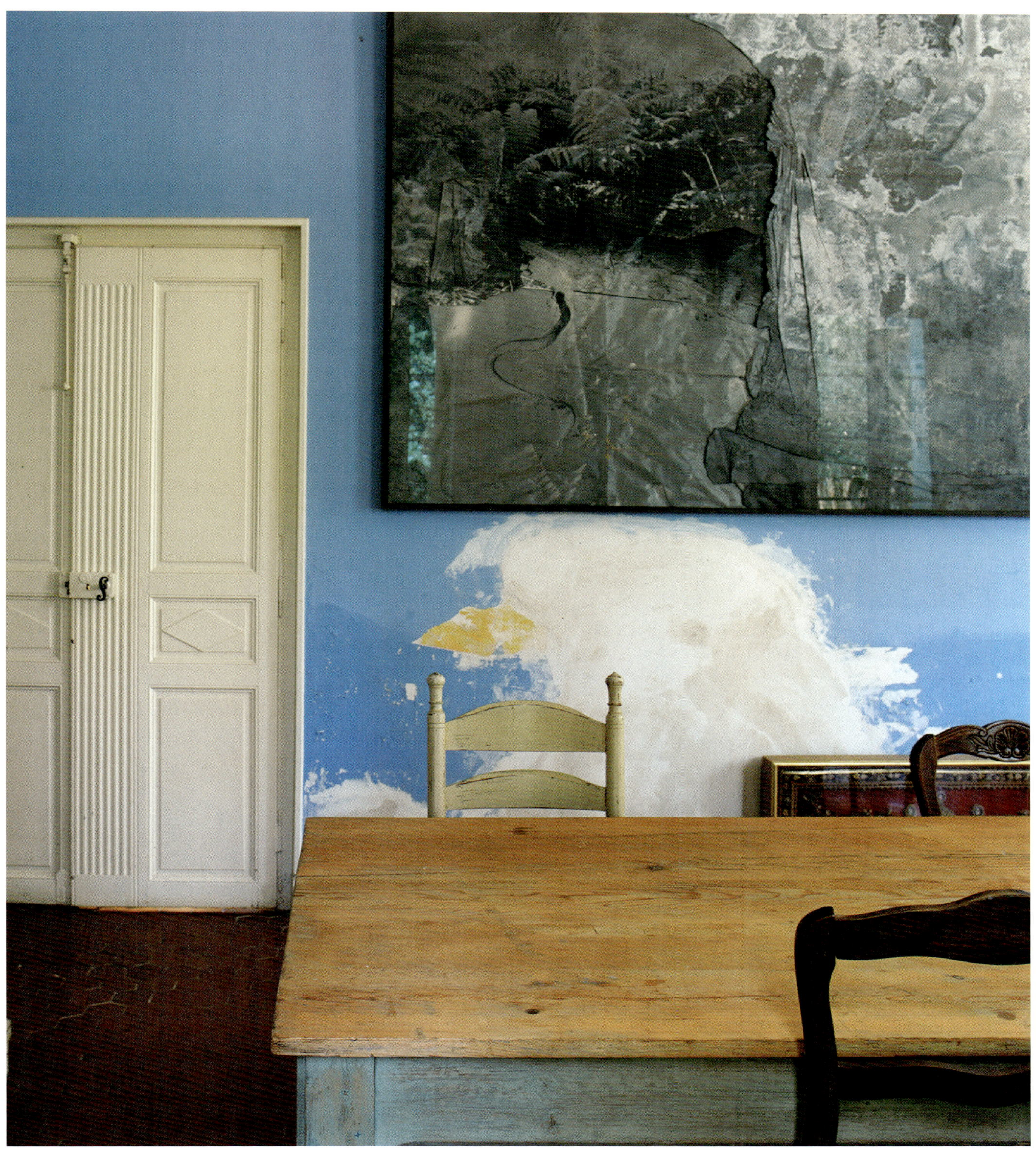

Modern Painting, 2003
cibachrome, 50 1/4 x 44 inches

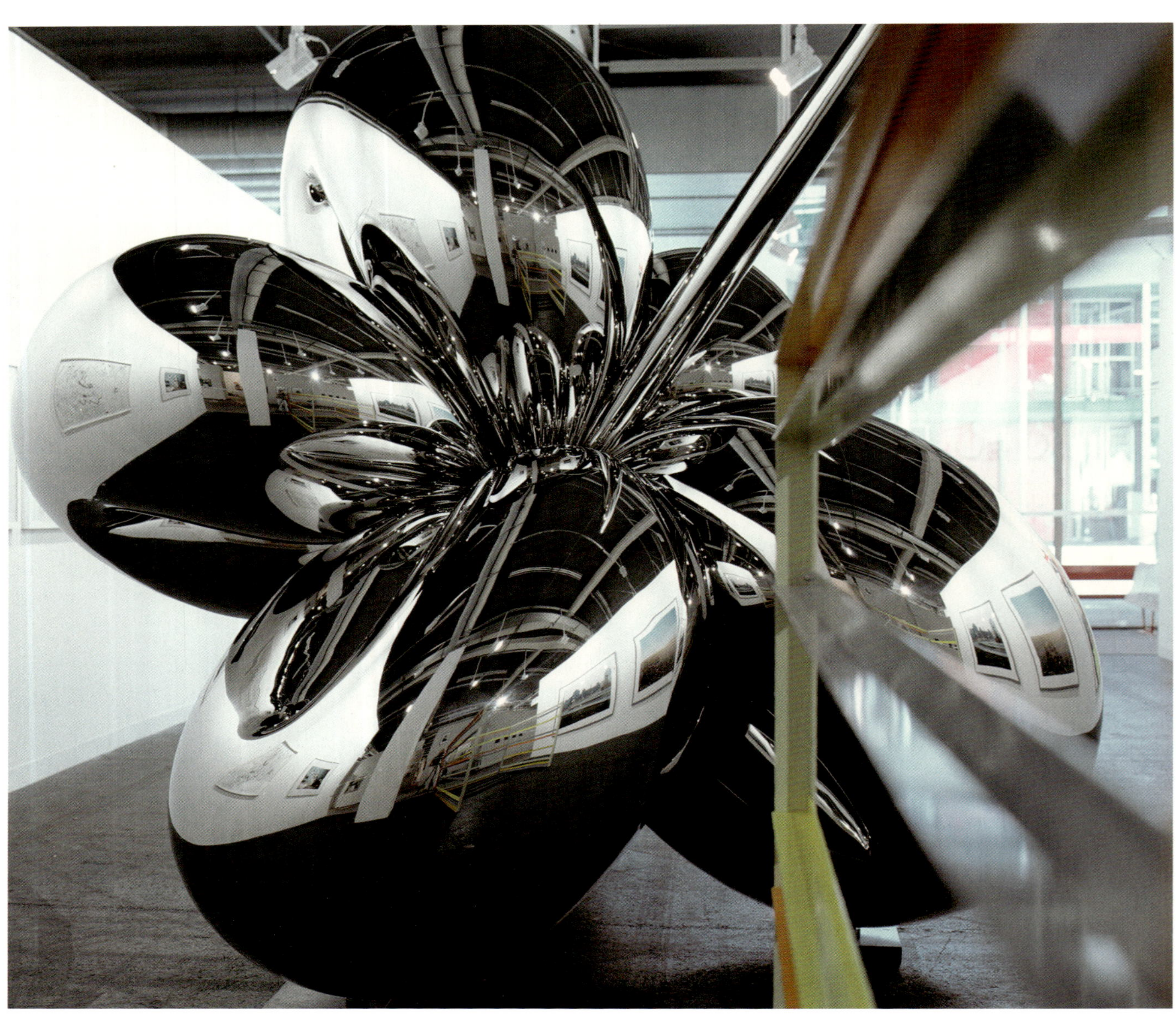

Blume, 2003/2004
cibachrome, 45 1/4 x 50 3/4 inches

CONTENTS

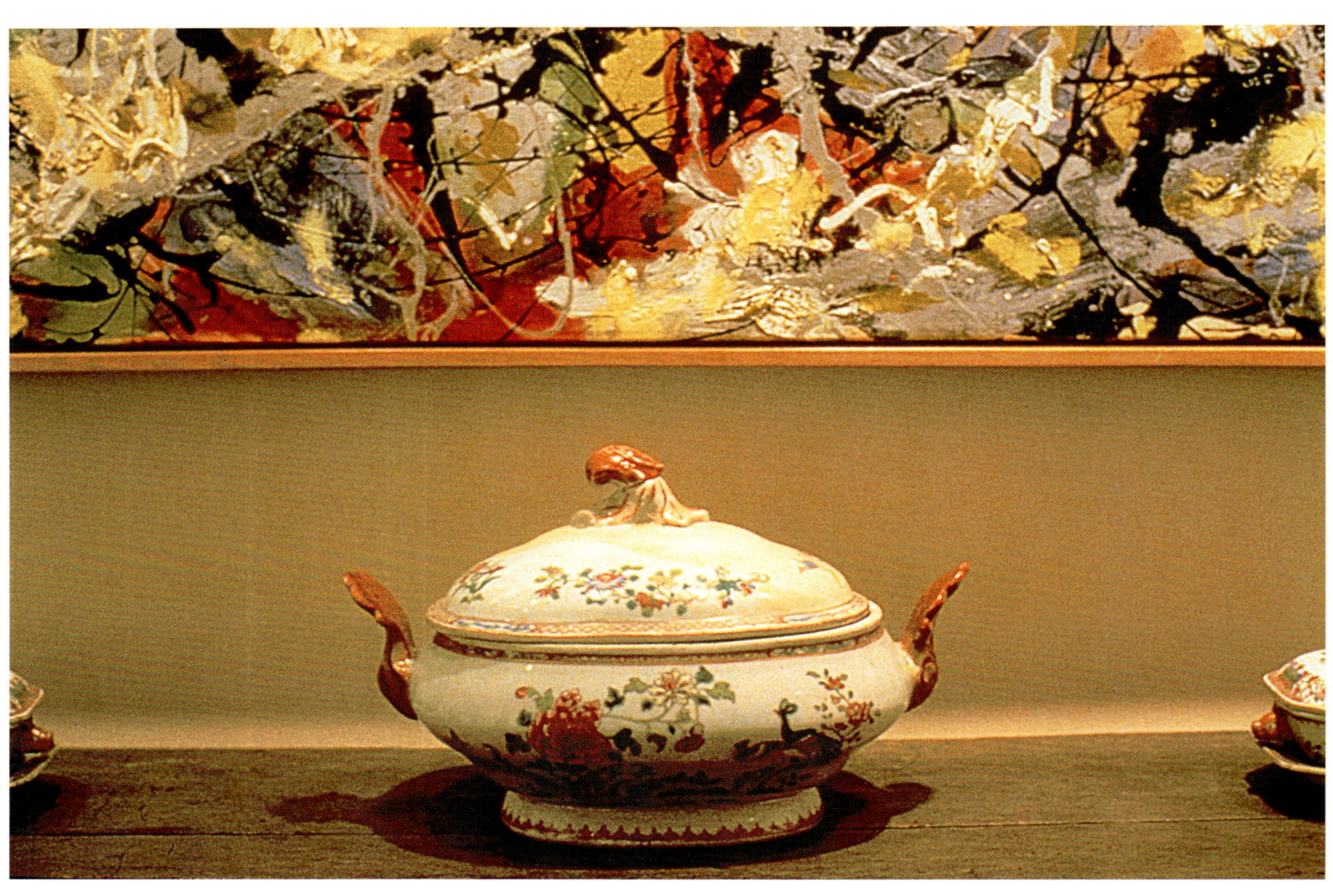

Pollock and Tureen, Arranged by Mr. and Mrs. Burton Tremaine, Connecticut, 1984
cibachrome, 28 x 39 inches

INTRODUCTION

Philipp Kaiser

And art is always a collaboration with what came before you and what comes after you.[1]

Louise Lawler

Louise Lawler does not exist alone. Her name becomes part of the title of the exhibition and catalogue *Louise Lawler and Others*, thus from the outset undermining the institutional desire to be the first to show a retrospective view of her works from the last twenty-five years. The title, which could equally refer to a band of musicians, aims first and foremost to challenge authorship. Lawler's conceptual strategy of (mainly photographic) appropriation met with an active artistic environment and a theoretical base in New York in the late 1970s and early 1980s, also as a result of the collaborative approach to work shared by critics and artists alike. Lawler was as uncompromisingly skeptical of subject-centered concepts of authorship as other artists of her generation, at the same time that Neo-Expressionist painting was flooding the North American and European markets.

In her first solo exhibition An Arrangement of Pictures at Metro Pictures in 1982, Louise Lawler arranged the works of the gallery artists (Cindy Sherman, Robert Longo, Jack Goldstein, Laurie Simmons, and James Welling) and presented the whole ensemble for sale as if she were an art dealer, even taking ten percent commission. Finally, she photographed these works from the gallery at the homes of the collectors, appropriating the "Metro Pictures style" for this purpose, a style that became her own distinctive signature over the years.[2] The different locations of art, the context of private collections versus the (more or less) public gallery exhibition, and the reappropriation of works that had been sold through their return to the gallery, all reflect the tautological structures of the institution of art.

The multiplication of these different roles of artist, publicist, curator, and art dealer sees art as a collective undertaking that does not differentiate between primary and secondary activities. In this way, Lawler relinquishes any privileged position of artistic identity, while at the same time attempting to break down institutional boundaries.[3] Her early collaborative work with Sherrie Levine, Allan McCollum, and others demonstrates this, as does her strategy of appropriating other people's works in order to locate her own work and to negate the production of art. Lawler does not produce, but rather documents, takes stock, and analyzes contextual interactions on a wide variety of different levels.

Given all of this, the idea of presenting Louise Lawler's works in a monograph exhibition project with a catalogue would seem somewhat dubious. It could be argued that the act of contextualizing and historicizing Lawler in art history would mean reducing her practice; yet on the other hand, not including her in the history of art would mean ignoring her.[4] This tricky, if not to say aporetic starting point is also illuminated by the history of the multifaceted reception Lawler's work has received. From the very beginning, her work has moved within a field of tension between institutional critique and Appropriation art, yet without deciding for one or the other. However, Lawler's work was often placed solely in the tradition of institutional-critical strategies in the style of Hans Haacke, Michael Asher, or Marcel Broodthaers, thus suggesting an analytical approach whose highest and only goal was the deconstruction of institutional parameters. Yet the fact that Lawler works "dedicate" themselves to Lawler, as described by Isabelle Graw in her contribution to this catalogue, is completely disregarded. Appropriation nearly always entails affection and is preceded by a personal decision. The aim is not to rob Louise Lawler's works of their fundamental critical nature, and yet the focus of attention on her work to date seems to have generated this aporia in the first place. The institutional approach to artistic institutional critique will always be problematic because the museum takes on the role of benefactor. Lawler's practice, however, has moved on from oppositional criticism of the institutional authority in the early 1970s, in order to systematically question this authority in the role of an accomplice.[5] She looks at the scenes and details that are not immediately apparent, and the framework, such as museum signs, press releases, logos, etc, all in order to make ideological and repressive conventions visible; and she also approaches the main stage of the exhibition space: but without differentiating between these various locations in a judgmental manner. When documenting situations that she has found, Louise Lawler decentralizes her view to focus on the margins of art and displays the circumstances in which they are presented, their dispositive. She focuses on the surroundings and boundaries, and shows the autonomous work of art to be a fiction that has always been caught up in a social, historical, and thematic context.

Seen from a conceptual angle, Lawler's works are symbolic acts of criticism and thus discursive in nature. They also reflect their mediality in the endless reflections of a Jeff Koons flower, for example, by becoming a metaphorical reference to the photographic mirror image of the world. Photography fragments, annexes, and is presented as literal, before merging once again in endless contextualized interconnections. All of Lawler's appropriated works of art therefore speak incessantly of the artist herself, of themselves, and of their context.

Some years ago, George Baker, who took part in an inspiring conversation with Andrea Fraser about Louise Lawler for this catalogue, called for her work to be historicized, so as to identify her as a key figure for Context art of the 1990s.[6] Andrea Fraser formulated her own artistic practice in the mid-1980s, taking Louise Lawler as one starting point, and she has also worked collaboratively with her. In this catalogue, Birgit Pelzer provides a comprehensive and precise view of the whole oeuvre of Louise Lawler, while Isabelle Graw elaborates on the discourse of Appropriation art. Graw's term "dedication" seems to have been unwittingly taken up by Jack Bankowsky, in order to shed light on Lawler's relationship to Andy Warhol, who appears in a large number of her works. Finally, Louise Lawler conceived this catalogue and worked in close collaboration with Mónika Sziládi, who designed the catalogue. Thus, Lawler has also moved artistic practice into this institutional sphere of influence.

Notes

1. "'Prominence Given, Authority Taken.' An Interview with Louise Lawler by Douglas Crimp," in Louise Lawler, *An Arrangement of Pictures* (New York, 2000), unpaginated.

2. Ibid.

3. Andrea Fraser, "In and Out of Place," *Art in America* (May 1985): 122–29.

4. Stefan Römer, *Künstlerische Strategien des Fake: Kritik von Original und Fälschung* (Cologne, 2001), 177.

5. Ibid., 179.

6. George Baker, "Paint, Wall, Pictures: Something Always Follows Something Else. She Wasn't Always a Statue," *Texte zur Kunst*, no. 26 (June 1997): 89–94.

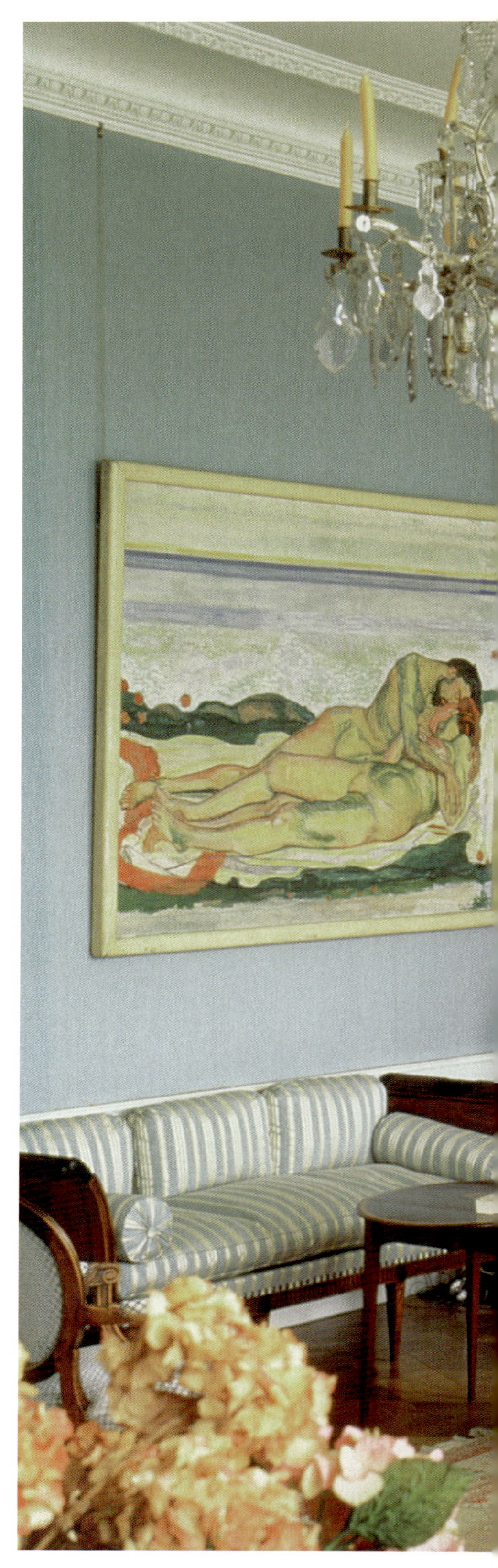

Salon Hodler, 1992/1993
cibachrome, $49^{1/4}$ x $58^{1/2}$ inches

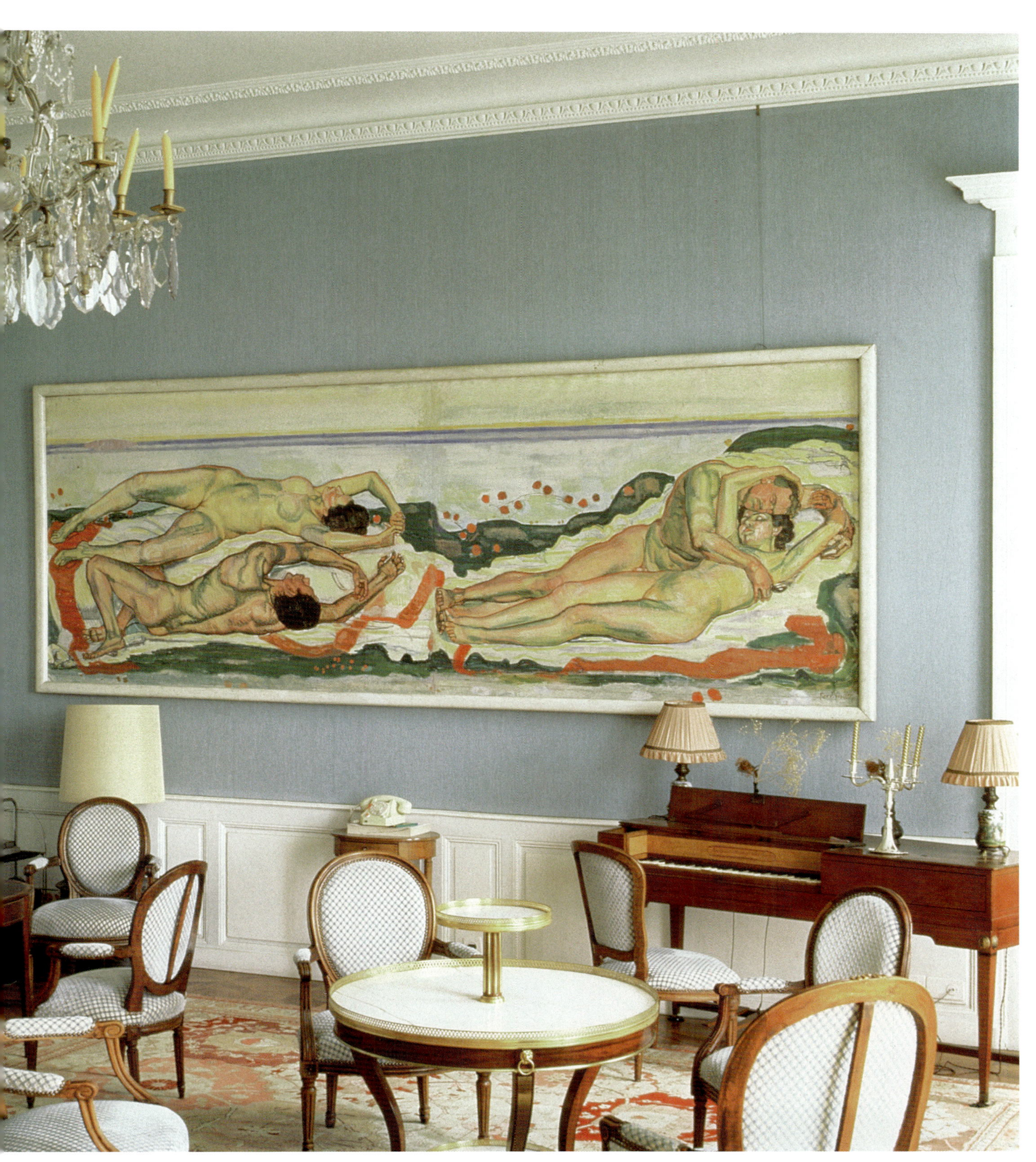

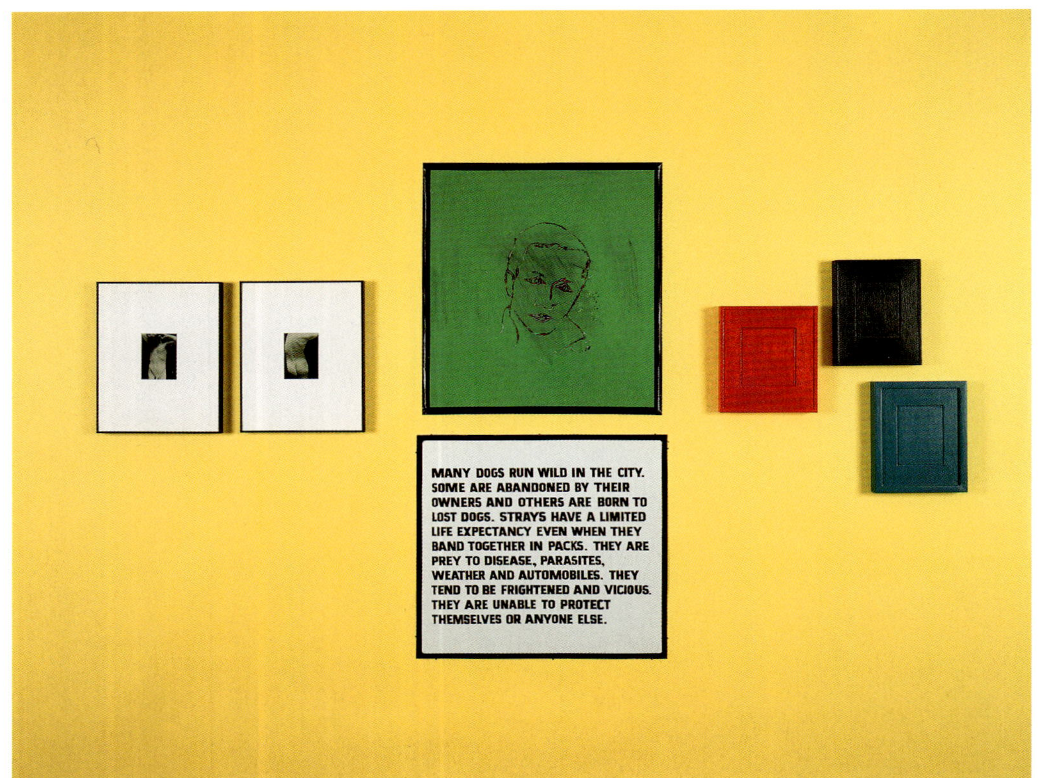

(Allan McCollum and Other Artists)
Lemon, 1981
cibachrome, $28^{1/2}$ x $37^{1/4}$ inches

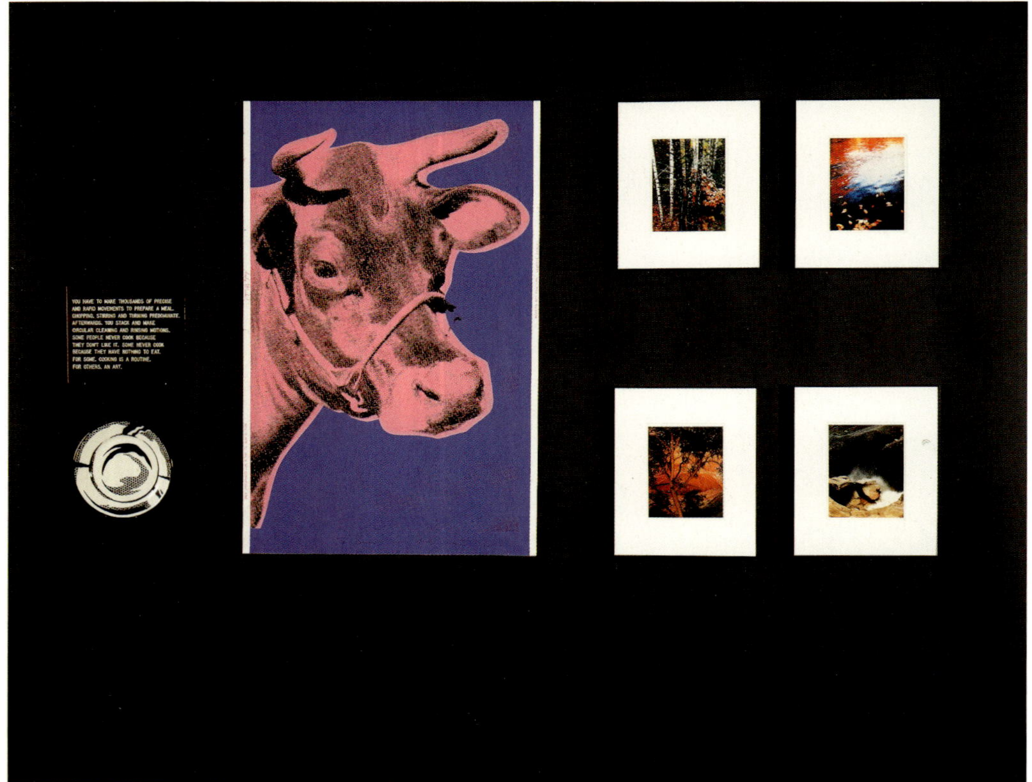

(Roy Lichtenstein and Other Artists)
Black, 1982
cibachrome, $28^{1/2}$ x $37^{1/4}$ inches

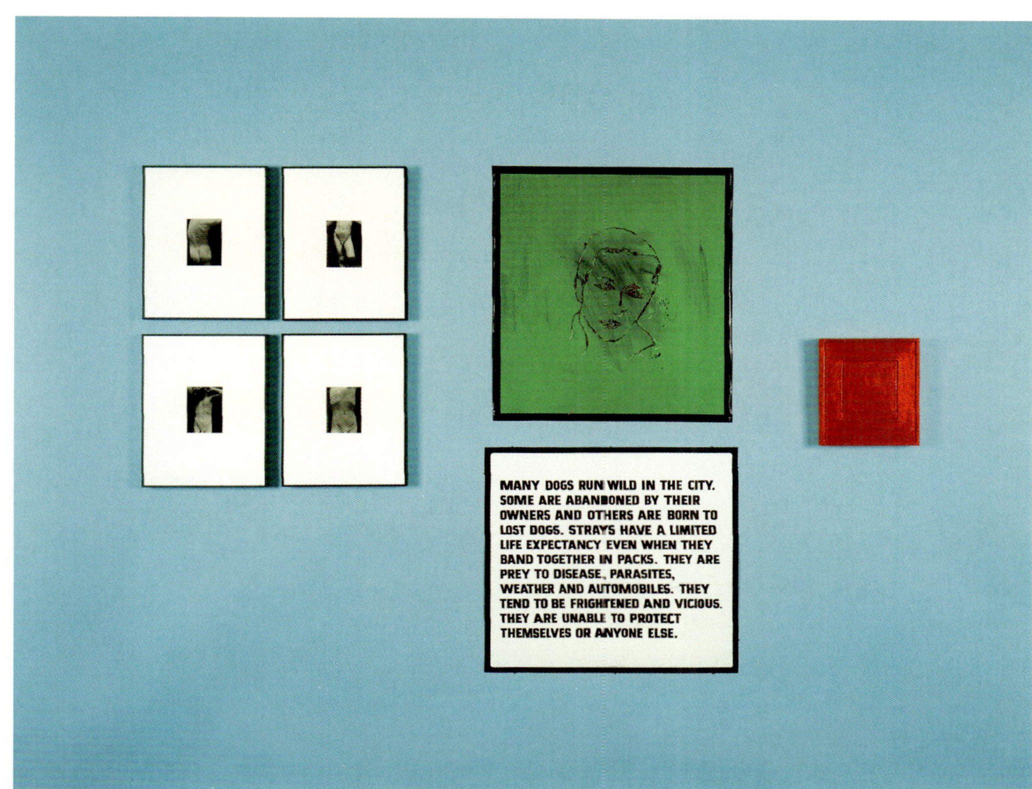

(Holzer, Nadin and Other Artists)
Baby Blue, 1981
cibachrome, $28^{1/2}$ x $37^{1/4}$ inches

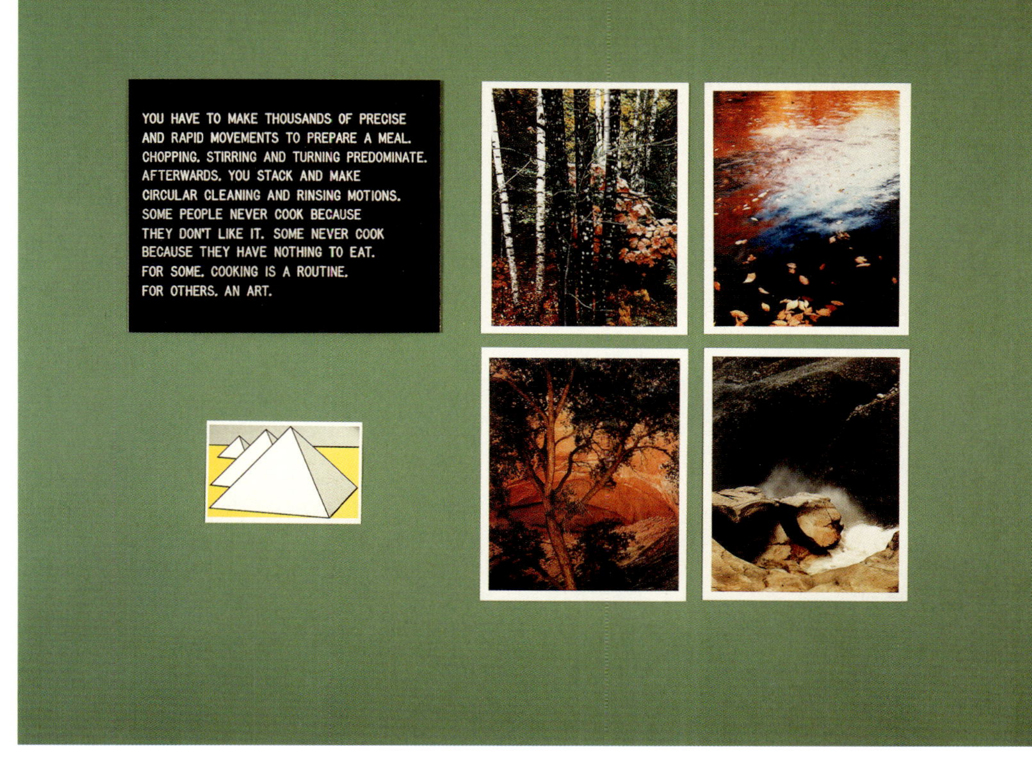

(Jenny Holzer and Other Artists)
Kelly Green, 1982
cibachrome, $28^{1/2}$ x $37^{1/4}$ inches

Pink and Yellow and Black III (Brillo) from **On a Wall, On a Cow, In a Book, In the Mail**, 1999
cibachrome, $68^{1/2}$ x 37 inches

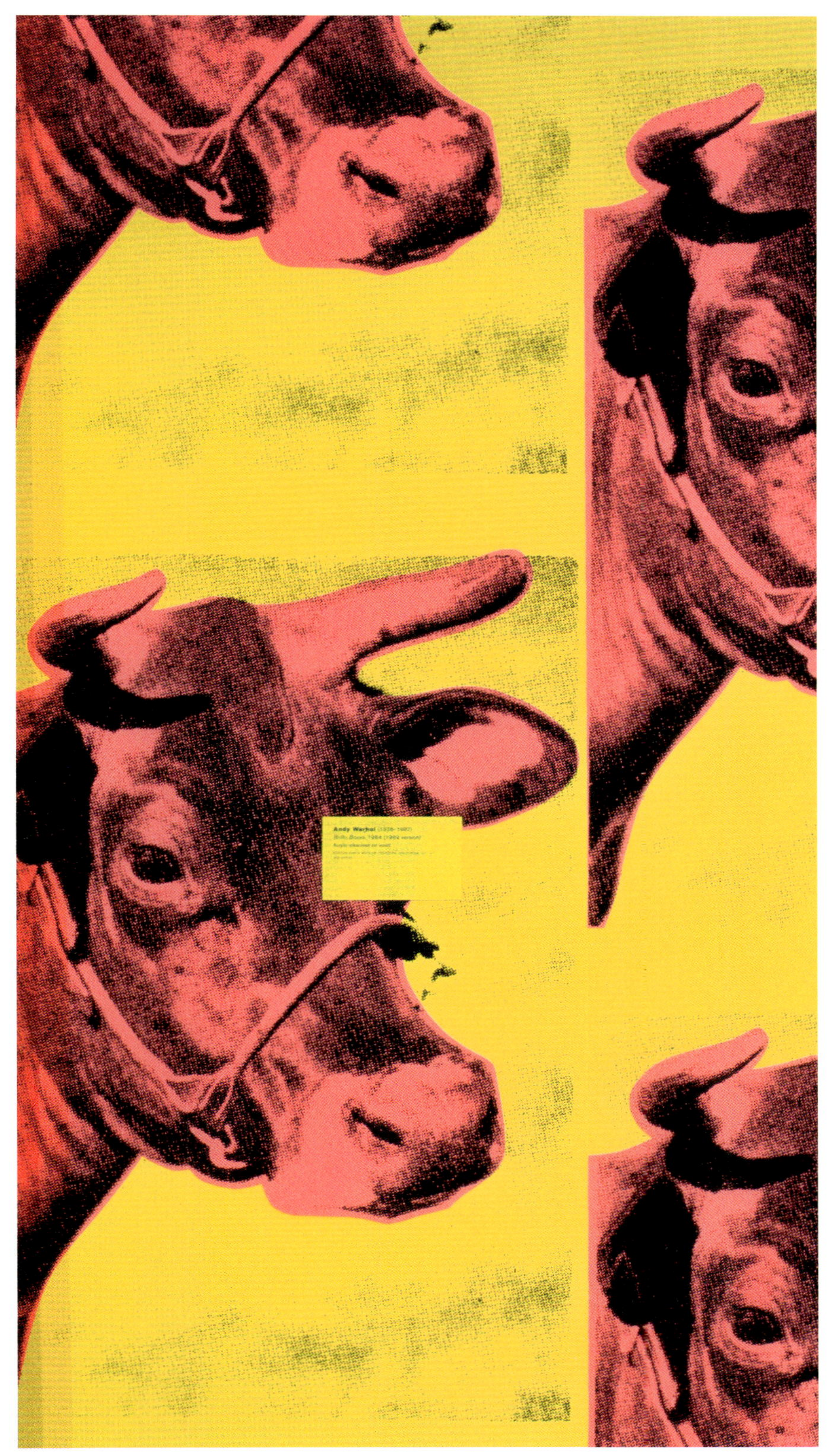
Andy Warhol

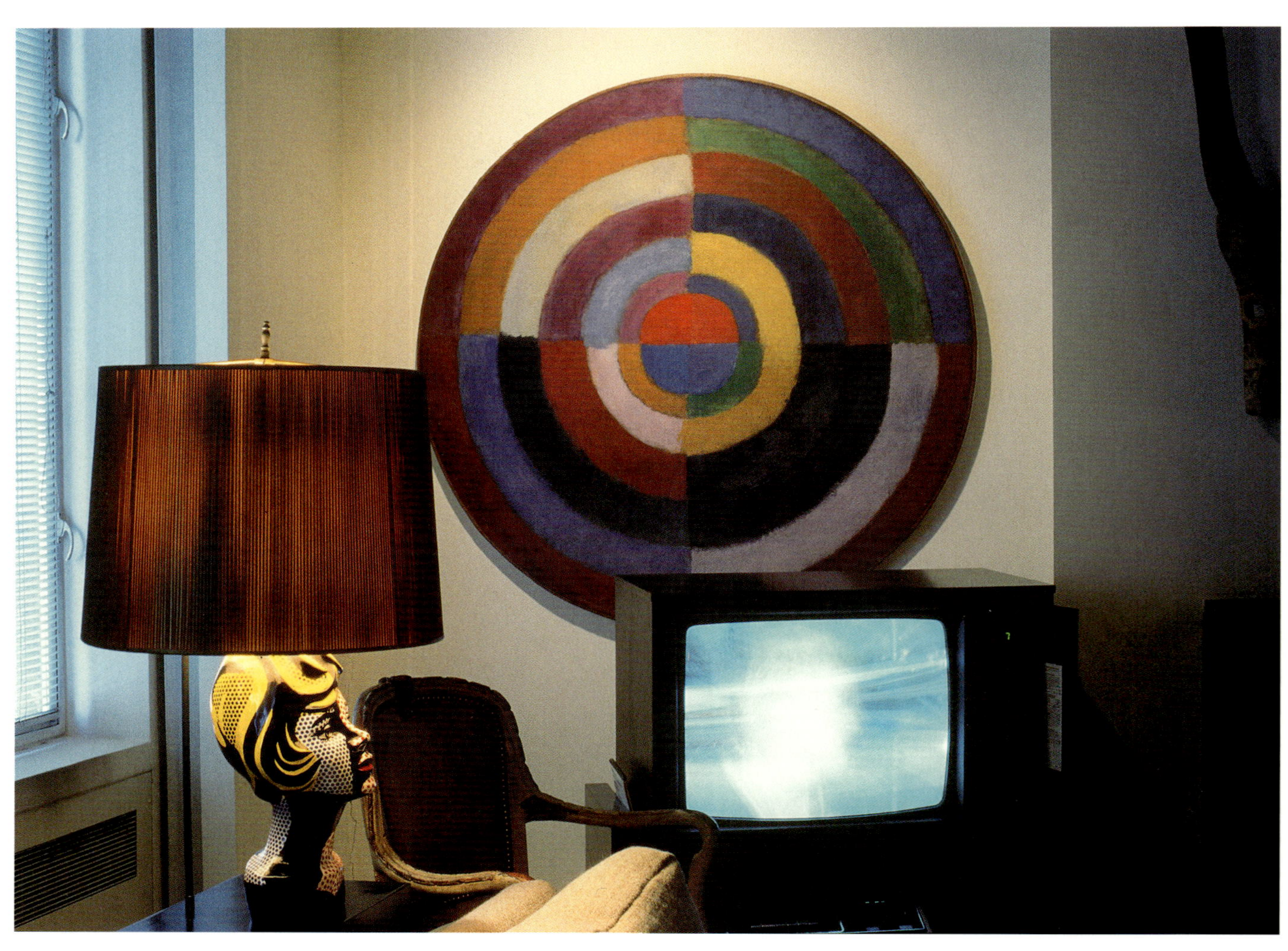

Living Room Corner, Arranged by Mr. and Mrs. Burton Tremaine, New York City, 1984
cibachrome, 28 x 39 inches

INTERPOSITIONS: THE WORK OF LOUISE LAWLER

Birgit Pelzer

The work of Louise Lawler comes to us via a seemingly forthright program bearing on the conditions, procedures and arbiters of the presentation, positioning, and circulation of works of art. Working within a continuous circuit of intelligibility, she photographs art and its spaces—but only in order to disrupt the economy of attention and affect so expertly channeled toward them. Her photographs and other interventions are characterized by a visual decentering intended to focus less on the works than on what surrounds them: on a set of relations that are at once rigid and loose, insistent and indeterminate and which, without being perceived for what they are, nonetheless mark out—in interactions that are elusive, opaque, and full of random contiguities—the forms of authority and power at work in the institutional setting. In this same setting the located constellation of influences—the resonance effect generating "reputations" and values—derives in part from the channeling and capitalizing of attention taken and given.

However, below the surface of this thematic program, combining a concern with "institutional critique" and methods of what is designated as "appropriation," lies a more fundamental question: that of the equivocality of our link to the other and to its different sites. This basic, insoluble equivocality is at the heart of Louise Lawler's photographs. An elemental impasse, this head-spinning equivocality magnetizes, via a process of discreet corrosion, an oeuvre spun out of interlocutions. The troubling acuity of Lawler's approach lies in the way it intensifies—as an "arrangement of arrangements"—the ambiguity of the chosen modes of statement. Using subtle procedures of mimetic disconnection/reversal/gearing-down to immobilize the prevailing operations of inclusion and exclusion, of unification and division, the "pictures," with their offbeat framings, reveal Lawler's way of relating to the work of others so as to make her own production of them.

In this appropriation and its play on identification with an overt cruelty, the frankly incongruous detail plays a crucial part. What faith can we have in a system founded on such readily reversible components? These photographs chop up established meaning. They feed off the presupposition of a body of knowledge already developed, indexed, and codified. What is Lawler showing us? In a world defined by the continuity of relationships, her photographs isolate climates, pointing out in their classifications and assemblages the "in-between" of art places and art objects: furniture, showcases, labels, signatures.[1] An arrangement is always linked to agreements between groups, to systems of subordination, coordination, alienation. Homing in on a detail does not mean looking for trivia, however; trivia

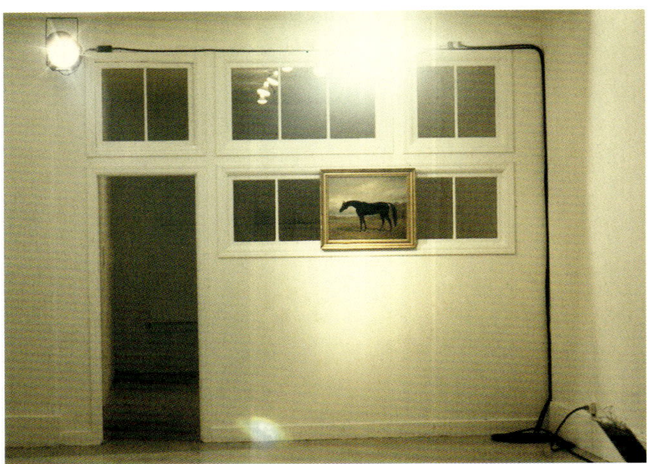

Artists Space, New York, 1978

Installation with oil painting (by H. Stulman, 1883) borrowed from Aqueduct Race Track, two VNSP par 64 1000 watt lights hung over the painting, one directed at the viewer, the other through the space and out a window, projecting across the street onto a building facade.

A logo was designed for Artists Space, used on the cover of the catalogue and produced as a poster (with no text). It was posted in lower Manhattan.

lead astray, while Louise Lawler's photographs are strictly focused, playing with the rigidity of the established code by introducing an element that clashes. It is the detail that counts, the detail that adds something, provides extra input. In the shift of contour it generates the suddenly dissociated detail testifies to the existence of a fringe to things, a penumbra oddly resistant to proof and fixed evaluation.

Faced with habitual modes of understanding, in-group consensus, and standard interpretations, Lawler's photographs rebound to generate a slight breach. Within the power system, with all its complicities, credulities, loyalties, and acknowledgement of credentials, they dodge and sidestep. The photographs and other interventions always belong to the interspace, to the "beyond" of intersection: between two canvases, two categories, two labels, two authors, two times. But the vacant space thus captured, and the details hidden as if of no significance—details found, checked off, detected, made to interact within the panorama of contemporary art and its offshoots—exact an intellectual volte-face. Nonetheless something of the subject finds a place for itself within the impalpable point of radical, in-between shift, seized upon in the proximal slippage of meanings/conventions/contextual confusions. The arrival of something indeterminate shakes up these scenes too full of meaning. Most striking of all is the elusive significance of whatever it is that insists so uninsistently. The impression emanating from the oeuvre is one of sophistication, grace, and a keen elegance. A poignancy.[2] Her method—sharp, antithetical, cutting, imponderable—is analogous to the movement of the knight on a chessboard: scarcely has he moved forward than he veers off, pulls back from the scene to observe, and makes the territory gained part of a prognostic splitting, a scornful distancing.[3]

What we retain of this defensive gambit—so discreet in these times of exhibitionist cacophony, so unexpected amid the disparate anesthesia of the art of today—is a tone: the pertinent, impertinent, light yet caustic tone of the epigram and the fable. Louise Lawler's evasive framings are tailored with utter precision to

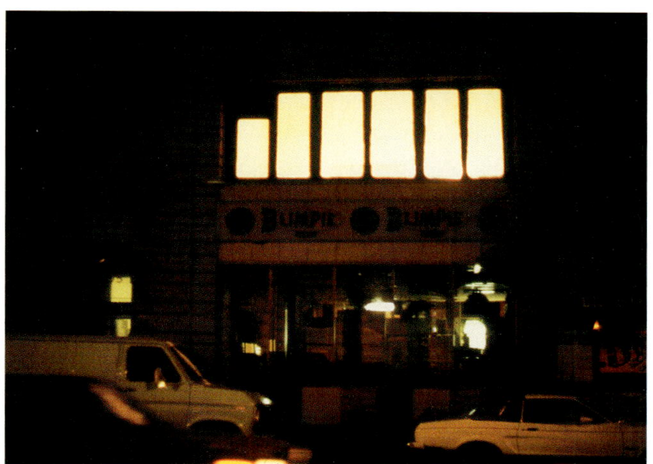

a felt sensation that seeks to distance itself from emotional confusion. How are we to create space for the irresistible need to exercise our faculty of judgment and recognition in a world where everything is aimed at depriving us of it, in a world of widespread, well-ordered confusion where the issue of recognition is simultaneously overexposed, denied, scrambled, made suspect, and usurped by rampant saturation with identitarian and other agendas? In addition to their challenge to the powers that be, to systems and to authority, there is the singular place these cool-headed analyses offer to the activity of the singular eye, to a sensibility free of pathos, nostalgia, regret, and militantism. This sensibility advocates no rallying to a cause, but rather a vision shot through with perplexity, a functional acknowledgement of the new approach to managing symbolic affairs, and the fragile adventures of a relationship with the present marked by distancing.[4] With its acute sense of the precariousness of our ways of inhabiting time—a sense of the ongoing misapprehension of influences and practices so readily rendered exploitative—Lawler's oeuvre indicates that on its own the obvious, visual or not, is obviously insufficient.[5]

As an approach to her way of working, I would like to look back at the early projects and thus home in better on the nature of her stance.

1. Louise Lawler's first New York exhibition was held in 1978 at Artists Space. In what was an incongruous displacement of context in a venue dedicated to the presentation of emerging art, she borrowed an 1883 painting of a standing racehorse from the New York Racing Association. She opted for lighting the space with two theater spotlights: one, placed above the painting, shone into the viewer's eyes, making the picture hard to see; while the other, directed across the gallery toward the outside, linked Artists Space to the street below.[6] Already then, Lawler was attempting to combine and decompartmentalize highly divergent places, arbiters, and communities of interest and style. The question was how to achieve the intersection of things not supposed to intersect—no situation ever being, she stressed, more than a part of something, or basically relative to something. Her photographs documenting the installation are marked "Detail."

Also involved was the interplay between elevation and depreciation of the object, the 1883 painting. The picture, which you had trouble actually seeing, was hung in the middle of a row of windows, a scenographic change that suggested a host of dissimilar notions: stalls in a stable, the landscape overflowing into the window area, a patch of painted sunlight echoing the glare of the Hollywood-style spotlight.

From the outset, then, Louise Lawler's approach concentrated intersection of contexts, impact of detail, incongruous connections/disconnections, and foreground and background in an artistic mise en scène. Already present were the issues of appropriation, of the limits it imposes and violates, of how in a group situation borrowing raises the question of being "in" or "out," of the nature of bonding and the social, mental, and imaginary distances governing it, and of what lies beyond boundaries, clubs, and cliques. In terms of agenda, this problematic of appropriation flies the flag of a certain discourse, one that came within the purview of recent contemporary art under the appellation of "institutional critique"—a term created in response to the highly different work mode adopted by artists such as Michael Asher, Daniel Buren, Marcel Broodthaers, and Hans Haacke in the late 1960s.

2. In 1980 Louise Lawler made a double-edged intervention in Amalgam,[7] an exhibition of works on paper at the prestigious Leo Castelli Gallery in New York. Her focus was on both the famous works on show and their labeling with names guaranteeing authority and acceptability. Once given permission to intervene, she hung her piece, a photograph titled ***Open***, among works by Jasper Johns, Cy Twombly and others. Responding to the ostentatious presentation of their names alongside their work, she labeled hers "Anonymous." ***Open*** is centered on the fold and margins of a book open at a short story by Alberto Moravia, and we can make out fragments of a circled text, whose opening words are: "I made my first mistake."

In proposing the institutional setting as something to be "read," this intervention lays bare Lawler's different angles of investigation. If the system relies solely on the interplay of difference and placement, and if the differences derive their value solely from their placement, then it is the symbolic order itself that raises the issue of place. Lawler's observation of the relationship between different places is aimed at discerning in it something usually not-seen. ***Open*** is a contextual intervention of an explicitly elliptical kind, in which she breaks the chain of names and its system of references by introducing the word "Anonymous" in place of her own name. In the photograph ***Open***, she singles out and defamiliarizes a recognized fragment of literature in the world of the recognized visual arts.

Open, 1980
black and white photograph, $6^{1/8}$ inches diameter

Nevertheless, singling out something that clashes—a fragment of literature—and inserting it into this framework upsets the hegemony of affiliations, provokes a shift in the implicit and the explicit, and brings about slippages of meaning in terms of contiguity. Targeting the joins/breaches in the symbolic order, Lawler introduces a hairline crack into the circularity of apparently closed systems. In place of the Other and the others, she injects into the imposing edifice of credence-seeking representations a discontinuity touching its multifarious points of junction. This itinerary through places marked and unmarked testifies to the extent—if place exists solely in the symbolic order—to which each symbolic mark engenders the void of the place it creates.

This is typically Louise Lawler terrain, with textual and visual effects intersecting at a crossroads which, despite its uncertain topography, clearly summons us to an act of reading: to the functions shared—maybe in terms of rival statements—by text and image. This could be a way of making photography the intermediary for a language. Aside from the importance of the titles of her photographs, an entire segment of Lawler's work has to do with inscriptions. Texts do not appear solely in relation to the photographs: the artist also places them on glasses, matchboxes, paper napkins, paperweights, writing paper, and the gift vouchers she began to make. Affixing them to these practical objects might be a way of indicating that everybody else counts too, and not just the attention-consuming art world.[8] The added benefit, she says, is that this allows for a displacement of artistic imperatives. Lawler sets real store by everything the art-institution framework produces, up to and including its humblest, most neglected ephemera: invitation cards, information sheets, captions, wall inscriptions, labels, and murals. Integral to the exhibition and circulation of art, these modest, marginal elements become separate vehicles for her work. Concerned to spell out the routes taken by the work of art, given that any such route involves launching ceremonies conducted in valorizing language, she homes in on the secondary cogs—rendered virtually intractable by their diffuse omnipresence—of art's presentation and marketing mechanisms. All in all, in these anodyne, hybrid objects—as at some implosive differential threshold—we find a concentration of forms of artistic expression, advertising seduction strategies, the media industry, the mechanisms of mass production, the slackening of critical standards, and the overwhelming dominance of the market. The opposite sides of the artistic field may also be co-present in these places. But are they co-presentable? What the artist seems to be saying, ironically, is that however hard you twist you can never turn a mere band into contraband.

3. Invited to present her first official exhibition in 1982 at the Metro Pictures Gallery in New York, Lawler responded with a mise en scène of works by its artists: Robert Longo, Cindy Sherman, Jack Goldstein, Laurie Simmons, and James Welling. The gallery represented a group of ideologically related artists whose strategy concerned the issues of appropriation. As Lawler explains: "A gallery generates meaning through the type of work they choose to show. I self-consciously made work that 'looked like' Metro Pictures."[9] The title she chose was Arranged by Louise Lawler, and, in a kind of Swiftian role-sharing tableau, there began a series of comings and goings. First she went to see collectors who had bought from Metro Pictures and photographed works by the gallery's artists surrounded by the everyday objects of their private or public settings. Then she blew the photographs up to "normal size" and exhibited them, but with titles like *Arranged by Barbara and Eugene Schwartz* or *Living Room Corner, Arranged by Mr. and Mrs. Burton Tremaine, New York City*. Thus she rounded off the generic "Arranged by..." with the names of the owners, tagging the latter with their own act of installation. This naming of the photographically sampled site simulates a reverse reappropriation. In these arrangements, caught on the hop and trapped by photography in the mirror of their own being-there, there is an ongoing interplay of planes with a canny trick at its core: the splitting of acts, an unresolved shifting between places of statement, between authors and operators, between proprietors and producers.

Arranged by Louise Lawler, New York City, 1982

Installation with works from the inventory of Metro Pictures, New York

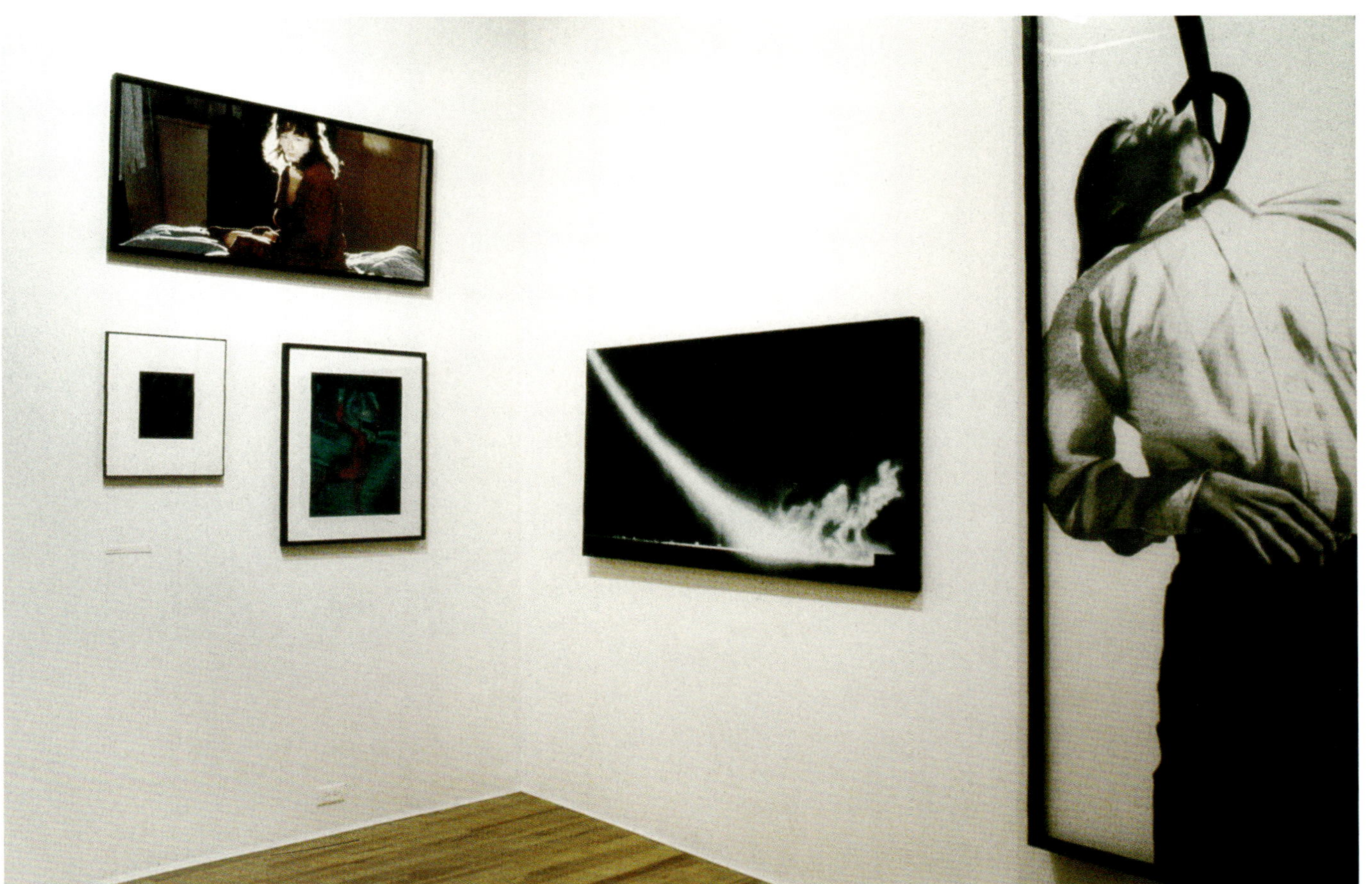

In the interview with Douglas Crimp that prefaces her book *An Arrangement of Pictures*, in which she looks back at the decisions taken for this exhibition, Lawler says, "The situation is always part of what produces the work for me." Insisting on the power of context, which for her implies a necessary shift in the notion of the author, she adds, "The work can never be determined just by what I do or say. Its comprehension is facilitated by the work of other artists and critics and just by what's going on at the time."[10] She also declares explicit and implicit collaboration as central to her work: "Collaborations can produce a shift in focus and concerns."[11] Thus she went on to work in conjunction with other artists, as in *A Picture Is No Substitute for Anything*, with Sherrie Levine, in which they adopt a sham gallery-owner role; in the *Ideal Settings for Presentation and Display* installation with Allan McCollum, which presented the gallery space as a life-size advertising venue; and with Douglas Crimp for his own book *On the Museum's Ruins*,[12] in which Lawler's photographs expand on and intensify the book's underlying thesis: that the significance of a work of art—largely based on unquestioned cultural consensus—is established in relation to the circumstances of its institutional framework. Once again a shift in the focus of our curiosity is generated by this challenge to the notion of the author and by an insistence on what someone else produces, on the effect of discrepancy, distance, and internal inconsistency, and on issues of adjacency, repetition, and the unusual. The effect is not where one expects it to be.

Lawler's initial act at Metro Pictures—responding to the gallery's invitation with an arrangement of works by its artists; photographing the works in question in the homes of the gallery's collectors; singling out her own work while titling it "Arranged by . . ." and adding the collectors' names; and then showing it in the same gallery—takes us into the mad whirl of merchandising and representation, into the closed system whose fundamental overkill she highlights with an act which is itself part of a game in which the circulation of goods is dictated by the rules of transitivity. The multiplicity of occurrences shown and re-shown pushes up the value of the objects concerned and simultaneously fuels their discourse. This is a tautological system in which every element is self-substantiating, in which "being amongst ourselves" spills over in endless circularity onto all concerned. Each resymbolized occurrence brings a profit: for the Metro Pictures artists, their collectors, the gallery owners, and the artist Louise Lawler. Added value is incorporated into a system of recognitions, identities, and rapid upward mobility. Likewise, this is the arena for photographing capital, for the valorizing of value. Louise Lawler, then, is interfering in the arena of the capitalization of benchmark sites.[13] And yet, in this game of incursions and references, her work's critical mirroring pumps up the runaway capitalist mechanism. And reinforcing all those octopoid ramifications, it boosts supply in the process. For in an exchange-based economy, denunciation plays its own unmistakable part, adding to the situation in that it is inevitably caught up in the mimetic, in the process of reciprocity. At the

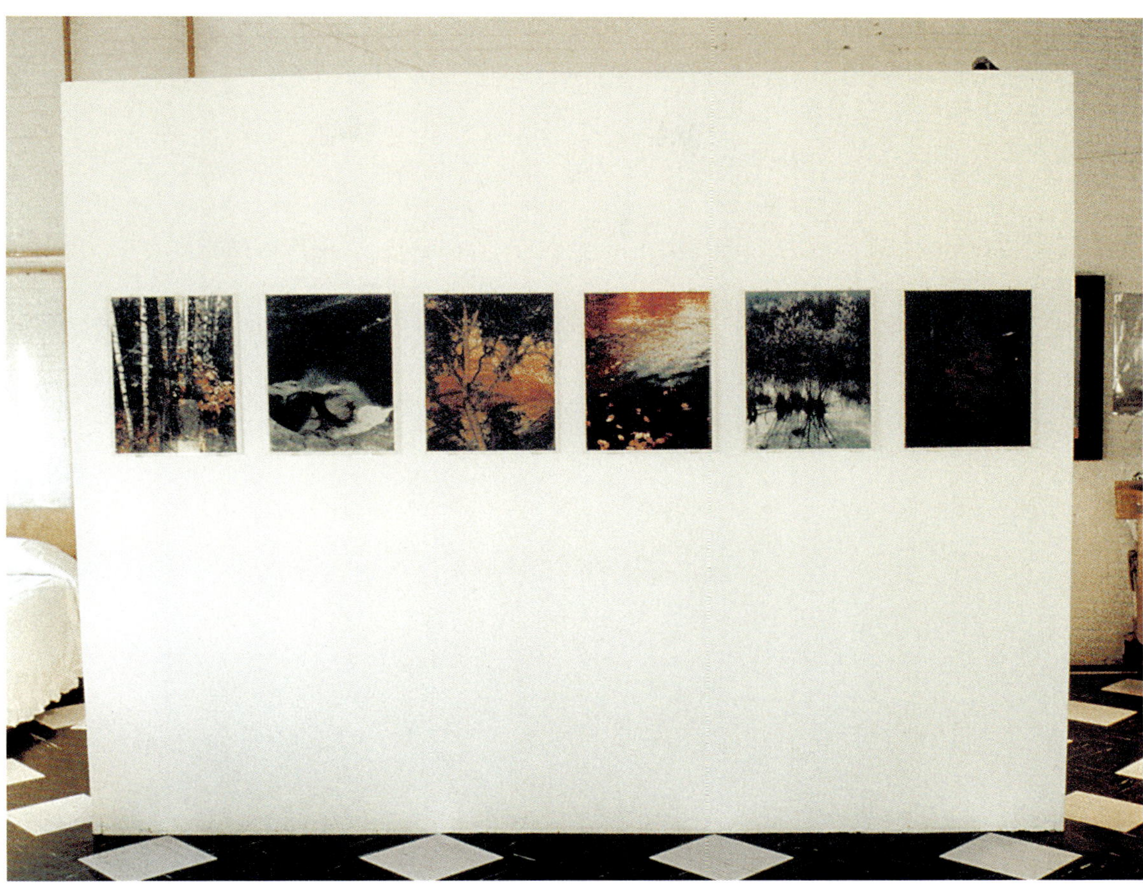

A Picture Is No Substitute for Anything, 1981

Works by Sherrie Levine, presented on Thursday, June 25, 1981, at Louise Lawler's, 407 Greenwich Street, New York

same time, denunciation is not the point. The point seems rather to be a focusing on the sequence of signs in their complex movement between stasis and fast turnaround, a game that stresses return on investment in a monopoly situation caught between deregulation and supplier confrontation as free market principles swing into action.

4. Lawler's oeuvre, however, cannot be reduced to a mere contextual act. There is more to her than just "institutiona critique." For a touch of indeterminacy remains. Continuing to be shown not as isolated works, but always in their context as statement, in their relationship to the venue,[14] her photographs set out to get a fix on where mimesis and reciprocity are coming from. Taking literally photography's specificity as a medium that registers by dividing, Lawler itemizes and cuts her way toward pointing up some imperceptible turnaround point. As if trying to draw such a point out of a state of passivation, this process of division teases out the thread running through the interplay of references and suppositions.

In this way the photographs seize the different states of positioning and

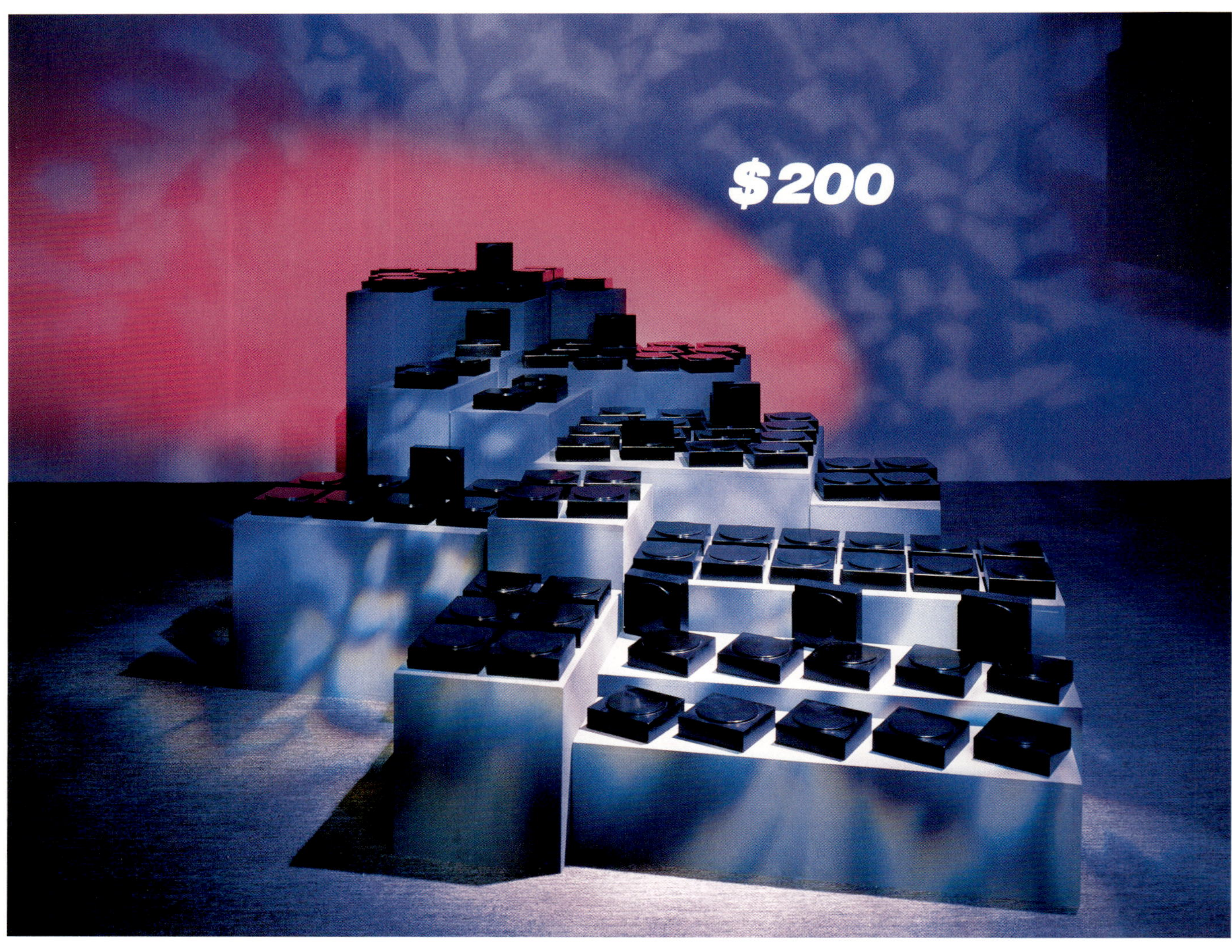

Louise Lawler and Allan McCollum

For Presentation and Display: Ideal Settings, 1984

100 or more hydrocal objects, bases, stage lights, with gels and template, and slide projection, Diane Brown Gallery, New York

visibility governing the way works of art are exhibited, stored, classified, packed, transported, unpacked, hung, related to each other, offered for sale, bought, and collected. Lawler surprises these objects in their oscillation between exposition and abandonment, in a process involving face and interface: on show, set back to back, turned to the wall.[15] The network that dictates the artistic sphere of influence becomes visible in the muffled violence of its imposed conformity, bogged down as it is in its parading of in-group insignia and the gustatory eclecticism of its status symbols; but also—via its adaptable, flexible, unfailingly-connected hold on things—in the display of its mobility as a profit factor. Here we find the porosity of the contemporary art institution, the erosion/fusion between art/market/advertising/lifestyle that points up the colossal jump in prestige of contemporary art within the culture industry, and the insidious, just as colossal shift by which the work of art becomes an exchange standard for investment across a range of cultural fields. This seems to be an art issue, but in fact the dominant problems have to do with a reorganization of cultural hegemony under the aegis of other imperatives. The titles accompanying the images also influence and displace the photographic agenda. They take different forms: direct description, quotation, challenge, enumeration, narrative opening, historical indication. Some provide a soundtrack for the scene photographed. Often interrogative in tone—raising the possibility of action, or a choice—Lawler's titles target authority figures, seeking out channels for a new and different mobilization of attention. Whether on the wall or on the photograph itself, the titles invoke the tradition of photographic captions—yet their content is not the kind of information that goes with documentary material.[16]

5. The issue of photographic documentation in the visual arts is taken up in the portfolios. After all, the place of the photograph is just as much on the pages of a book or newspaper as on the walls of a museum or gallery. Moreover, in a catalogue or art book, it tells as much about the absent work as about its adjacencies and added extras. In this way it seems to line up perfectly with one of the modern aporias of the work of art: the space of its immobile mobility, of its disappearance and dispersion. Created for issue 26 of the review *October* in 1983, the artist's first portfolio highlights the manifest paradox: the scale imposed by the page generates an analogy with documentary, with sequence, with inventory. To take an example, one double-page spread juxtaposes four photos, each presenting a kind of taxonomic accumulation. A reduplication takes place within this semblance of classification, a quotation of quotations that is specific to Lawler's photography. The portfolio makes concrete the extent to which photography gives rise to comparison, autopsy, and verification. It also emerges that in this concern with inventory, photographic recording tends to reduce works of art to nomenclatures of signs and catalogues of indices that are readily and rapidly recognizable. Applied to works of art, the sequential character of photography—together with its inherent reactivity—is revealed to us as inducing a certain viewing mode, which is part of a system of references and thus convertible: we are never faced with a single object, but always with an endlessly combinable series of comparable, potentially identical signs.[17] The descriptive sampling process is revealed, at worst, as rendering the works unreal, paradoxically contributing to the organization of their invisibility. Here order is established. The Louise Lawler portfolio produces an arrangement of arrangements, an echo of the adaptation of something already adapted, so as to home in on the process behind the opaque exactness of the adaptations produced by culture. Drawing on the inherently specular nature of photography as a recording procedure, Lawler reflects back at the art system the image of its own activities, of its function as framework. In a conversion of time scales the system can see itself from the outside, hear itself with a time lag: "I think art is part and parcel of a cumulative and collective enterprise, viewed as seen fit by prevailing culture."[18]

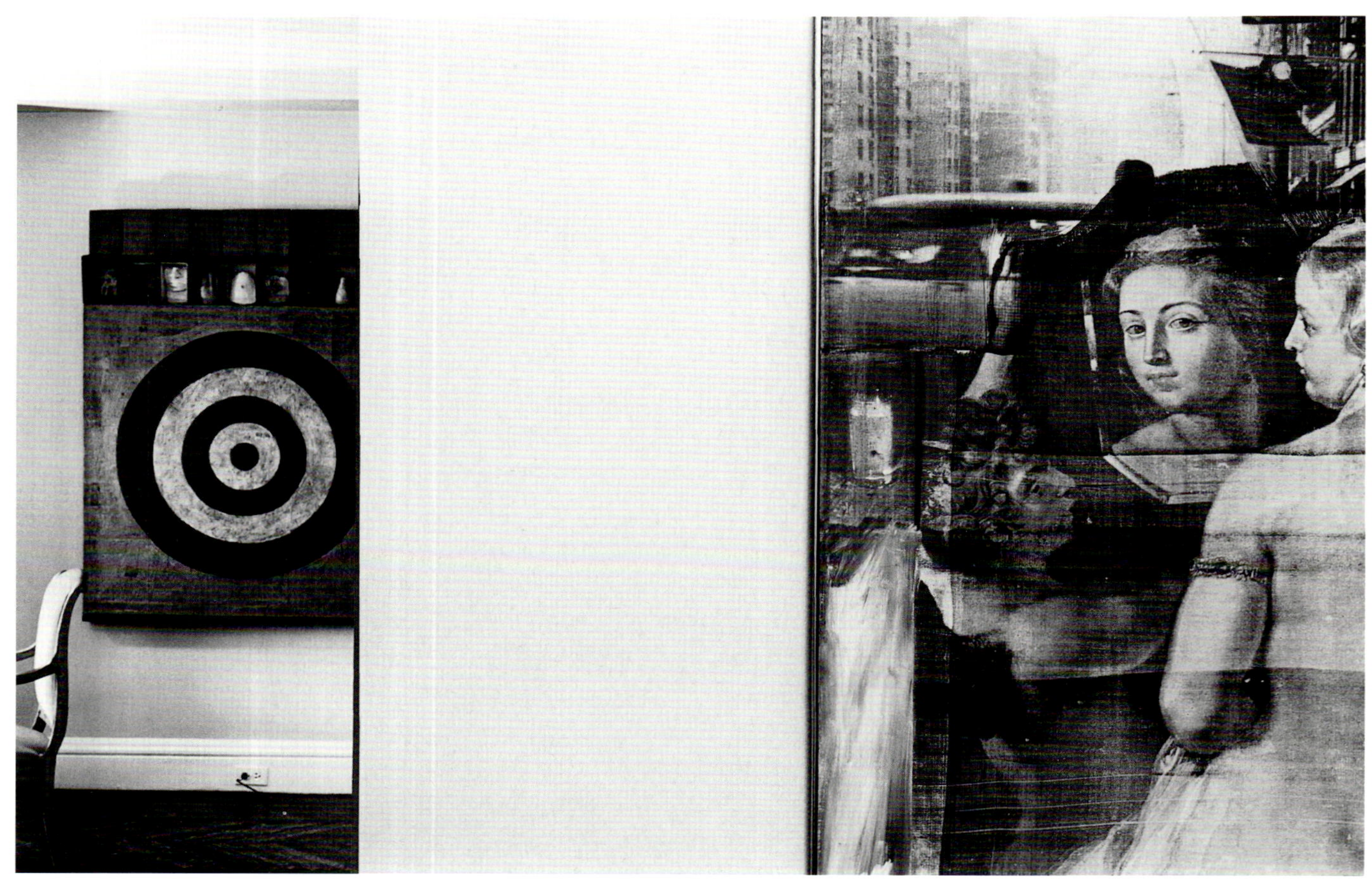

From Here to There, 1990
black and white photograph with title as text on mat, $15^{1/2}$ x 23 inches (image)

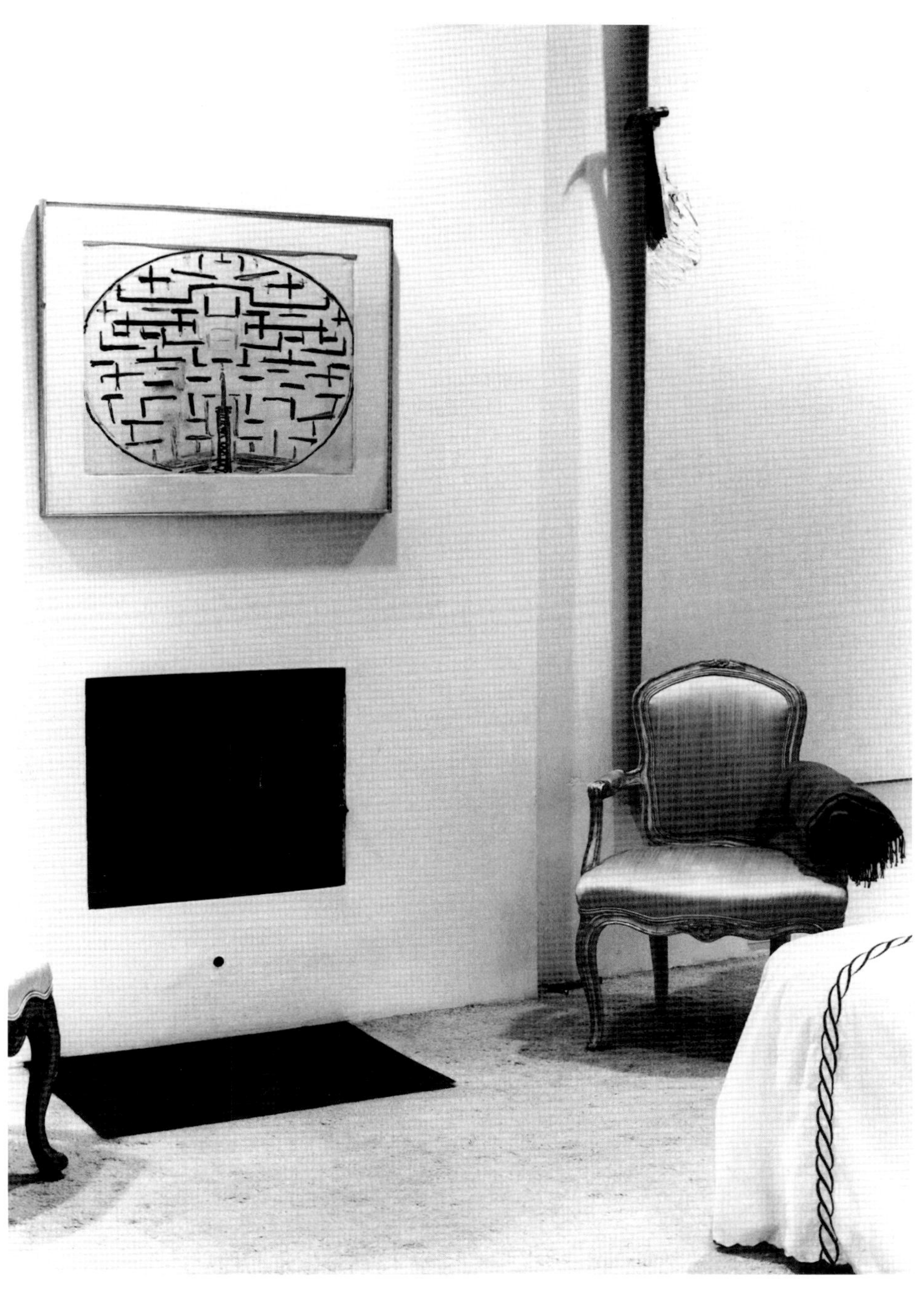

Bedroom with Fireplace, Arranged by Mr. & Mrs. Burton Tremaine Sr., New York City, 1984/1989
black and white photograph with title as text on mat, $21^{1/2}$ x 15 inches (image)

Lawler's implicit montage of quotations simultaneously conceals and reveals its intentions. Has art been caught out? Has it taken things to excess? There is an implosive dose of derision in these scrutinies of compositions seized, cropped, rendered unstable, defined, in which a breach gives shape to what is missing. The impact—notably the emotional impact—of Lawler's photographs springs from a cluster of cancelled-out particularities, whose disappearance is at work without our realizing it. The edited-out clues are there almost negatively, in the ghostlike details, with the real issue being played out somewhere between vanishment and an attempt to establish solid points of reference in the face of this elision, and in the face of chance, conjecture, disorder, and noise.

The representational system applied in her photographs is akin to stage design, registering the way works of art function as scenery in the atmospheres created for them. In these out-of-frame framings and their dilation of different time frames, Louise Lawler plays on a dual space: the exhibition as stage, and that stage's wings, its reserve collection, with the separation between the two serving to codify and enhance not so much the theatrical illusion as the boosting mechanism in itself, the valorizing of value. In these subtle hingings of shot and out-of-shot, concrete expression of the compromise between the openness and closedness of different worlds, she immobilizes areas of unstable motion, a change of level, a pivoting of those worlds. In its preciosity and free-floating "baroquism," the very off-centeredness of her agenda pinpoints the growing importance accorded to what was initially no more than a technical approach to the presentation and coordination of the works in question; and in doing so it stresses the extent to which the significance assumed by the "arrangement" and the "installation" presupposes a theatrically spectacular spatial model. Lawler is out to locate the differential, nowhere indemnified and sometimes described as the "elusiveness" of an atmosphere—yet an elusiveness utterly dependent on this precise occupation of space. Her approach, then, can be seen as using interference and interposition to give concrete expression to this "impalpable": to the surplus stemming from the difference between places.

Notes

1. "The Sites of Art: Photographing the In-Between" is the title Johannes Meinhardt gave to his article in Louise Lawler, *An Arrangement of Pictures* (New York, 2000), unpaginated. This is one of many enlightening articles by Meinhardt on Lawler's work.

2. See "'Prominence Given: Authority Taken.' An Interview with Louise Lawler by Douglas Crimp," in Lawler, *An Arrangement of Pictures* (see note 1), unpaginated.

3. The image is used by Vladimir Nabokov to describe the writing of Jane Austen in his *Lectures on Literature*, ed. Fredson Bowers (New York and London, 1980), 57–58.

4. Rosalind Krauss, in her analysis of the *Paperweights* series as a miniaturized paradigm of the multistoried interaction between work/context/spectacle/appropriation/preservation, seeks to pinpoint the specific character of Lawler's point of view, its state of being stunned by the mirage it transmits to us. Krauss calls it "the strangely stunned but tender neutrality that one would have to identify as her 'style'," concluding that while Lawler's camera documents all sorts of arbiters influencing the work, especially in terms of dominance, it reveals something else as well: "It also—in the very stillness and distance of its gaze—puts wonder in place. No matter how temporarily and with what ambivalence." See Krauss, "Louise Lawler: Souvenir Memories," in *A Spot on the Wall*, ed. Hedwig Saxenhuber, exh. cat. (Cologne, 1998), 35, 39.

5. The artist has pointed out that her aim is neither subversion nor interference, strategies by now tried, tested, and accredited to the point of being academic, if not downright sterile: "It is no longer a matter of trying to subvert or intrude. Those strategies are now recognized and invited. Now it is a matter of finessing, which is certainly not enough." See Martha Buskirk, "Interview with Louise Lawler [May 20, 1994]," *October*, no. 70 (Fall 1994): 106. Thus Louise Lawler is out to avoid overkill and outright provocation. The injunction issued by the inventory is subdued, low-key, discreet. We find ourselves part of a revealing tableau in which the nature of the revelatory data, despite the latter's obviousness, remains elusive.

6. See Benjamin H. D. Buchloh's description and analysis in "Allegorical Procedures: Appropriation and Montage in Contemporary Art," *Artforum* (September 1982): 48–50.

7. See Louise Lawler's account of this intervention in the interview with Buskirk (see note 5), 107.

8. See the interview with Crimp (see note 2), unpaginated.

9. Ibid.

10. Ibid.

11. Interview with Buskirk (see note 5), 106.

12. Douglas Crimp, *On the Museum's Ruins*, with photographs by Louise Lawler (Cambridge, 1993).

13. These capitalization effects in their museum-related form—where they signify simultaneous accumulations of prestige, donations, tax benefits, and a civic-minded sociability in which private passions turn out to be convertible into public virtues—were indirectly addressed in 1994 in The Label Show exhibition at the Boston Museum of Fine Arts. Louise Lawler's contribution involved the joint presentation of a piece from the museum's collection—eighty-eight ornamental thimbles in their Chippendale display case (legacy of Louise D. Alden) and twelve black and white photographs of the same thimbles, each accompanied by words—"just desserts," "rich rewards," "loot"—inscribed on the passe-partout. See Abigail Solomon-Godeau, "'The Label Show.' Contemporary Art and the Museum," *Art in America* (October 1994): 53. The work was originally produced for and installed in The Enlargement of Attention: "No One Between the Ages of 29 and 35 is Allowed" at the Boston Museum of Fine Arts (1991).

14. The critical literature on Lawler's work is largely made up of essays providing carefully detailed descriptions of the relationship—freshly pinpointed via a tactical displacement—between works of art, their context, their functions, and their values. See notably Andrea Fraser, "In and Out of Place," *Art in America* (June 1985): 122–29; and more recently Dietmar Elger, "Behind the Art Scene with Louise

Lawler," and Thomas Weski, "Art as Analysis: On the Photographic Works of Louise Lawler," both in *Louise Lawler: For Sale*, ed. Dietmar Elger (Ostfildern, 1994), 47–52 and 59–63; also Helmut Draxler, "Art into Culture: Exhibition as a Social Convention," in *A Spot on the Wall* (see note 4), 70–72. A common feature of these interpretations is their emphasis on decoding in terms of sociological contextual categories—data which Lawler's work makes specific use of, but to which it cannot be reduced. Over time a surplus emerges in the subtle admixture of disquiet, uneasiness, cheeky nonchalance, and humor in this critical inversion of representer/represented—an admixture whose precise make-up it would be far from easy to explain. The surplus seems to lie in the tension produced in the slightness of insubstantial things, a tension that renders palpable a discountenanced embarrassment: in the intimation of indecision and perplexity, like a held note that one still hears when the sound has dissipated. All in all we find ourselves faced with an "oeuvre" that in turn creates a semblance—Louise Lawler's *maniera*, which confers a presence on that which does not exist or exists in that place only—or at least a remnant that cannot be absorbed into the sociology of the data, the history of taste and the chronicles of common sense. In the Piercean terms Panofsky uses in setting out to locate aesthetic content, we are back with "that which a work betrays but does not parade" (Erwin Panofsky, *Meaning in the Visual Arts: Papers in and on Art History* [New York, 1955], 14). Whatever the level of derision directed at proper names—as attested by, in addition to *Open*, her *Birdcalls* in which the names of artists are distorted into the sounds of birds—and whatever the pointlessness of the proper name as pure index, as singular statement of a one and only, unequivocally recognizable existence, it nonetheless remains true that via his or her work an artist renames singular: in a non-deducible singularity not precisely describable in terms of the properties of the nameable, these latter being marks of conformism.

15. As George Baker emphasizes in his piece on Lawler's work at Metro Pictures in 1997, the new series of photographs presented for the occasion plays with an identical oscillation between abandon and apotheosis—but this time as applied to exhibition venues in themselves, empty of works: in this case, the very space of the gallery, thematized via its change of site and accompanying renovation. See George Baker, "Paint, Wall, Pictures: Something Always Follows Something Else. She wasn't Always a Statue," *Texte zur Kunst*, no. 26 (June 1997): 88–93.

16. In 1985, for example, an exhibition titled Interesting was followed by another—with slides viewable only at night—called Slides by Night: Now That We Have Your Attention What Are We Going to Say. The proliferation of interstices may reflect not so much an affirmation as an incongruent reflexive stance. In 2000 the installation *More Pictures*, a set of variously colored, variously hung/slanting photographs of Andy Warhol's *Silver Cloud* cushions, bore the title *Something About Time And Space But I'm Not Sure What It Is*.

17. A sly echo of the proliferating recording of images as hesitant indices of consecration by a visual culture on the qui vive, Louise Lawler's "pictures" reflect, in passing, the problem posed by the inordinate diversification of contemporary art. The broadening of its staging encourages an ultimately sociocultural standardization revelatory less of the irreconcilable singularity of the works concerned than of their excessive compatibility. The presence of the work and the very goal of the artistic act both seem buried in a history that is increasingly forgotten, mangled, and abrogated.

18. Interview with Buskirk (see note 5), 106.

MoMA napkin, 1999

Produced for the exhibition The Museum as Muse, The Museum of Modern Art, New York. The five categories printed in black were conceived by Kynaston McShine, the curator of the exhibition. Used at the opening cocktail reception and intended to be available in the cafeteria for the duration of the exhibition.

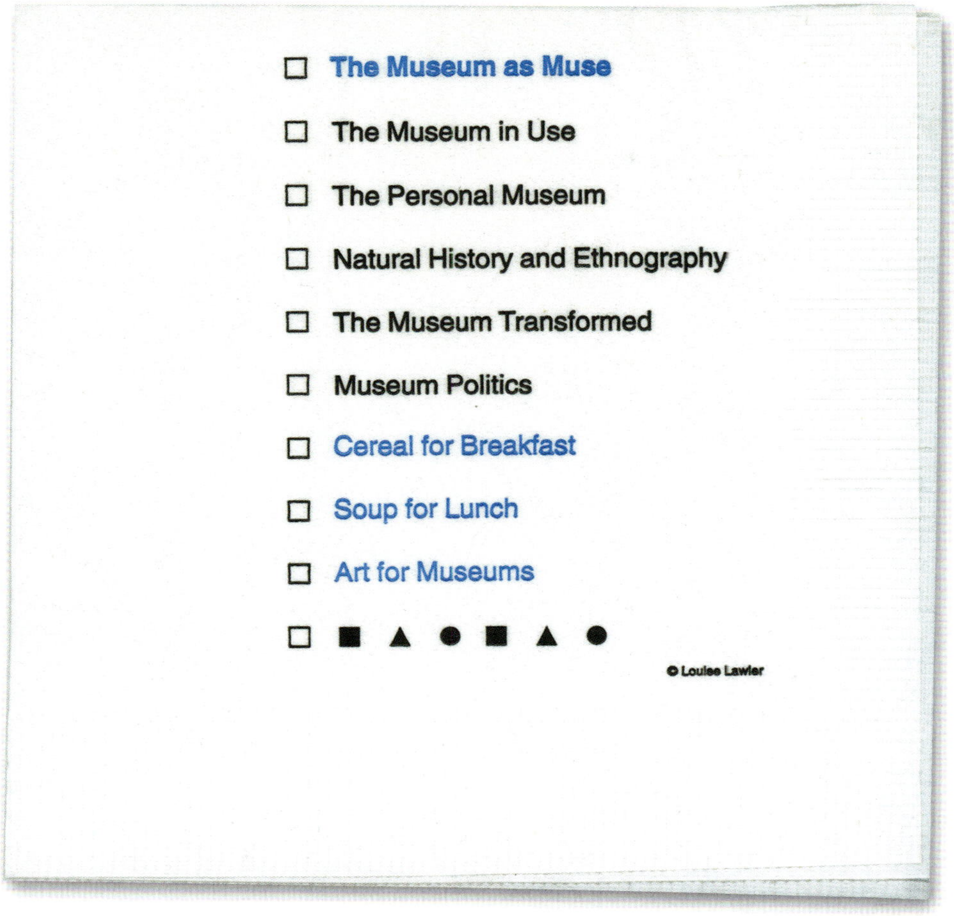

☐ The Museum as Muse

☐ The Museum in Use

☐ The Personal Museum

☐ Natural History and Ethnography

☐ The Museum Transformed

☐ Museum Politics

☐ Cereal for Breakfast

☐ Soup for Lunch

☐ Art for Museums

☐ ■ ▲ ● ■ ▲ ●

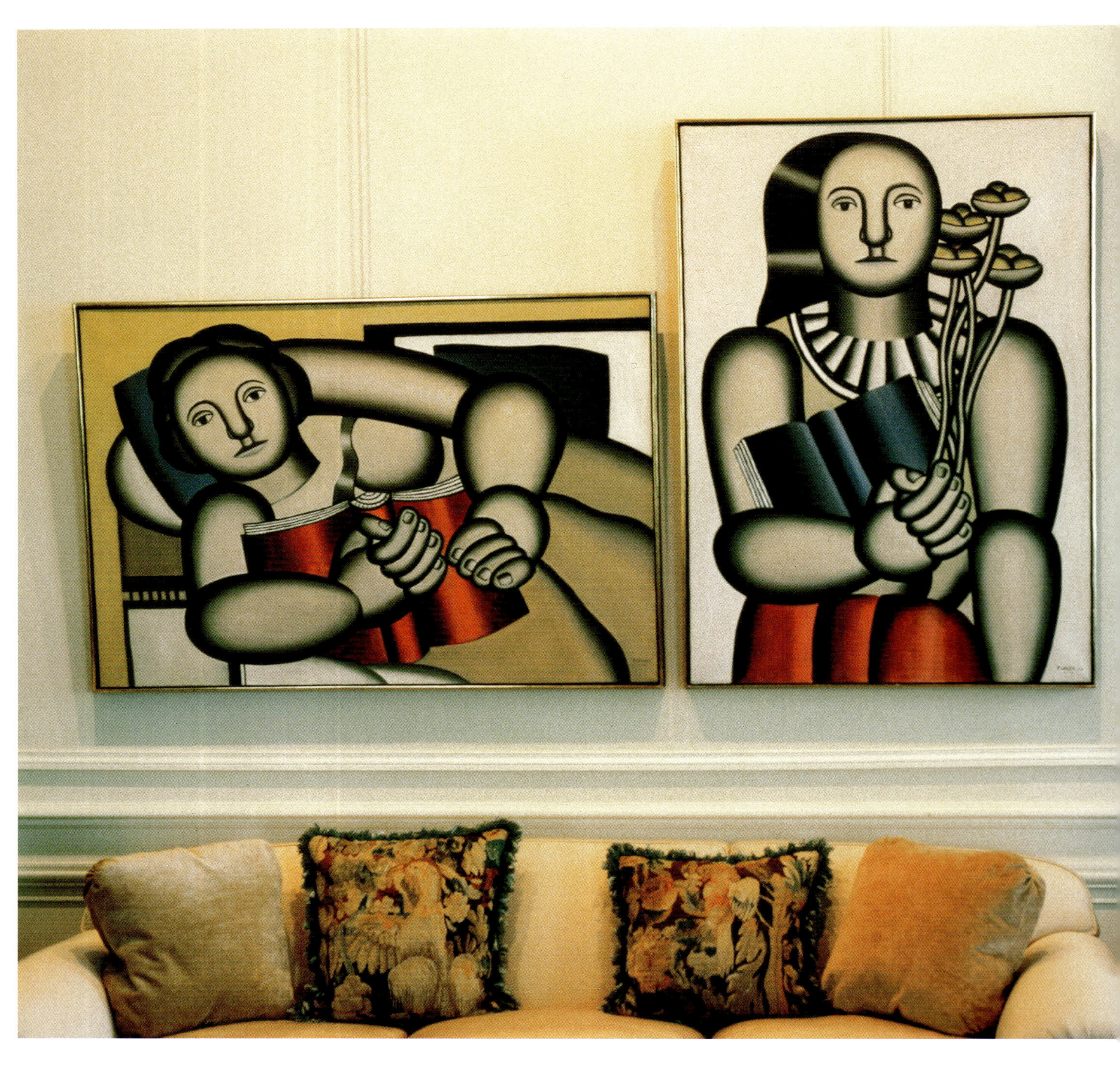

La Lecture, 1924, Femme au Livre, 1924, Positioned together, Tous les Deux, ensemble, New York, 1985
cibachrome, 26 1/2 x 38 1/2 inches

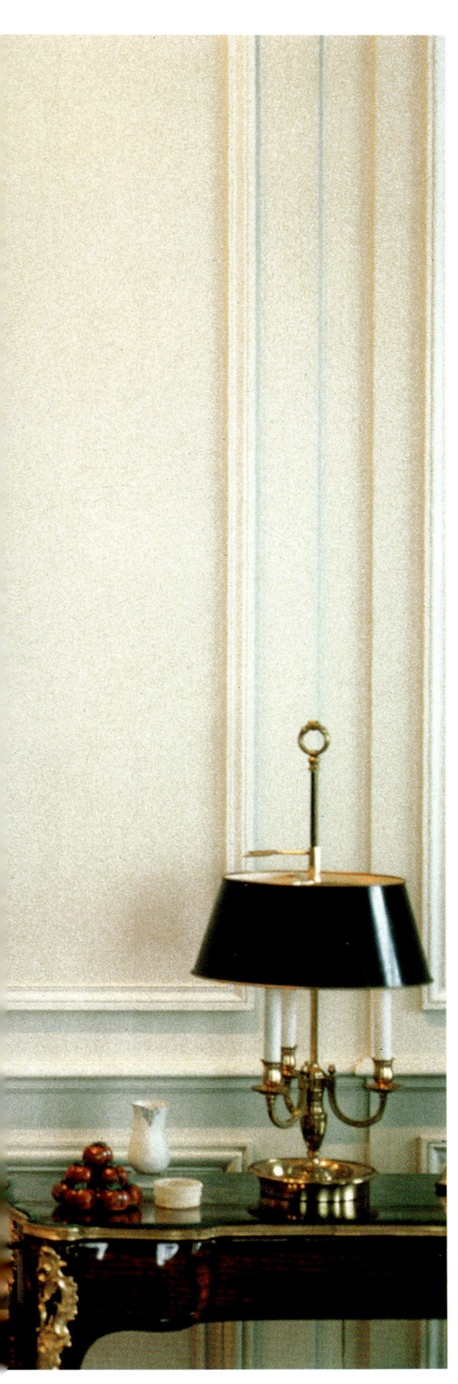

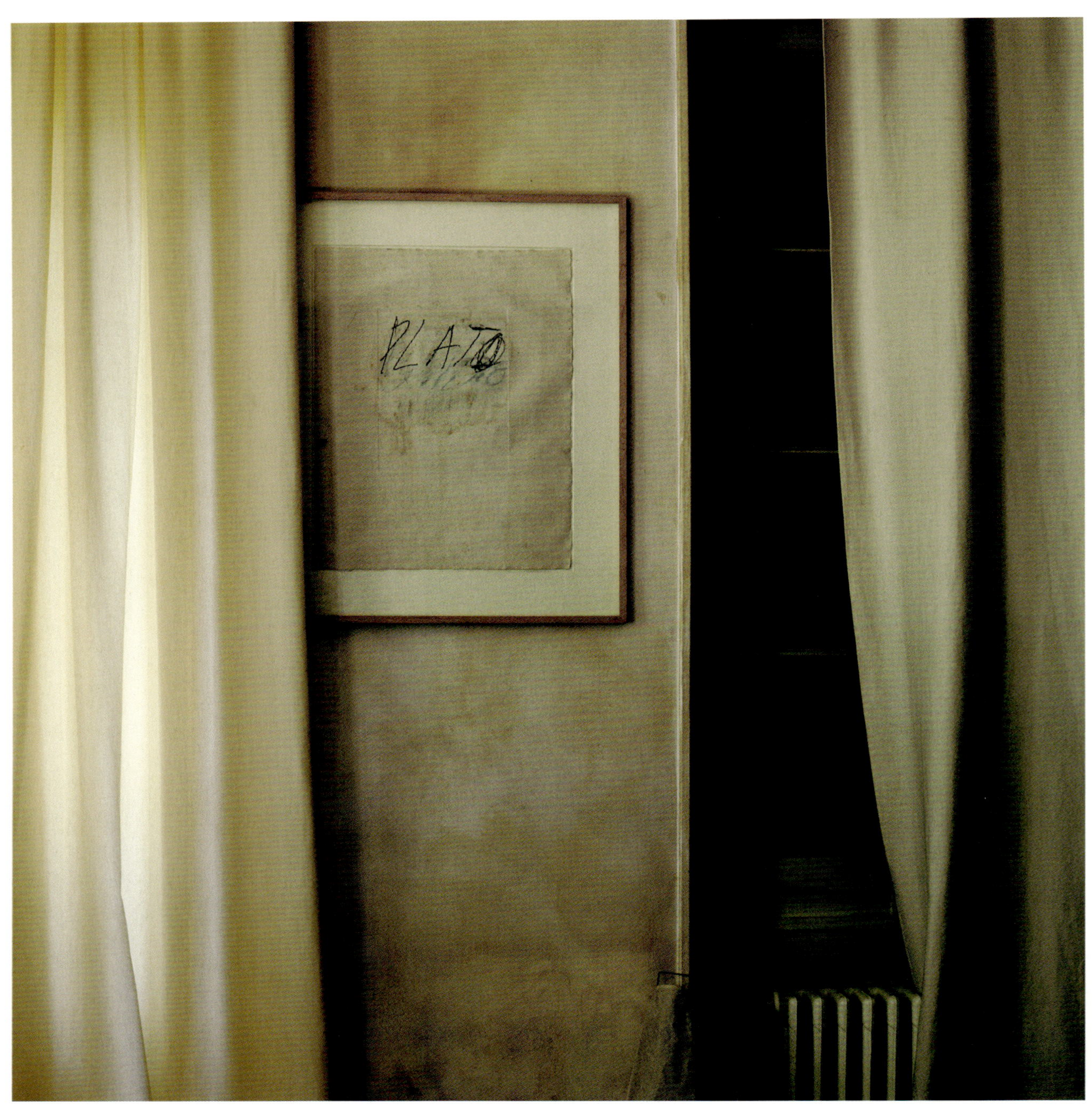

Plato, 2001/2002
digitally produced cibachrome, matted, 26 x 25 inches (image)

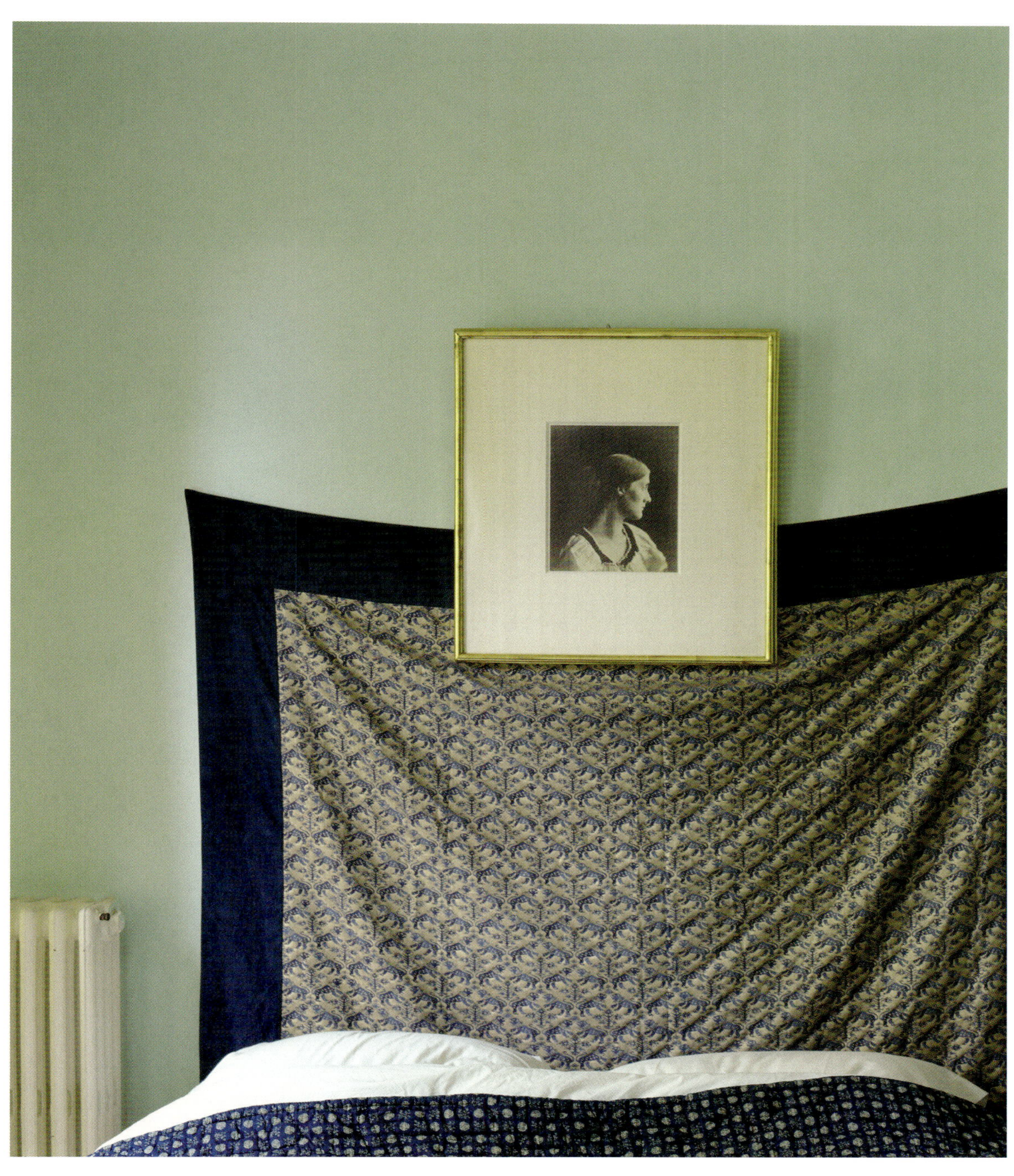

War Is Terror, 2001/2003
cibachrome, 30 x 25 3/4 inches

Still Life (Candle), 2003
digitally produced cibachrome, 13 x 10 3/4 inches

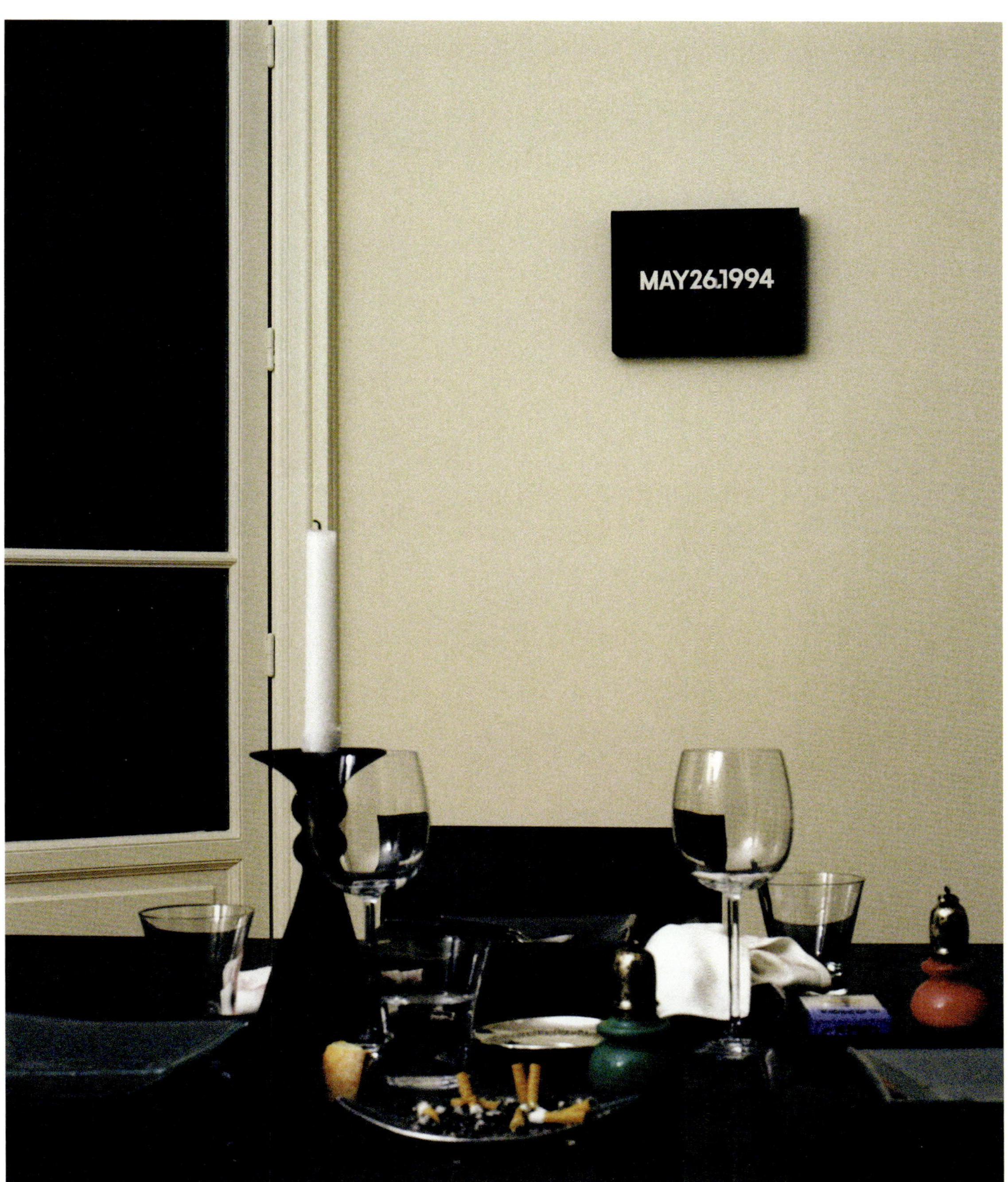
MAY26.1994

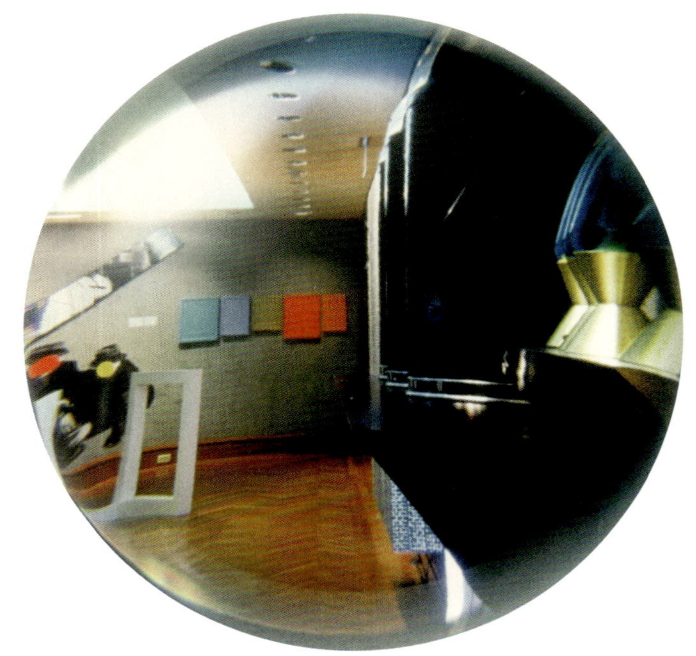

She made no effort to rescue art from ritual

☐ yes ☐ no

Untitled (Happy New Year), 1991/1993
paperweight: cibachrome, crystal, felt, 2 inches high, 3 1/2 inches diameter

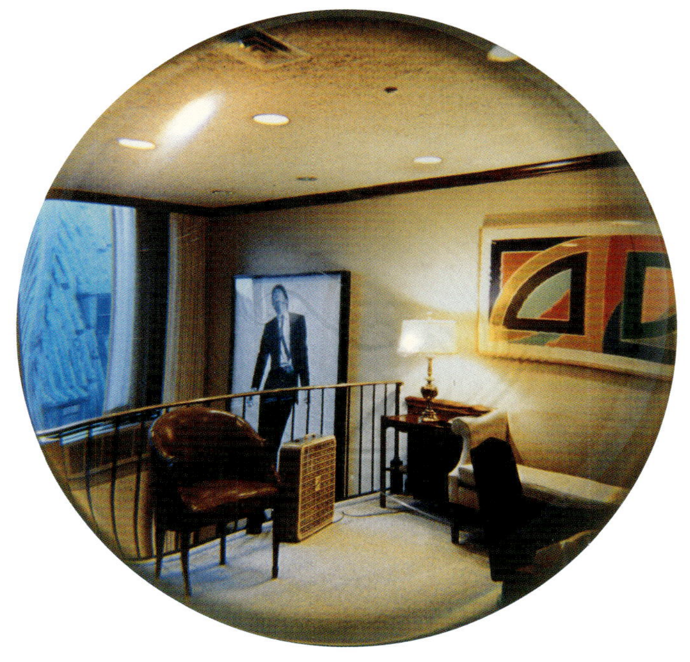

Longo, Stella

Repetitive, purposeful and intentional behaviors which are designed to neutralize or prevent discomfort

Untitled (Reception Area), 1981/1993
cibachrome, crystal, felt, 2 inches high, $3^{1/2}$ inches diameter

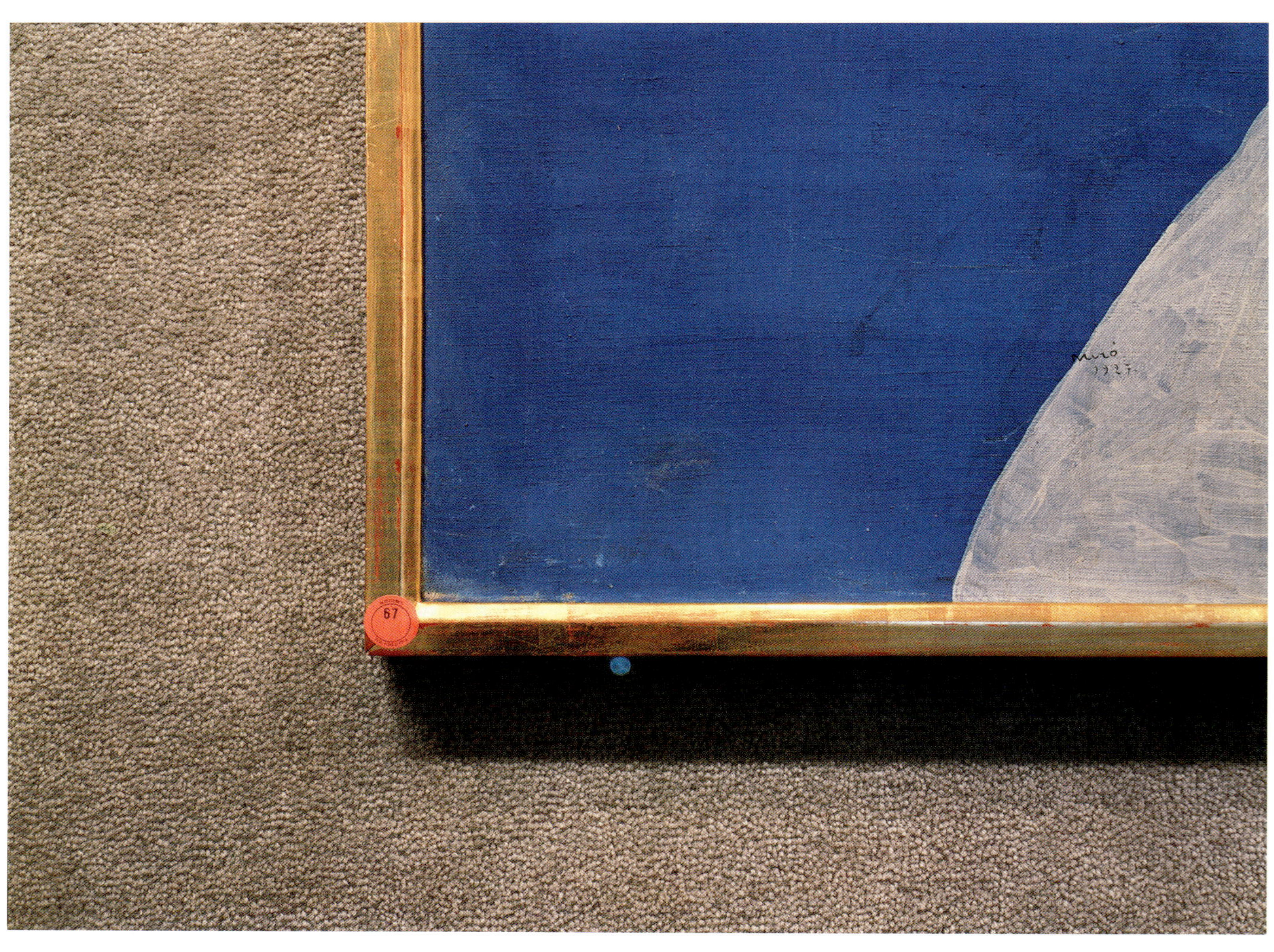

Blue Nail, 1990
cibachrome, 40 x 50 inches

DEDICATION REPLACING APPROPRIATION: FASCINATION, SUBVERSION, AND DISPOSSESSION IN APPROPRIATION ART

Isabelle Graw

1. Active Formation or Parasitic Behavior?

Appropriation is a precondition of artistic work. Appropriation, in the literal sense, is the process of making something one's own property. The Renaissance artists, whose legends were collected by Giorgio Vasari, spent a great deal of time appropriating technical skills and artistic standards, with the aim of surpassing these standards and skills while assimilating them. The majority of them received instruction from teachers: appropriation became organized in the crucial institution of the teacher-pupil relationship. The classical academic study of art can also be interpreted as a lesson in practices of appropriation, considering how much time is spent copying pictures. Copying a picture means no more than to appropriate it by reproducing it, and to thus internalize the knowledge contained in the image. However, this form of appropriated reconstruction remained—still in modernism—oriented toward the production of "originality." When, as a young man, Picasso, for example, copied the Old Masters, this was considered to be a kind of preparatory study, which, although already showing signs of his own handwriting, would at some point be replaced by an "original" visual expression. A work of art that feeds only on appropriation, and even makes this explicit, would have no chance of acknowledgement in this scenario. Something must to be added, something more than simply appropriation that could be described as the artist's own achievement. This system of values, however, was shaken up radically in the 1980s in the course of postmodernism with its questioning of the significance of authorship and originality. Postmodernism was a quotation culture (Fredric Jameson). The definition of art began to change as the notion of genuine creation was lost in favor of "pastiche"—the method that reassembled what was already to be found that Fredric Jameson declared to be one of the main characteristics of postmodern practices.[1] The image of the artist also underwent radical changes: artists were no longer outstanding individuals but instead fell back on an existing stock of images, "making their nest" there. A model of appropriating, parasitic behavior replaced the model of the strong subject that creates something new using its own resources. The artist fed on cultural symbols and was to a large extent dependent on these, while at the same time possessing enormous subversive potential. Biologistic and viral imagery enjoyed considerable popularity both in postmodern theory and in art critical theory and artistic statements.[2] In the case of Peter Halley, this went so far that he wanted his abstract half-tone images to be understood as "cells and conduits," which were meant to visualize the viral dispersion and networking logic of society, and he drew on theorists such as Jean Baudrillard and Michel Foucault as evidencing their existence.[3] According to Halley, these painted cells were intended to be a reference to real cells such as residential buildings or hospital beds, connected to power lines just like these, lines through which vital fluids are able to leave and enter.[4] This analogy between painting and a society based on molecular structures made it possible for painting to lay claim to a close reference to society—a kind of history painting. Subversion metaphors also followed this viral scheme—in the 1980s, the image of the Trojan horse was widespread. The artist duo Clegg & Guttmann stated in an interview that good art should function like a Trojan horse: enticing enough to be let in, and subversive enough later.[5] Thus art disguises itself in order to be able to infiltrate enemy terrain. When it reaches its goal, it unfolds its power to degenerate—like a virus that has infected its host organism. It should be noted that Clegg & Guttmann make no mention of the nature of this subversion and how it is achieved in an artistic context.

2. Extending the Zone of Appropriation

The first break with the prevailing modernist system of beliefs that still continued into the 1980s, and in which appropriation to a certain extent ranked as a preliminary stage before the development of an individual signature, was esteemed to be Duchamp's readymades, and the diverse Duchampian effects of the twentieth century (Pop art, Minimal art, Conceptual art, Appropriation art). Readymades, industrially manufactured objects that have been taken from their functional context and declared a work of art by artists, represent a form of artistic appropriation—a particular type of artistic appropriation to be more exact—which has a special role. Artistic appropriation in this case means to select and take possession, or to declare the object to be one's own work. However, a readymade is not the result of arbitrary selection, as is often alleged. It results much more from the choice of a particular object, and this chosen object is appropriated and taken possession of all at once. Selection and appropriation go hand in hand and each readymade is the embodiment of this appropriating selection. The readymade owes a debt to the appropriating gesture of the artist, and it bears witness to this gesture—to a specific artistic sensibility. The artist has not chosen a random object, but a specific one—in the case of Duchamp the famous pissoir. The object is manipulated in such a manner that it is able to reflect artistic "sensibility." In the case of readymades, something is thus added, for example the title that Duchamp gave to his work of art, which the art historian Thierry de Duve, with good reason, compared to the effect of a color.[6] Readymades are colored with the help of titles, and artistic expression survives in the titles. Thus, on the one hand we can say

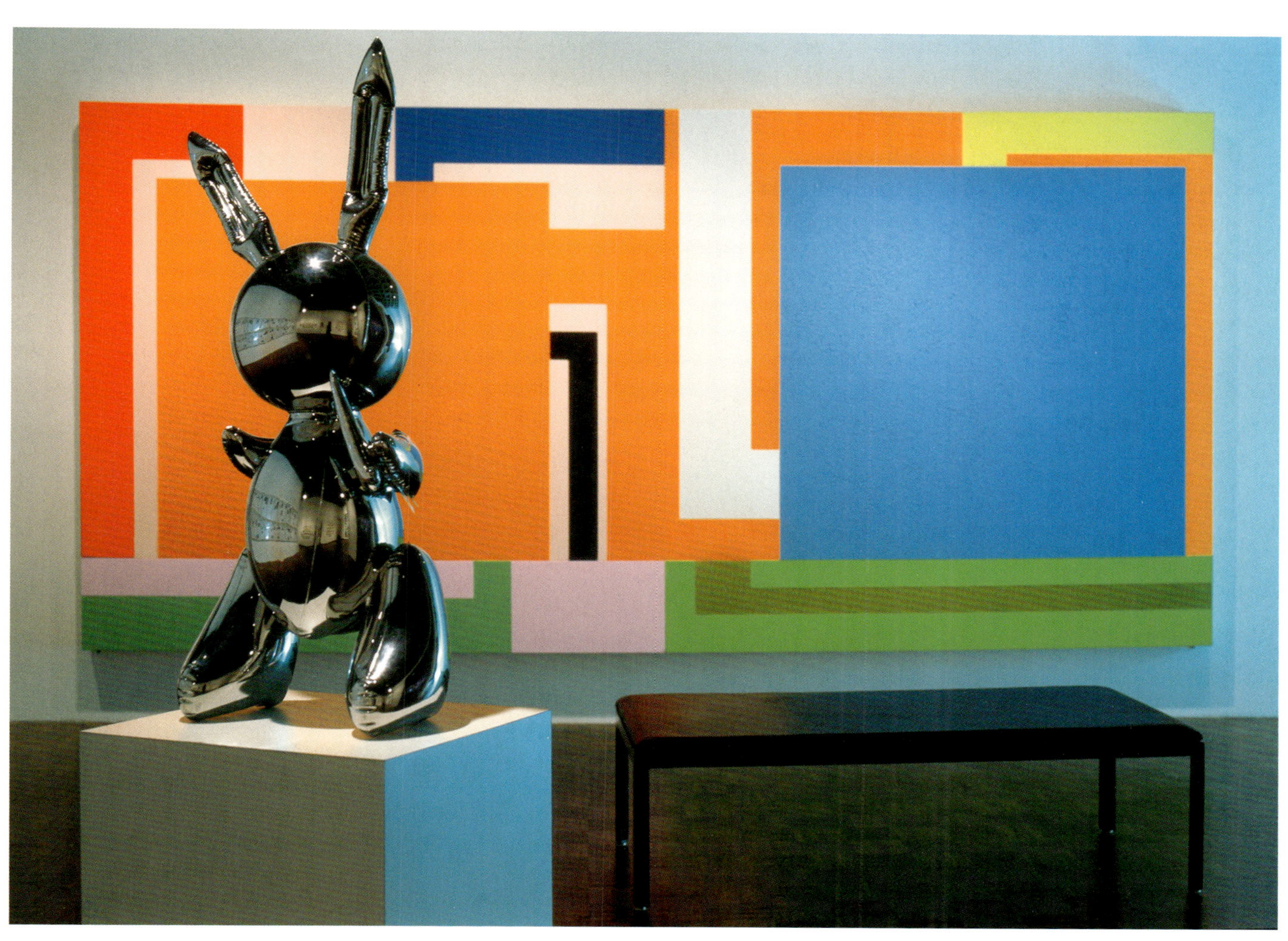

(Bunny) Sculpture and Painting, 1999
cibachrome, $47^{1/2}$ x 66 inches

that Duchamp's readymades historically mark the extension of the zone of appropriation in that they extended the possible area from which objects can be appropriated, while on the other hand, it must be noted that their claim to an individual signature is in no way revoked. The indications for this signature have merely been pushed to the edges of the artistic work. Singularity can no longer be located "immanently," as in the brushstroke. It becomes manifest on the level of the appropriating selection, for example as a signature that has been added to the readymade, or, in the case of Duchamp, a title that suggests a particular meaning. The assumption made by postmodern art critics well into the 1990s, that Duchamp's readymades signaled the "death of the author," cannot really hold its ground when viewed from this perspective. There are too many indications of an active creative author. However, Duchamp's readymades have once and for all broken with the classic expressive ideal that postulates the idea of artists who express themselves in their artistic work. The appropriating—in the sense of selecting and taking possession—artists do not express themselves directly, should they ever have done this at all. On the contrary, they have decided on a particular system of experiments, have set out on a (probably casual) search for an object or a situation that they find worthy of appropriation. Such situations as appear in the works of the artist Louise Lawler—which have been appropriated in a particular manner—are a good example of this. It is appropriate to describe them, in analogy to the Surrealist "objets trouvés," as "situations trouvées" (Johannes Meinhardt).[7] This is because the situations photographed by Lawler are the result of a choice to the extent that the artist came across or found them. They quasi fell into her hands. The idea that, in an artistic practice which is primarily based on appropriation, we are dealing exclusively with goal-oriented action by an active artistic subject with intents and purposes, must be qualified in the light of this perspective. However, the problem is that the majority of art-theoretical appropriation discourse is based on this premise of voluntary action.[8] This does not take into account the fact that the appropriating artists are also pulled along by their object.

3. Appropriation as an Antimodernist Antidote

In one of the primary texts on this subject, the art historian Benjamin Buchloh described appropriation as an "act." The choice of this term is significant, not only because every action obviously requires a subject. More than that, an action assumes a subject that has decided to carry out a particular action and who knows what he or she is doing. Consequentially, a whole heap of cognitive and theoretical intentions and performances is imposed upon this "act": "Each act of cultural appropriation therefore constructs a simulacrum of a double negation, denying the validity of individual and original production, yet denying equally the relevance of the specific context and function of the work's own practice."[9]

Although Buchloh is talking about "cultural appropriation" in general here, these ideas contain the basic art-theoretical claims that were made for artistic appropriation in 1980s, beginning with the negation of "individual and original production" that the "cultural appropriation" is supposed to automatically provide, and leading to the view that this appropriation is in fact a simulation, and is thus merely feigned, a notion that was very widespread at that time, due to the popularity of subversion and simulation theories (Jean Baudrillard, Michel de Certeau). Buchloh's objection that appropriating gestures ignore the context also proved to have prophetic qualities.

The Buchloh quote is enlightening in three respects. Firstly, it stands for the notion that appropriation is an act that can have sociocritical functions imposed upon it. Secondly, the word "simulacrum" points to the at the time remarkably widespread—and today hardly conceivable—influence of Baudrillard's simulation theory, based on the notion of reality made up only of signs, out of control and no longer able to be influenced.[10] Thirdly, with his reference to the disregard of the context that accompanies cultural appropriation, Buchloh formulated a problem that the Context art of the 1990s faced by declaring the context to be an integral part of artistic work.

For progressive American art critics of the late 1970s, the slogan of the time was to challenge autonomy, and "appropriation" was a concept that could be used to contest the hegemony of modernism, embodied by critics such as Clement Greenberg or Michael Fried.[11] In view of a modernist ideology, which assumes a given, immanent law that applies to art, the concept of appropriation was in a position whereby it could become a bearer of new hope. It allowed the modernist claim to immanence to be challenged inasmuch as something "extrinsic" is always added to art in the process of every artistic act of "appropriation." The "immanent" in art can no longer claim to be visibly evident: the boundaries between "internal" and "external" are in a state of flux.

4. Infected by the Object

In the 1980s, the image of an appropriating artist was of someone who encountered a world that only existed as a simulation with a practice of simulation (Peter Halley), an act of appropriation thus always situated on the level of the system of signs.[12] Halley wanted his abstract, colored, cellular pictures to be a representation of this stage in social development, in which the signs float freely and constantly create and reproduce themselves. Like many other artists of his generation, Halley made sure, by means of written statements, that this "content" would be read into his pictures, which led to the most obvious features being disregarded—these were, when it came down to it, variations on the modernist theme of the grid. It was expected even more so of artists that they would take

next page:

Bought in Paris, New York, Switzerland, or Tokyo, 1987
Stella/Brass (detail) *Les Indes Galantes IV*... purchased from a banker, now located on the Blvd. Victor Hugo, 1966/1986

5 cibachrome photographs, transfer type on wall, 23 x 15$^{1/2}$ inches (each image)

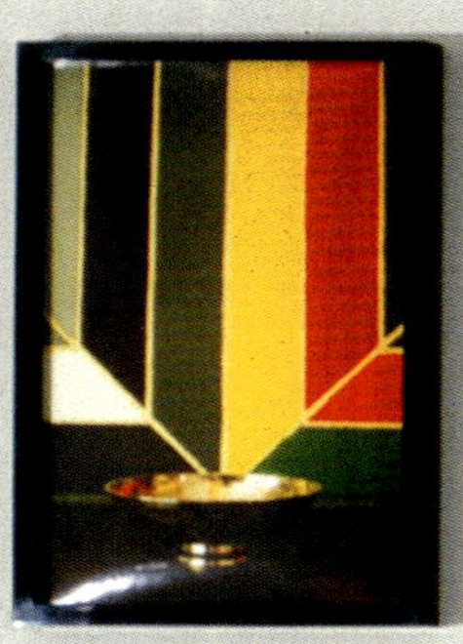
BOUGHT IN

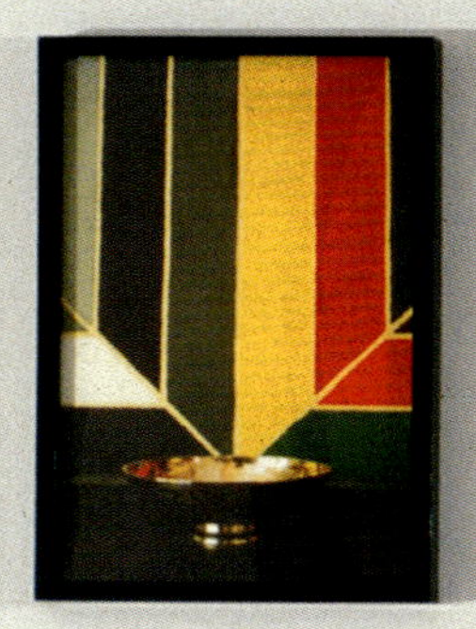
PARIS,
NEW YORK,

SWITZERLAND,

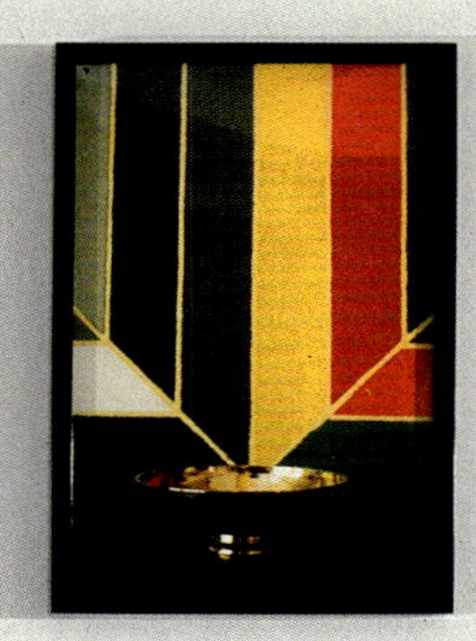

Now located on the Blvd. Victor Hugo
OR

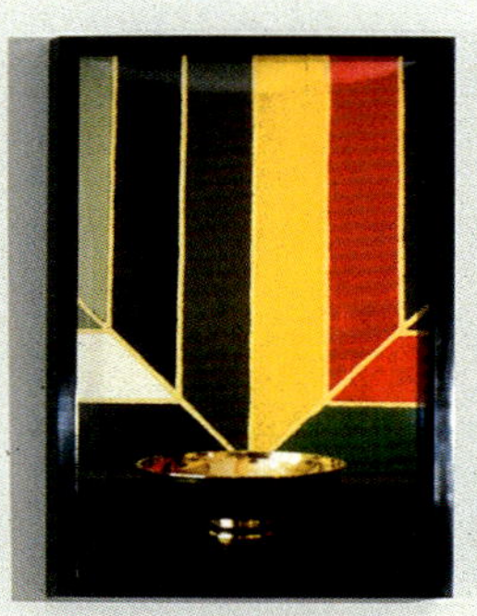

1966/1986
TOKYO

part by means of appropriation in society's generation of signs, although for theorists such as Baudrillard this generation of signs was synonymous with society itself. The objections to this simulation theory, which claimed that society still generated real effects such as exclusion or discrimination, were not voiced until the late 1980s, favoring identity-political approaches. For the time being, people imagined the artist drawing on the diverse forms of "mass culture"—nowadays one would speak more specifically of a "visual culture"—as a source. The central problem of the prevailing understanding of artistic appropriation can be seen precisely in the fact that an instrumental relationship between the appropriating artist and his or her visual material, was, and is, assumed. This began in the 1980s with the idea that the appropriating artist "subversively infiltrates" existing media images, to use a viral metaphor that was common at that time. This operation was considered to be successful at the moment when it had managed to "permeate" the "immune system" of the "body" like a stealthily spreading virus. One example for the viral metaphors that were widespread then, and still are now, can be found in an entry in a dictionary of art historical terminology, which reads: "When an appropriation does succeed, it works silently, breaching the body's defenses like a foreign organism and insinuating itself within, as if it were natural and wholly benign."[13] The possibility that this body would activate its powers of resistance and fight back against that which the artist had appropriated, was not taken into account at all. Instead, the artistic subject and its power to act were, with hindsight, incredibly overrated. This even went so far as to say of the appropriating artist that he or she was intervening, an association that drew parallels to state intervention. Every time a work of art seemed to suggest that an artist could also perhaps be fascinated or even overwhelmed by his or her material, then this was seen as a danger, perhaps even the greatest danger of appropriation.[14] The appropriating artists who allowed themselves to be overwhelmed by their own material had given up and joined the enemy camp, so the theory went. The idea that the "enemy" who had been infiltrated could also to all intents and purposes be stubborn, had no place in the theory of appropriation prevalent at the time, in which appropriation was seen as a unilateral act. To allow the appropriated material even a minimum of own momentum would have meant falling back on modernist premises, and this, as already indicated, was to be avoided at all costs. For this reason, neither the appropriated material and its specific character, nor the process of appropriation itself was examined in detail.[15] After all, the belief that something emanated from the material, and that it made certain claims of its own, was the modernist credo par excellence—a credo which was to be rejected due to its mystical connotations. In order to avoid misunderstandings: I have no desire to promote a return to modernist premises; however, in my view, the modernist conviction that material has its own ambience can be seen productively and in a way that is not mystical. Rather than regarding appropriation as a process controlled by one side only, it can be seen as a process of mutual influence, in which the dynamic of

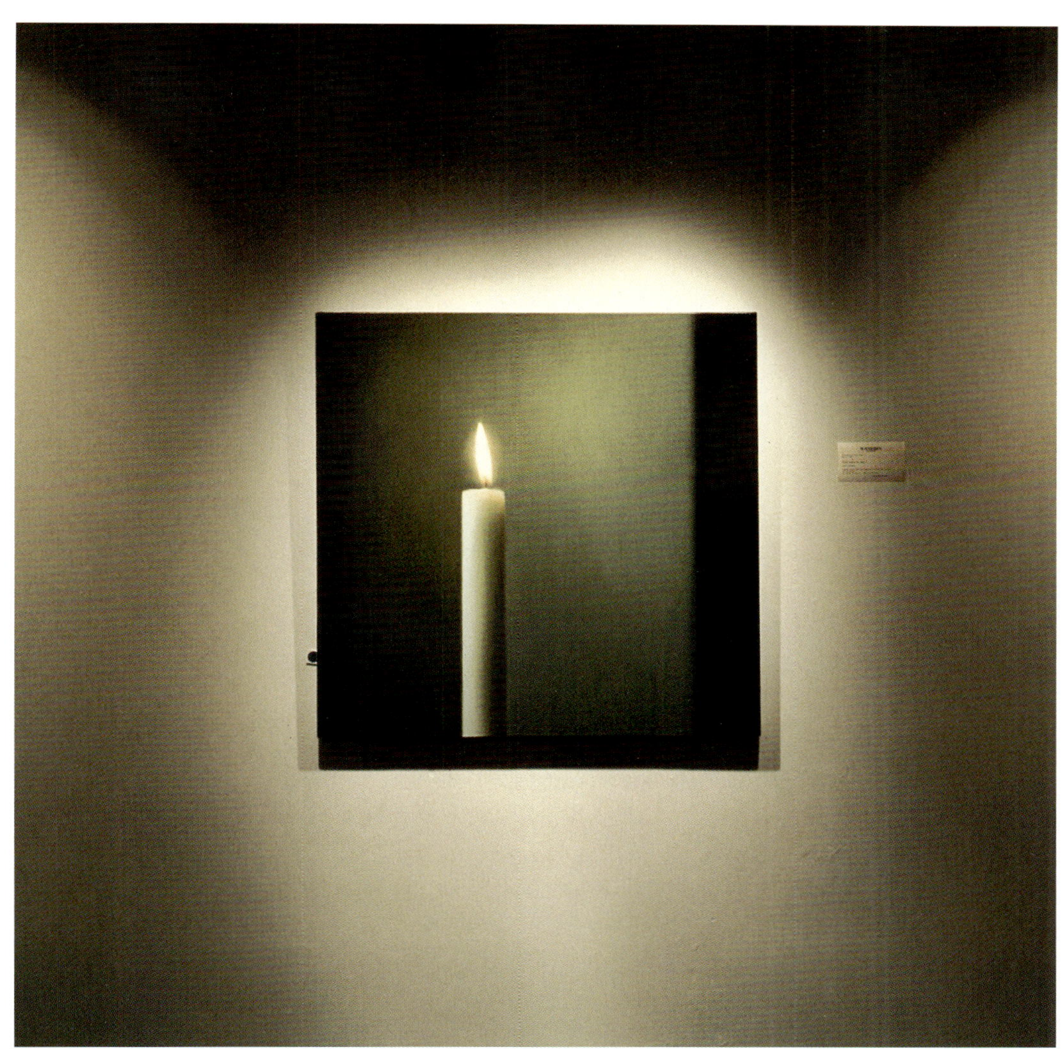

What Else Could I Do, 1994
cibachrome, 24 x 24 inches

the appropriated material is transferred to the appropriator.

Thus I would propose an interpretation of artistic appropriation that allows the appropriated material a certain momentum, and in which the possibility that the artist is enthused by this dynamic is feasible. This material can also have the form of an institution with which artists see themselves confronted, if for example they have an exhibition in a gallery. Institutions have particular specifications, especially for practices that are circumscribed with terms such as "institutional criticism" or "location specifics." Thus one could say that the institution-critical approach—such as that of Michael Asher—continues to be led and influenced by the appropriated institution. Louise Lawler pointed out this power held by the appropriated institutions in an interview, when she said that her early exhibition An Arrangement of Pictures (in which she appropriated the work of other artists from the gallery, by photographing or presenting them) was virtually molded by the gallery Metro Pictures. "I self-consciously made work that 'looked like' Metro Pictures," she says.[16] Thus when situations not only make particular specifications but also generate methods of appropriation, this must have an unavoidable effect on the term appropriation. Appropriation must now be understood as a form of dedication—because the situation appears to be dedicated to the appropriator—it is a situation with which the appropriating artist is confronted as if it were meant to be. This kind of reconstruction of the concept of appropriation is particularly useful for artistic production. Because the moment an artist appropriates something—be it an illustration from advertising, or the situation in the home of a collector—then this something has, in a certain way, fallen into his or her hands. This can be clearly demonstrated using the example of the history of readymades. When Duchamp selected and appropriated everyday objects, these were supposedly products of a chance encounter; at least that is how he himself depicted it, as if these objects—which could be a cellaret or a comb—had forced themselves upon him unexpectedly while he was walking through department stores or strolling past shop windows in Paris. Apart from the fact that such statements by artists, which have also been made by contemporary artists such as David Smith or Christopher Wool, are variations on the topos of "inspiration"—the classic myth of the artist—they also record something fundamental: the other face of appropriation, the moment of dedication ascribed to it. A person who appropriates an object is also faced with something that emanates or appears to emanate from that object. The object infects the person and something transfers from it to the person. The advantage of this view is that it refers specifically to artistic production. Whereas abstract and schematic subversion theory declared the artist to be the only agent of subversion and paid no heed to the tension resulting from the appropriated material, here appropriation becomes a process in which the artistic subject bargains with something that has unpredictable consequences.

Another advantage of this reformulated concept of appropriation for investigations of contemporary art is that it allows art to be thought of as a complex interactive relationship. By this I do not mean that art is sufficiently described by the idea of a relationship of appropriation, or that art consists entirely of this relationship. However, if appropriation implies both the conscious formation by the subject as well the subject's dependence on something external, then this describes a tension that is generally present in artistic work. Every work of art in which appropriation plays a role—and it can be assumed that in works of art nowadays, the artists make no secret of their uses of appropriation, but rather display them—shows traces of subjective formation and also visible traces of the effects of extrinsic laws. The latter can result both from the model of the appropriated material and from institutional constraints. Yet this understanding of appropriation as interaction amounts to a necessary break with the perception common since the 1980s that appropriation was an instrumental relationship to the world—a perception that is even more remarkable for the fact that it is completely contrary to poststructural theory at the time, which heavily influenced art theory. At that time, instrumental reason was being challenged, as was the notion of a subject with the power to act autonomously. Thus, according to this, every act of appropriation would amount to putting the subject in its place. It generates dependency and amounts to a surrender to something. Being infected by something leads to a loss of control.

5. The Appropriation of Appropriation Art

The term appropriation has been through countless stages in cultural history—from a negative to a positive coding. Initially, it stood for something that should be rejected, for a colonialist appropriation of the world or control by the art market or culture industry. In the 1980s it gained a new, more positive meaning in the light of the artistic practices, mainly in New York, that were subsumed under the label Appropriation art.[17] Before this, Pop art had extended the appropriation principle of the readymade, so that it seemed as if the appropriating artists potentially had everything—the entire collection of images in our visual culture—at their disposal. Appropriation art continued from this point, except that now the clearly visible artistic manipulation of media images, such as in Warhol's screen prints that he later painted over, were no longer a criterion, or, more to the point, were no longer supposed to be a criterion. The dictionary defines Appropriation art as having "the strategic appropriation of other images as the largest common denominator."[18] By definition, appropriation should thus always be strategic, implying goal-oriented behavior and a confident subject in control. Another notion of the subject, which sees the subject as being divided or as having failed, has no place in such an understanding of appropriation, and the fact that something might happen to the artist during the process of appropriation is also not taken into account.

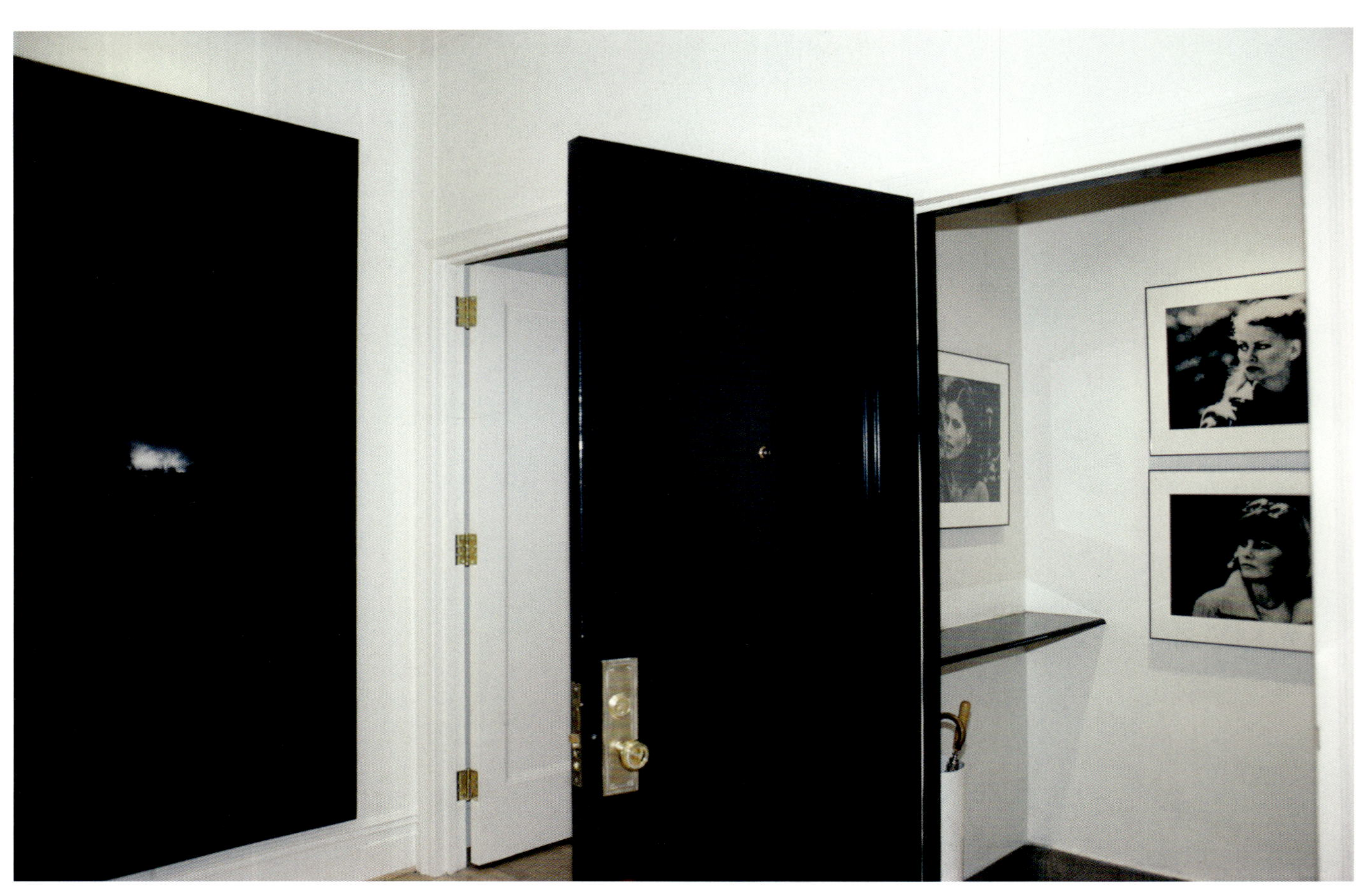

Arranged by Barbara and Eugene Schwartz, 1982
cibachrome, 30 x 40 inches

Artists such as Sherrie Levine, Louise Lawler, and Richard Prince are—with good reason—considered to be pioneers in this field; Prince had already begun to photograph publicized advertisements as far back as the late 1970s, in a manner that further enhanced their glamour. He presented these "re-photographs" as his work. Louise Lawler's works are based less on the media, but rather the concrete public and private location of art. Her works are a photographic glance into interiors, a glance that seems detached, yet at same time fetishizes. Sherrie Levine on the other hand specialized in the different means of reproducing works of art that have become famous—for example the photos of photos by Walker Evans, or drawings by Egon Schiele that have been torn out of catalogues or photocopied. Levine's appropriating practice in particular seemed to depend a great deal on the cultural significance of the appropriated originals. Yet in the same way that she drew artistic legitimacy from the respective artist's names (Feininger, Schiele, Evans), these culturally charged originals were whisked through a specific artistic process: with titles for the pictures (*After Walker Evans*) and delicate passe-partouts which framed them in an unmistakable manner—a visual signature that initially went completely unnoticed in the reception of Levine's work, for reasons which had to do with the previously mentioned phobia toward modernism.[19] What counted were the political implications of her work that people automatically wanted to see in the "denial of authorship and production."

Production and reception have never been as intertwined as in New York in the late 1970s and early 1980s. The exchange that took place between the fine artists and the art historians who appreciated their work was very intensive.[20] The artists and critics spoke the same language, read, according to Levine's recollections, the same books by poststructural authors, and cooperated with one another. A reflection of this was the regular cooperation for example between Louise Lawler and Douglas Crimp—an art critic who earned a reputation as a writer on Appropriation art very early on. Thus a collective point of reference was created, and Roland Barthes's essay "The Death of the Author" was one of the most important reference parameters. Theory and practice were constituted interactively, and nowadays it is difficult to say what was there first: the concept of appropriation or an artistic practice that first and foremost wanted to determine itself via appropriation and favored the transformation of appropriation into an allegorical figure of criticism. It is, however, certain that two things came together at the same time: artists who took recourse to media originals in the tradition of Dada and Pop and seemingly left it at that, and critics who combined a particular approach with the concept of appropriation—the antimodernist repoliticization of art. There was also a common foe—Neo-Expressionism—a synonym for the up-and-coming *wilde Malerei* that people believed should be fought against because it seemed to be taking over the art market. Painters such as Julian Schnabel or David Salle were seen as a threat because their paintings did not hide the fact that they were based on particular other original paintings (Polke, Picabia). Attempts were made to discredit

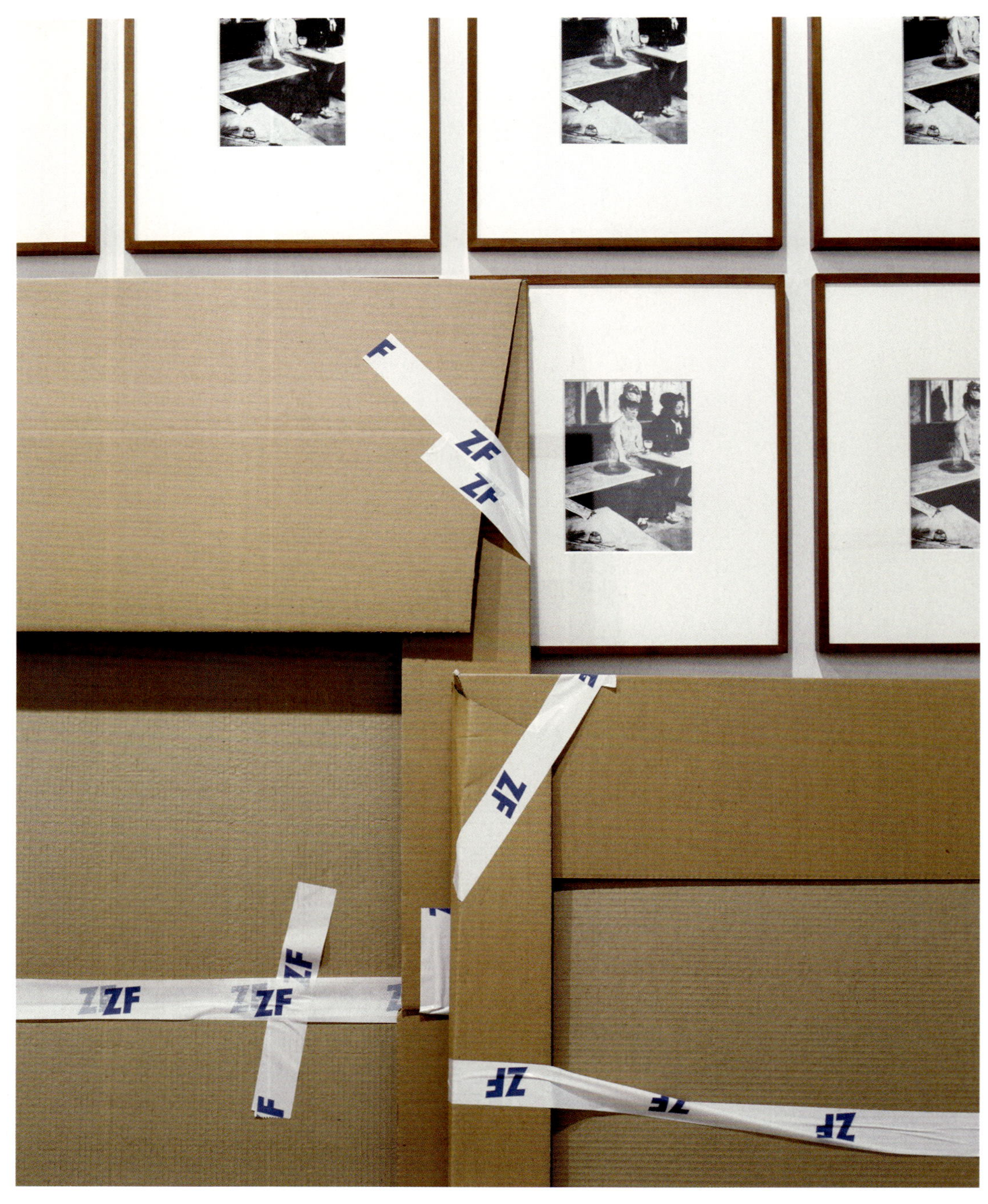

Absinthe, 2003/2004
cibachrome, 30 x 23 3/4 inches

this form of painterly appropriation by dismissing it as pastiche. In the heat of the battle, however, there was a failure to distinguish between very different painting practices. Everything was thrown into the same pot, from Salomé through to Baselitz and Kippenberger, and written off as Neo-Expressionism. Believing oneself to be surrounded by an enemy—which nowadays can no longer be clearly defined—had the advantage that it unified the protagonists. The publication *Art After Modernism* is a witness to this unity between the theorists (Rosalind Krauss, Benjamin Buchloh, Douglas Crimp, Craig Owens) and the artists (Martha Rosler, Thomas Lawson) in the struggle against modernism and *wilde Malerei*.[21] Louise Lawler was responsible for selecting and arranging the images for this book in collaboration with its editor, Brian Wallis.

6. Appropriation as Subversion, a Criticism of Language, and Replacement

Since the 1980s, scarcely any distinction has been made between "artistic appropriation" and "appropriation" in the sense of a fundamental way of relating to the world. The question of what is specifically artistic about appropriation ceases to be valid if appropriation is seen as critical (in the sense of a criticism of language) or subversive per se. The general understanding of Appropriation art is still influenced by this critical-subversive emphasis today; this even goes as far as the current lexical definitions that describe the act of artistic appropriation itself as "re-coding" or a "shift in meaning."[22] This means that a shift in meaning takes place purely due to the fact that an original image has been appropriated. The interest in how artistic appropriation takes place did not begin until the end of the 1980s, because then it became necessary to differentiate between "good" and "bad" appropriation. With such a large number of artists—such as David Salle, Julian Schnabel, Philip Taaffe, Jeff Koons, and Haim Steinbach—all riding the ticket of appropriation, a set of criteria was required. The critic Douglas Crimp, who had more or less "given birth" to Appropriation art with his legendary exhibition Pictures, admitted that critics had made things a little too simple for themselves by maintaining that appropriation was per se critical.[23] The scheme that he now offered, however, was no less arbitrary and also tended to quick conclusions. Crimp suggested that a distinction be made between a simple appropriation of style and an appropriation of the material, whereby the latter was to be accepted and the former rejected. This "criterion" also seemed to remain abstract, not taking into account the concrete aesthetic phenomena and not making strong enough distinctions. Is it not the case that every "appropriation" inevitably adapts the style of the original, whatever kind that original might be? And, if style cannot be avoided, what would be so bad about that? Could the appropriation of a style not lead to the open display and emptying out of the style, as is demonstrated in David Salle's pictures in their appropriating reference to Picabia or Polke? The works of

Sherrie Levine or Louise Lawler can also be seen to over-answer to a certain extent the style of the art they have appropriated. The fact that the artist might not have an entirely critical and detached view of the originals was an idea that did not easily go hand in hand with the main critical assumption, not least because criticism implies a critical distance. On closer examination, Levine's careful, if not affectionate, copy of a drawing by Egon Schiele indicates a relationship charged with obsessive fascination, which would presuppose another critical term. This applies equally to Louise Lawler's photographs, which also witness a relationship based on fascination.[24] Here, the object is seen both casually, while at the same time through the eyes of a lover. The idiosyncratic, detached perspectives, and pictures of installations which seem to have been taken in passing, and the arbitrary and seemingly abrupt sections all speak for the gaze of a connaisseur.[25] Richard Prince's photos were all the more suspect for progressive critics the more they were clearly indebted to personal fascination, as for example the photos in *Biker Girls*.[26] In the case of Levine the logic of subversion was taken to extremes: even as far as to celebrate her work as theft, and thus to confuse it with a criminal act.[27]

"Confiscation" was another very popular metaphor for appropriation, one that is characteristic inasmuch as it bestows on the artist the confiscating power of a state authority.[28] This metaphor also marks the lack of interest in the appropriated object.

7. Appropriating Dispossession

It cannot be said often enough that the understanding of appropriation in the 1980s was based on the Marxist interpretation of the term. In retrospect, it really does seem as if capital was deliberately made of the Marxist background, for example when the artist Sherrie Levine was celebrated for the fact that she dispossessed the male artists whose work she appropriated.[29] In the *Manifesto of the Communist Party*, Marx and Engels had proposed the "abolition of property" as the first measure to be taken,[30] and more that a hundred years later, such a method of dispossession was believed to be possible of artistic works. It was as if Levine had robbed the male artists of their male privileges and their status of genius. Artistic appropriation became a legitimate, in this case feminist motivated, countermeasure. In the same way that the Marxist background played into the understanding of appropriation, the concept of appropriation was also subject to significant changes in the course of its usage in Appropriation art. It increased in value and took a turn for the better. Whereas appropriation had been the central problem of society for Marx—the *Communist Manifesto* contains an appeal to break with existing forms of appropriation—it was now the case that artistic appropriation was ascribed sociocritical power. While for Marx appropriation was simply the form in which exploitation took place, because capital appropriated alienated

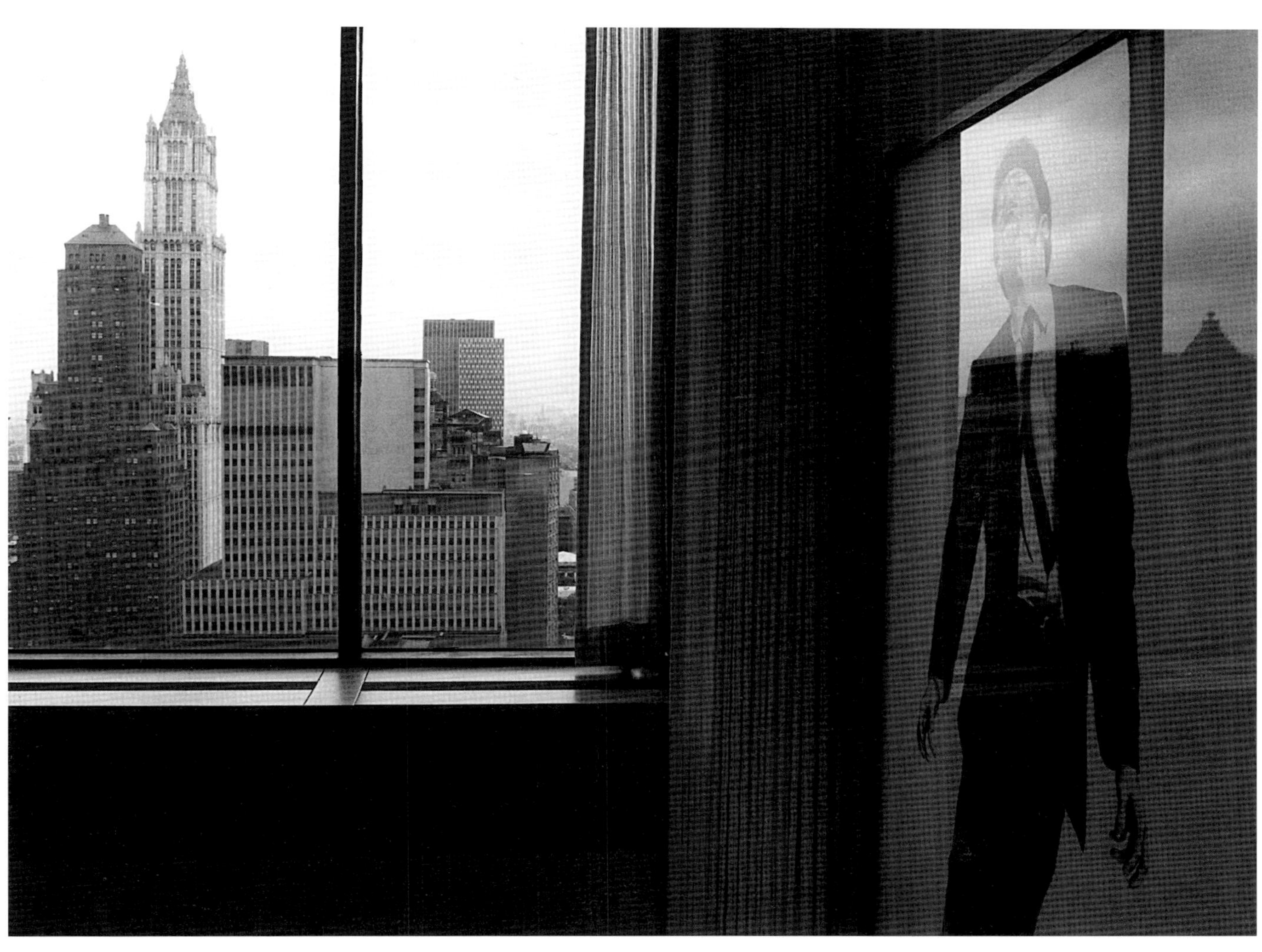

Arranged by Donald Marron, Susan Brundage, Cheryl Bishop at Paine Webber Inc., 1982
black and white photograph with title as text on mat, 17 1/4 x 23 1/4 inches (image)

labor, alienating and dispossessing the workers from their own appropriation of the product of their labor, artistic appropriation of Appropriation art now—under conditions of private property, alienation, and totalized spectacle culture—became a legitimate and necessary method: a kind of self-defense. That which Marx believed should be abolished, in order to achieve "real appropriation," was now one of the inevitable preconditions that could at least be artistically appropriated.

The objection at this juncture could be, with good reason, that artistic appropriation is something completely different to the Marxist understanding of "appropriation through labor." Is it not the case that artists, in contrast to workers, have the possibility to transfer the appropriated object naturally into their work, for which they can then claim authorship? And is their work not in principle less alienated—even under conditions of the art market and the productions of commodities? This is certainly the case, whether the artist experiences his or her work as alienating or not. Even those artistic attempts to programmatically stylize art into an externally determined or impersonal venture—such as Conceptual art—ultimately come to be seen as a product of their "creator."

Referring to Feuerbach, Marx had pointed out that work could not function without its objects.[31] However, he did not pay any particular attention to these objects or their potential for resistance. Under the conditions of the abolishment of private property, he imagined "real appropriation," in which the worker would no longer be dispossessed through his or her product and in which alienation was eliminated. The concept of appropriation today also continues to be determined by this ideal of "real appropriation"—inasmuch as there was scarce interest in the appropriated objects, with instead a concentration on the appropriating subject of the artist and the question of whether or not this subject had committed the act of appropriation with an affirmative or a critical intention. It was the artistic subject that was important; the subject should also be in the position to give appropriation another (critical and subversive) direction. In other words, this means that the appropriating artist was seen as not only having the power to appropriate particular objects or situations (beyond their concrete resistance and momentum), but in addition, the object or situation that was dispossessed and now appropriated could even experience a transformation of meaning. Appropriation became a method that one assumed would stand up to alienation. This was due to the concept of a strong artistic subject, which ultimately would remain in control of the situation. And yet the signs of alienation, which restricted the power to validity of the subject, were unmistakable. Private property, for example, was more than just intact in New York in the 1980s. This was the period of the real estate boom, frenetic consumerism, and high growth rates. Nonetheless, the artist was supposed to be able to master this situation by engaging with it and giving it more potency.[32] The notion of a strategy of surpassing began here, and since then this strategy has been frequently drawn on in art theory debates. This strategy also assumes a powerful artistic subject that fights back using the same methods and attempts to

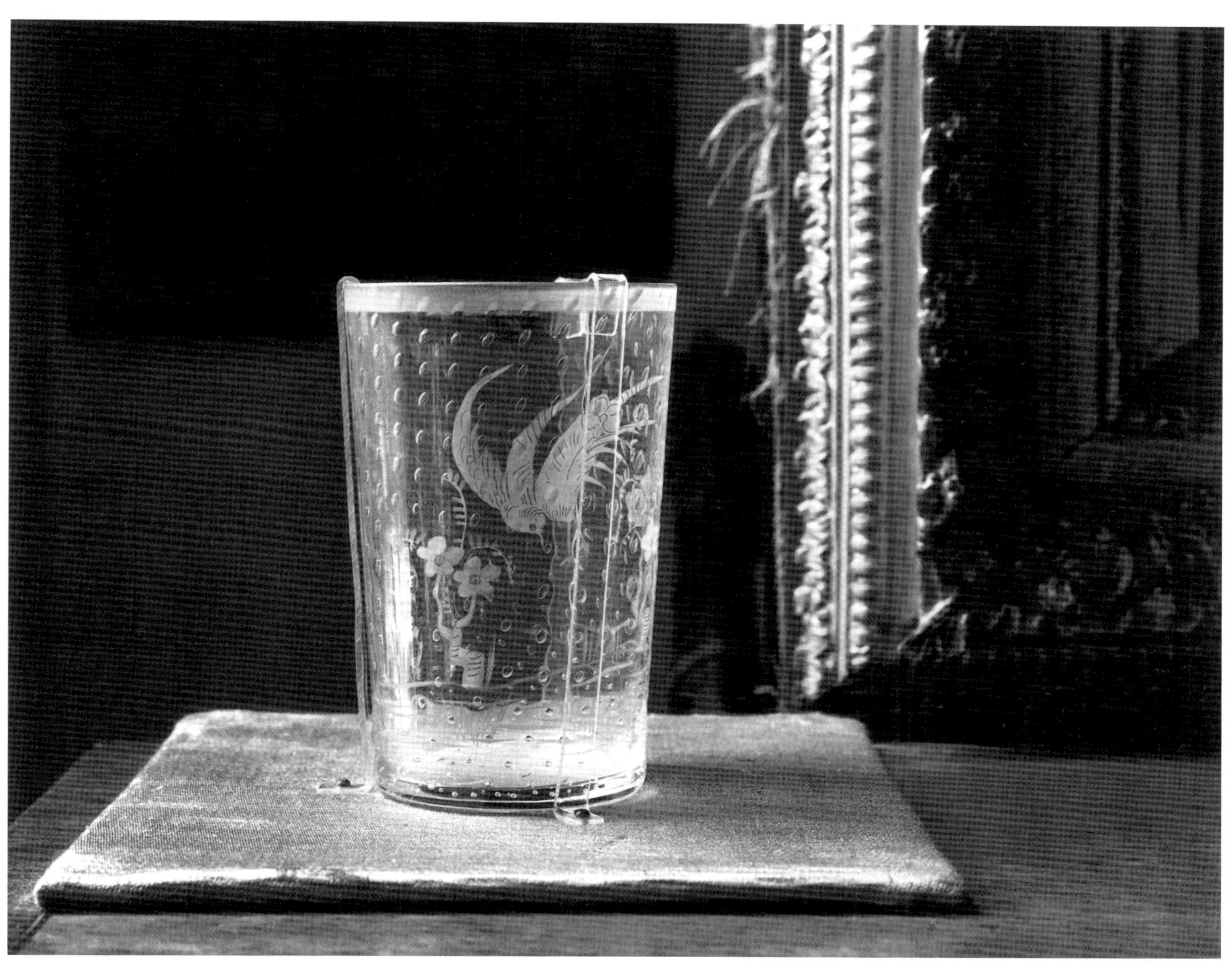

A Drinking Glass, 1989/1990
black and white photograph with title as text on mat, $9^{15/16}$ x $12^{5/8}$ inches (image)

surpass that which it struggles against. It is true that appropriating artists continue the logic of the appropriated object where appropriate, particularly since the object is approached from an artistic angle. However, here it is also necessary to concede that the object always displays a moment that is extrinsically determined. Yet it is exactly this idea of a confrontation between the subject and its alienation that is played down in favor of a concept of appropriation, which—as had already been the case in Marx—is seen one-dimensionally as a process of "taking," and, what is more, then goes a step further by claiming that this "taking" is automatically critical. That artists who appropriate also subject themselves to the object has been blotted out of this scenario, where in the long run only the assets count.

It was the Italian philosopher Giorgio Agamben who further twisted the spiral of appropriation, with his suggestion that alienation itself could be appropriated.[33] He put forward this theory in the book *Means Without End*, raising the possibility that humankind may appropriate their own historical being, their alienation, themselves. Seen from this perspective, the idea of not being in control of oneself is a status quo that cannot be reversed. Appropriation provides the possibility to find a stance vis-à-vis this status quo, to appropriate it. Yet whatever is appropriated in this manner will always remain alienated. According to this, there is no possibility to come to oneself, something that Marx still believed in, and something that was implicitly taken up by the apologists of Appropriation art. On the other hand, this theory makes it possible to work from this point of alienation, to work with it. Alienation becomes a premise that cannot be shaken.

Aside from the questionable tendency to make alienation a kind of law of nature, this model has the advantage of being able to draw appropriation and alienation together and take into account the fact that they are interdependent. Numerous artists in the 1990s have used this as a starting point, by either appropriating the alienated identity that has been ascribed to them (Renée Green), or by allowing the boundaries between the real and the alienated to constantly shift, as Andrea Fraser does in her performances. In the end, however, these options remain within the logic of property that Marx wanted to abolish. Are they therefore ultimately accomplices of the idea that capitalism is here to stay? To propose this would amount to assuming an intention, which artistic work cannot be reduced to in any case. These approaches rather represent an attempt to find a productive attitude toward a situation that no one believes can be unilaterally changed. After all, this situation has influenced us all too. But at that moment when it is artistically appropriated, and an attitude toward it is found, something has changed. What has actually changed can only be determined by investigating concrete, specific works. In a society that is based on private property—and it is this kind of society that we are dealing with at the moment—it appears that there is no way around this "appropriation of dispossession."

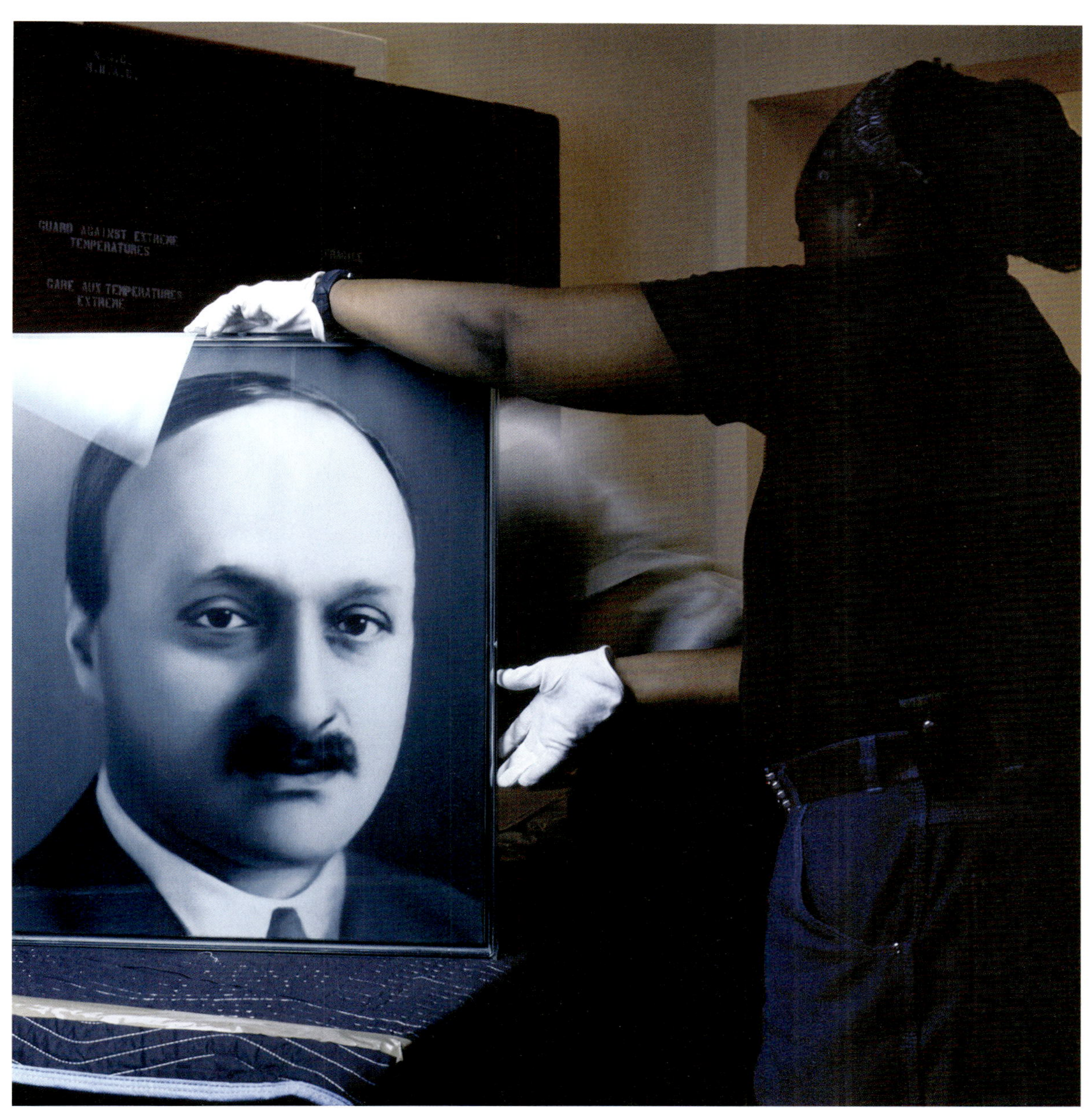

White Gloves, 2002/2004
cibachrome, 29 x 27 1/4 inches

Notes

1. Fredric Jameson, "Postmodernism and Consumer Society," in *The Anti-Aesthetic: Essays on Postmodern Culture*, ed. Hal Foster (Seattle, 1984), 113.

2. See Brigitte Weingart, "Viren infizieren! Die Topik des Viralen und der Diskurs über die Postmoderne," in *Ansteckende Wörter: Repräsentationen von Aids* (Frankfurt/Main, 2002), 75–103.

3. Peter Halley, "Notes On The Paintings" (1982), in *Collected Essays 1981–87* (Zurich, 1988), 23.

4. Ibid.

5. Clegg & Guttmann, "Interview 86," in *Collected Portraits*, exh. cat., Württembergischer Kunstverein Stuttgart (1988), 29–32.

6. Thierry de Duve, "Die Farbe und ihr Name," in *Pikturaler Nominalismus: Die Malerei und die Moderne* (Munich, 1987), 165–99.

7. Johannes Meinhardt, "The Sites Of Art: Photographing the In-Between," in Louise Lawler, *An Arrangement of Pictures* (New York, 2003), unpaginated.

8. See the entry on appropriation by Robert S. Nelson, "Appropriation Is not Passive, Objective, or Disinterested, but Active, Subjective and Motivated," in *Critical Terms for Art History*, ed. Robert S. Nelson and Richard Shiff (Chicago and London, 1996), 162.

9. Benjamin Buchloh, "Parody and Appropriation in Francis Picabia, Pop and Sigmar Polke," in *Neo-Avantgarde and Culture Industry: Essays on European and American Art from 1955–1975* (Boston, 2000), 349.

10. See Jean Baudrillard, "Zum Verständnis einiger Begriffe," in *Kool Killer oder Der Aufstand der Zeichen* (Berlin, 1978), 6.

11. Foster 1984 (see note 1) can serve as an example for the virulence of the antimodernist mood.

12. See Craig Owens, "Sherrie Levine, A & M Artworks," in *Beyond Recognition: Representation, Power, and Culture* (Berkeley, 1992), 115: "She does not photograph women, or landscapes, but pictures of them, for we can approach such subjects, Levine believes, only through their cultural representation."

13. Nelson 1996 (see note 8), 164.

14. See Craig Owens's criticism of Jeff Koons: "Interview with Craig Owens by Anders Stephanson," in Owens 1992 (see note 12), 315: "It is not coming out of a critical dissatisfaction and attempt to understand a set of production relations." Owens here implicitly criticizes Koons's fascination for his object.

15. A remark by Owens is symptomatic of this: "The appropriated image may be a film still, a photograph, a drawing." Further distinctions were not deemed to be necessary. See "The Allegorical Impulse: Toward a Theory of Postmodernism. Representation, Appropriation and Power," in Owens 1992 (see note 12), 54.

16. Douglas Crimp, "'Prominence Given, Authority Taken.' An Interview with Louise Lawler by Douglas Crimp," in Louise Lawler, *An Arrangement of Pictures* (New York, 2000), unpaginated.

17. See Stefan Römer, *Künstlerische Strategien des Fake: Kritik an Original und Fälschung* (Cologne, 2001), 99.

18. Stefan Römer, "Appropriation Art," in *DuMonts Begriffslexikon zur zeitgenössischen Kunst*, ed. Hubertus Butin (Cologne, 2002), 15 (translated).

19. See Römer 2001 (see note 17), 86. He claims here that Levine's photgraphic reproductions display no noticeable medial differences to those of Evans. In fact they have their own specific framing.

20. See John C. Welchman, "Introduction. Global Nets: Appropriation and Postmodernity," in *Art After Appropriation: Essays on Art in the 1990s* (Amsterdam, 2001), 10: "The first wave of postmodern appropriation correlates with the arrival and dissemination in New York of poststructuralist theories of reproduction and repetition."

21. *Art After Modernism: Rethinking Representation*, ed. Brian Wallis (New York, 1984).

22. The entry on "Appropriation Art," in *Prestel Lexikon: Kunst und Künstler im 20. Jahrhundert* (Munich et al.,1999), 20 (translated).

23. Douglas Crimp, "Das Aneignen der Aneignung," in *Über die Ruinen des Museums* (Dresden and Basle, 1996), 141. See also Isabelle Graw, "Der Kampf geht weiter: Ein Interview mit Douglas Crimp über Appropriation Art," *Texte zur Kunst*, no. 46 (June 2002): 34–44.

24. See the following comments by Louise Lawler in conversation with Douglas Crimp. Here a relationship of fascination may be assumed, although of course the artist's statements are not to be taken as the "truth" or the "meaning." Image, text, and programmatic statements are to be seen as forms of artistic articulation that belong together, without having to be treated on one—intertextual—level: "When I am working, I take lots of pictures. It's a way of working that's fairly flatfooted in that I have a sense that something is worthwile documenting, but the pictures that work are those that are affecting in some other way." It is clearly the pictures that affect the artist that are the pictures that work.

25. See Isabelle Graw, "Leistungsnachweise: Cindy Sherman, Barbara Kruger, Sherrie Levine, Louise Lawler," in *Die bessere Hälfte: Künstlerinnen des 20. und 21. Jahrhunderts* (Cologne, 2003), 64–78.

26. See Isabelle Graw, "Der Hausmann: Ein Interview mit Richard Prince," *Texte zur Kunst*, no. 46 (June 2002): 44–60.

27. See Douglas Crimp, "Pictures," in Wallis 1984 (see note 21), 185: "Levine steals them [the works of art] away from their usual place in our culture and subverts their mythologies."

28. See Craig Owens, "The Allegorical Impulse: Toward a Theory of Postmodernism. Representation, Appropriation and Power," in Owens 1992 (see note 12), 54: "Allegorical imagery is appropriated imagery; the allegorist does not invent images but confiscates them."

29. See Craig Owens, "The Discourse of Others: Feminists and Postmodernism," in Owens 1992 (see note 12), 182: "She expropriates the appropriators."

30. See Karl Marx and Friedrich Engels, "Manifest der Kommunistischen Partei 1848," in *Karl Marx, Friedrich Engels. Studienausgabe*, vol. 3, ed. Iring Fetscher (Frankfurt/Main, 1990), 59–89.

31. See Karl Marx, "Ökonomisch-philosophische Manuskripte" (1844), in *Studienausgabe*, vol. 2, 38–128 (see note 30).

32. See Jean Baudrillard, "Die absolute Ware," in *Die fatalen Strategien* (Munich, 1991), 144–48.

33. See Giorgio Agamben, "The Face," in *Means Without End: Notes on Politics* (Minneapolis, 2000), 91–100.

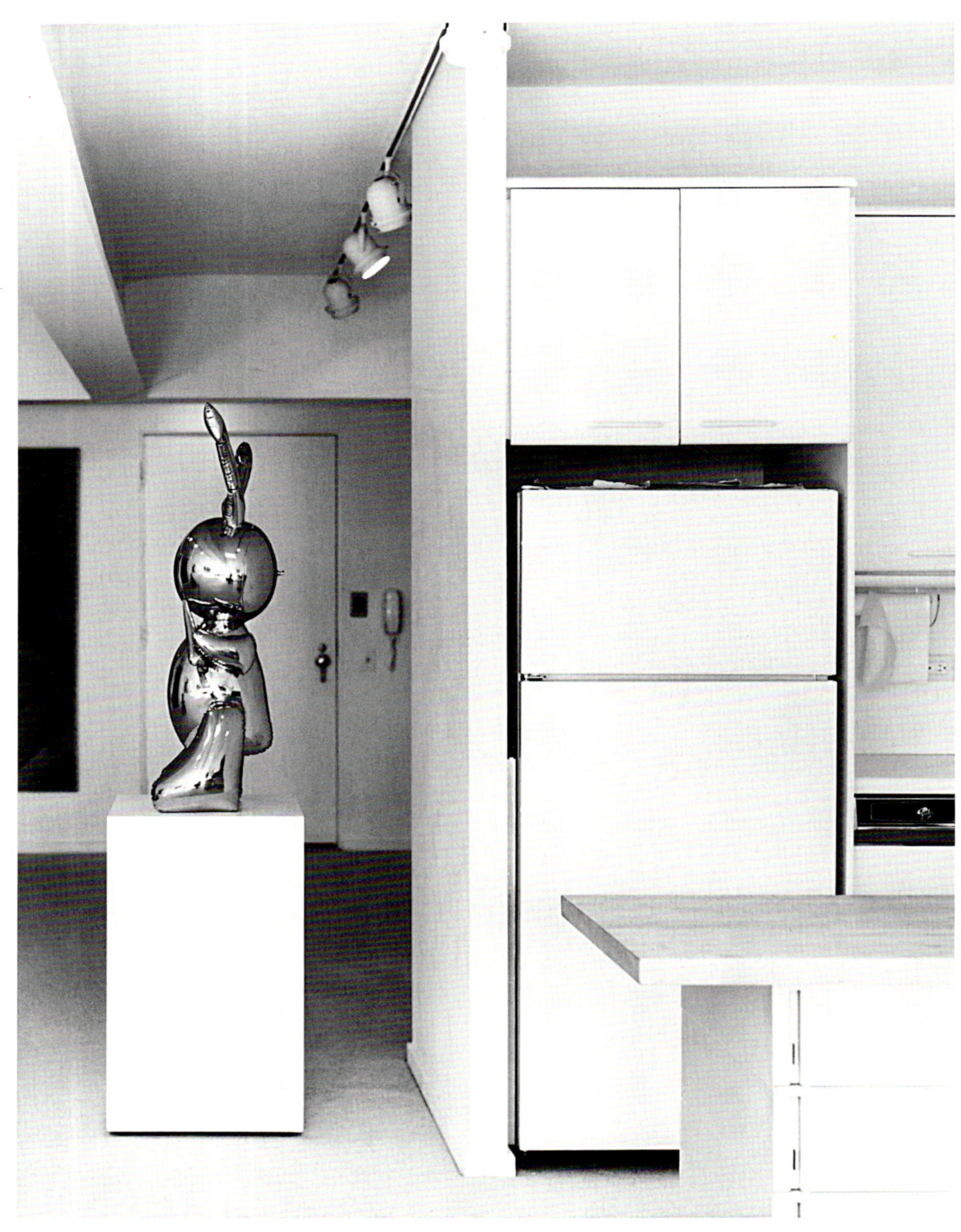

Foreground, 1994
black and white photograph with mat, $3^{5/8}$ x $2^{3/4}$ inches (image)

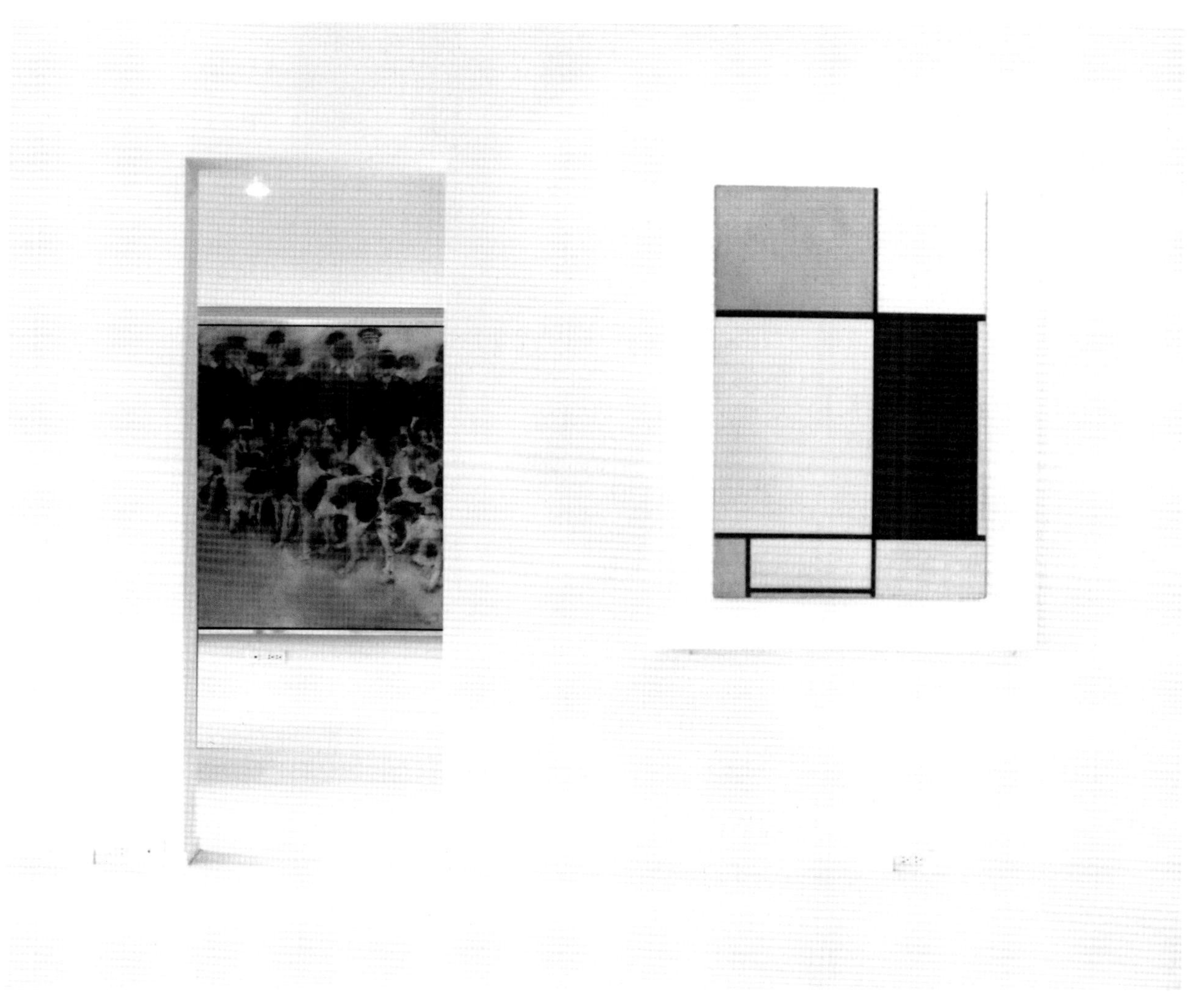

Background, 1994
black and white photograph with mat, $10^{1/2}$ x $11^{3/4}$ inches (image)

Pink and Yellow and Black I (Red Disaster) from **On a Wall, On a Cow, In a Book, In the Mail**, 1999
cibachrome, $32^{1/2}$ x 25 inches

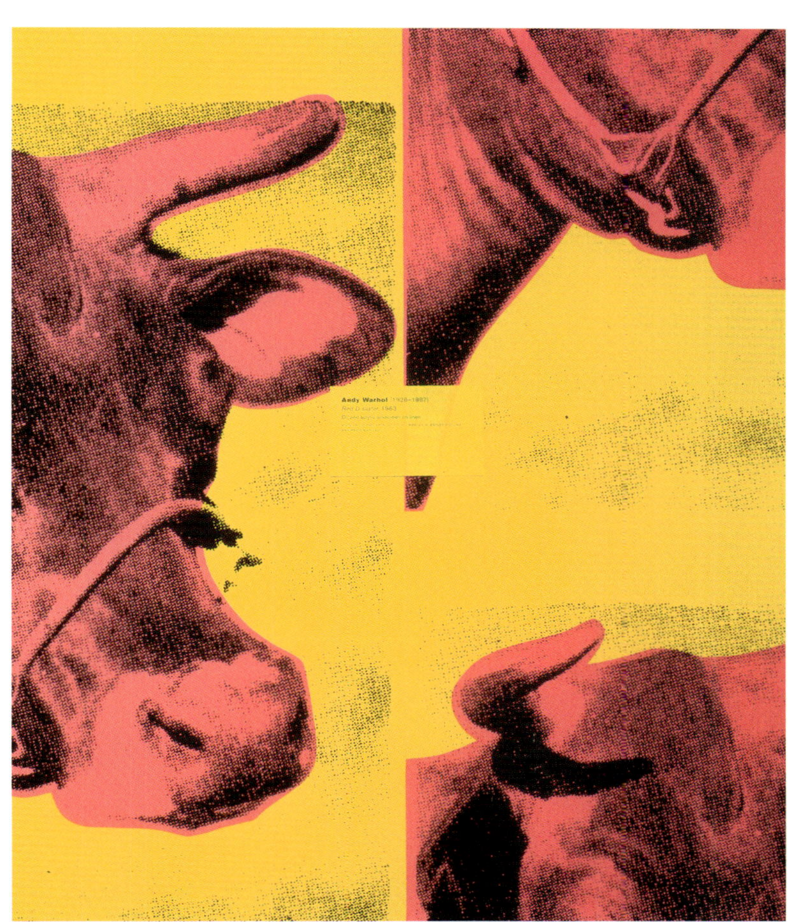
Andy Warhol

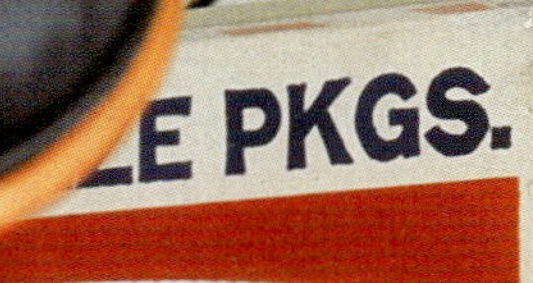
LE PKGS.
New!
Brillo
soap pads
WITH RUST RESISTER
SHINES ALUMINUM FAST

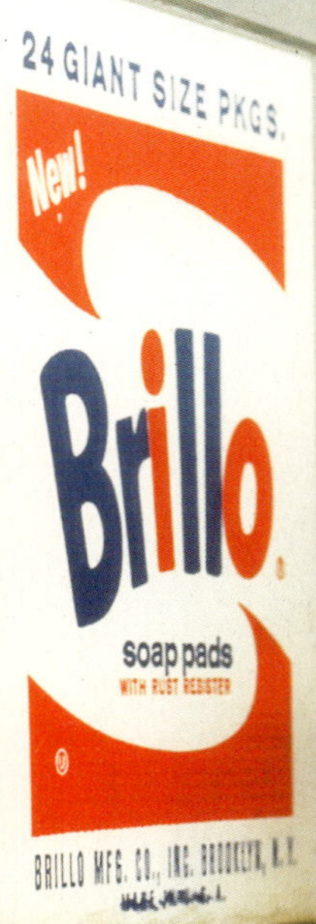
24 GIANT SIZE PKGS.
New!
Brillo
soap pads
BRILLO MFG. CO., INC. BROOKLYN, N.Y.

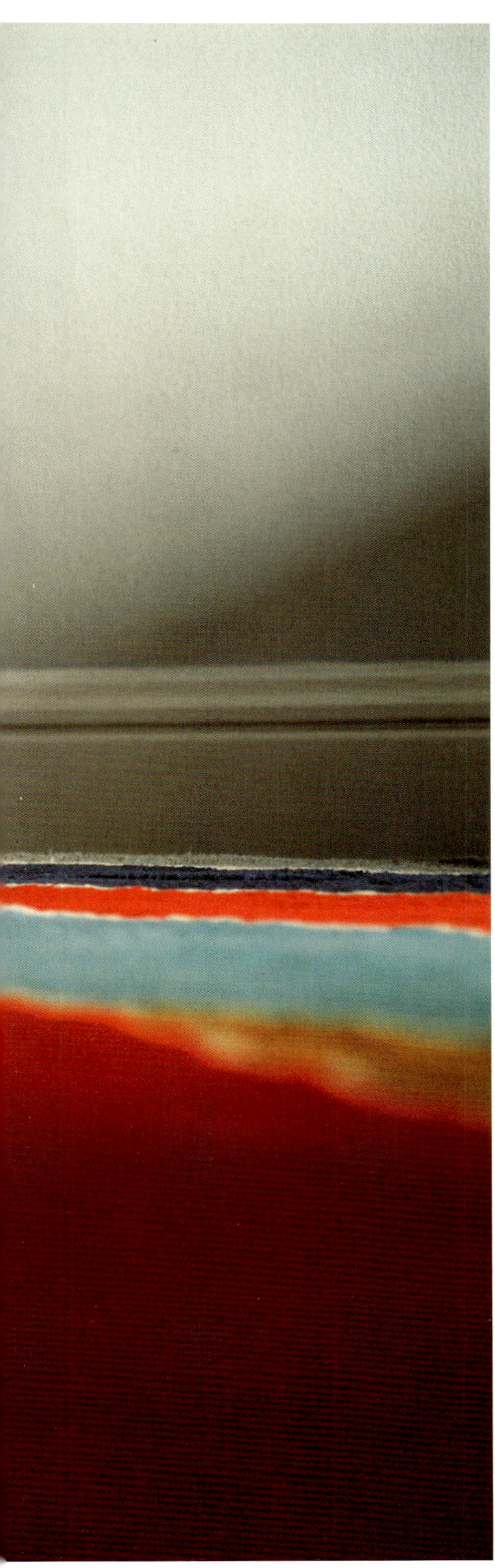

I-O, 1993/1998
cibachrome, 19 5/16 x 23 3/8 inches

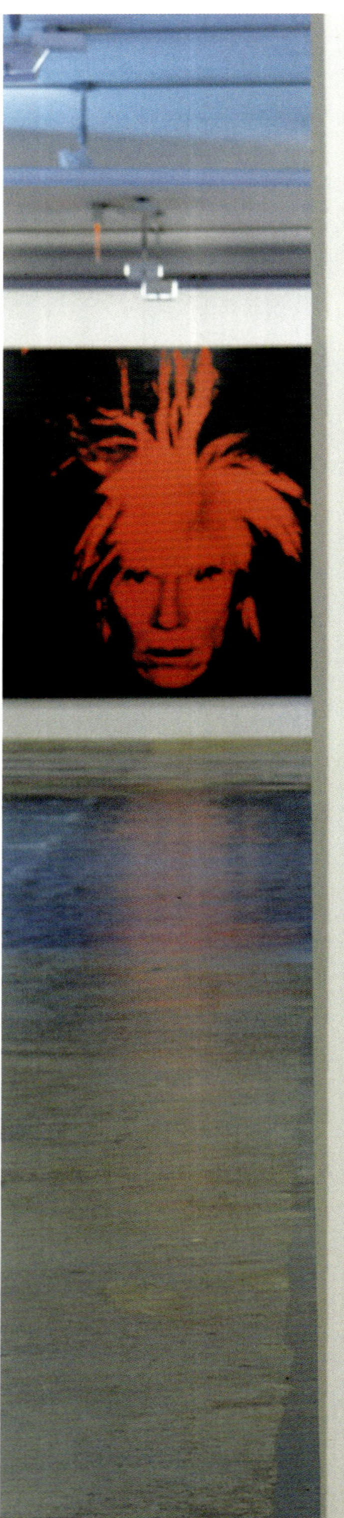

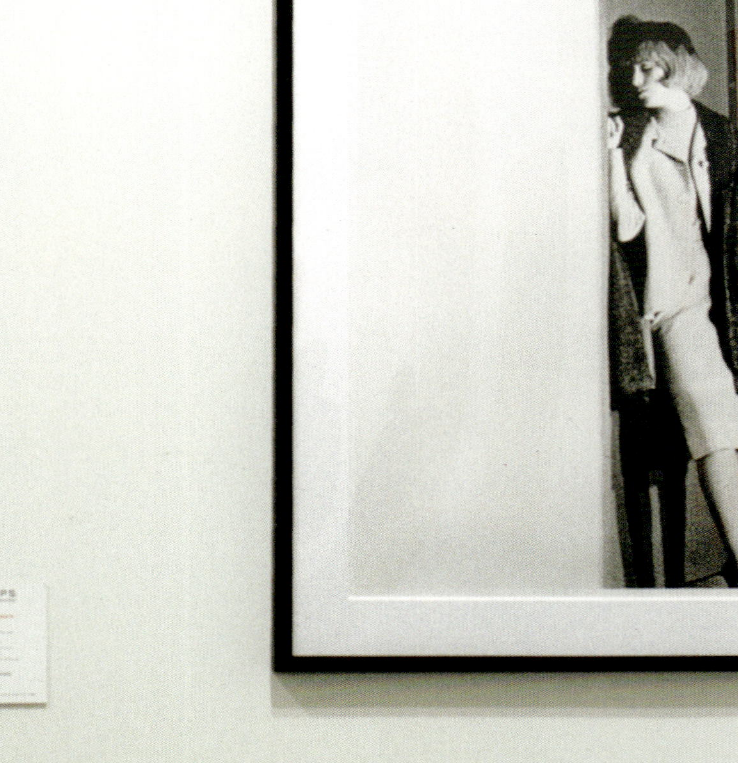

DOES LOUISE LAWLER MAKE YOU CRY?

Jack Bankowsky

Some people take pictures of people, some of trees or fruit; Louise Lawler takes pictures of artworks by Andy Warhol—I mean, she takes pictures of art by lots of artists, but it is Andy (ever in character) who shows up the most. In fact, Warhol's art explicitly appears in some forty-one individual Lawlers. That's easily twice as often as her next most photographed subjects: Lichtenstein and Koons follow at eighteen and thirteen cameos, respectively, with Richter, LeWitt, and then Johns running close behind.

One may reasonably object, of course, that my handicapping is beside the point: Lawler does not really make art about other artists, or even about other artists' art; she makes art about the institutions through which art passes—tricks out the determining conventions at the sites of its display and consumption—and so her attentions to Andy and his oeuvre might be seen as little more than incidental. Warhol—a uniquely celebrated and uniquely prolific contemporary artist, after all—would, as mere matter of course, lead the pack in the showrooms and salons where art resides and changes hands.

Still, forty-one works is a lot of works (all the more in an oeuvre as restrained as Lawler's), and, one way or another, a careful look at just what it is that Lawler does with Warhol's art promises to open out onto her practice more generally. One should scarcely need resort to special pleading to make the point that her *sujet fixe*—even more so, Warhol's inevitability as such—would all but guarantee the complexity of her projections and investments. But the point I'm getting around to, is that our reading of Lawler's art—or, in any case, its appreciation with anything like a nuance equal to what is on offer—has been somewhat hobbled by the critical branding efforts that helped bring it to visibility in the first place: I mean first, of course, "appropriation," and then "institutional critique." This much I hope might be proposed without my partaking in the almost phobic reaction that the latter rubric in particular has provoked in certain belletristic quarters. My wager is that a careful look at the kinds of questions Lawler puts to her seemingly inexhaustible precursor—the questions she puts to us through him—not only complicates the catechisms that threaten to reduce her own oeuvre to a social-studies one-liner but at the same time reveals her to be something like Warhol's best, most prescient, "reader."

Cindy and Andy, 2002/2003
cibachrome, $24^{1/2}$ x 19 inches

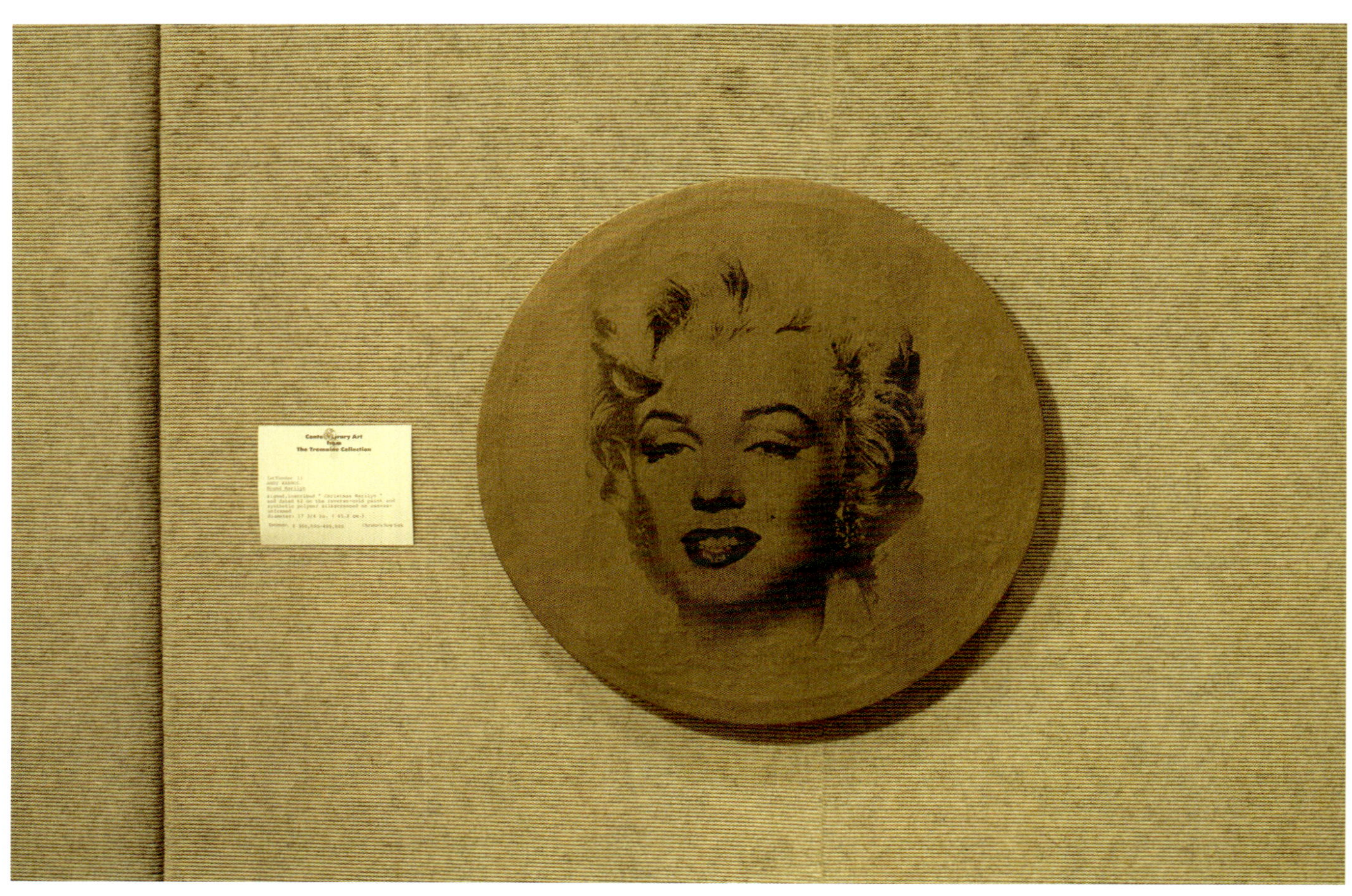

Does Andy Warhol Make You Cry?, 1988
cibachrome, plexi wall label, $27^{1/4}$ x 39 inches

An identical image exists with the title ***Does Marilyn Monroe Make You Cry?***

Does Andy Warhol Make You Cry?

Lawler poses the question in a 1988 work, for which it also serves as title. It's a good question. Better, in fact, than its pendant query: Does Marilyn Monroe make you cry? The twin interrogatives appear on wall tags of the sort that customarily identify art objects in a museum or gallery, each positioned next to an identical photograph of Andy Warhol's *Head of Marilyn Monroe* (1962), one of his celebrated gold tondi, "captured" against a fabric-covered wall that pegs the setting (at least within professional and collecting circles) as the viewing rooms of the international auction concern Christie's.

The first question is better because it is more complex. With the lesser query Lawler asks about a movie star; in the better version, about an artist who painted a picture of a movie star that she has photographed. With the lesser question Lawler sets up an expectation against which the better one asserts first its equivalence, then, and more tellingly, a difference. But why should Andy, perhaps not a sentimental favorite, make us cry? Not for the reasons Marilyn makes 'em cry: because she is a victim, a pure symptom, her evanescence leveraged in some dark pact of "the star system." Andy is often thought of as a pure symptom too, certainly a sign of his times, but he is not normally seen as a victim. More a vampire. Does Andy make you cry? Does Marilyn? The sum of the questions is more telling than the parts; indeed, posed together, they set in motion a musing on the varieties of contemporary celebrity that is the work's most disarming return.

This is fertile territory. To parse, to preserve such differences would be to understand no small amount about our contemporary condition. Warhol certainly thought about the contrast of famous people and not-famous ones—the screen tests, the mug shots versus paparazzi glamour, the superstars who were not so super—and out of that consideration came his copious poetry, toxic to some, but equal to our age.[1] But what, Lawler seems to ask, of the subtler varieties of celebrity? What of the difference between a Marilyn and an Andy? Marilyn was just the sort of celebrity Warhol was always on the make to meet, though he would not manage it as she died, inconveniently, in 1962 on the night after the last day of his first big show (the celebrated soup-can exhibition) and well before he was famous enough to rub shoulders with the likes of her. As the royalest of Hollywood royalty, Marilyn was unimpeachably A list; Andy was A minus. Well, by the end, he was a real A, and on the rise, but she was always triple A. Of course the years may change all this. Andy may ascend into the stratosphere as a bona fide immortal, and Marilyn may someday seem as obscure as the silent stars of yesteryear. Lawler, if true to form, will make a work about these fickle judgments of time—about the meaningful havoc they must wreak on her own infra-slim interventions.

Art Stars vs. Real Stars

If *Does Andy Warhol Make You Cry?* invites us to ponder two types of stardom, real stardom (Marilyn) and art stardom (Andy), *It Could Be Elvis* (1994) complicates the array. Andy was one of very few art stars who could have counted himself a real star, and so in fairness he is a star variety unto himself. In this lineup Joseph Beuys (as a 1980 portrait by Warhol) steps in to fill the art-star spot and round out Lawler's disorienting trinity. Elvis/Andy/Beuys: three distinct myth-types on the mass-to-high culture arc, plotted against the silver standard of the title. Where the earlier work "captured" Marilyn during a brief layover in her life as a painting on the auction house wall, here we discover Beuys rather more comfortably settled in the opulently appointed digs of a Geneva collecting couple. In *It Could Be Elvis* (but in fact it's Joseph Beuys!), a cropped face—the face-value explanation for the identity confusion cued by the title—butts in from the top of a shot. Warhol's painting is one eviscerated treasure among many in a pan-cultural, panhistorical hoard: The Regence console table is eighteenth century; the lamp, combining an African wood dish and a collar of animal teeth, is the work of Parisian artist Claude de Muzac (second half of the twentieth century); the carved wood mushroom inlaid with ivory and copper (probably the base of a sculpture) is Japanese nineteenth century; the love seat at bottom right is covered in vintage Fortuny; the screen, one of a pair recounting the tale of the 101 poets, is Japanese eighteenth century; and, finally, the painting is late twentieth century—a portrait by an art star (who is also a real star) of an art star (who is not perhaps quite a real star), and, as echt-Wagnerian shaman, a fair antipode to the artist who painted his picture. Such are the estranging effects of Lawler's slice of well-heeled domesticity, that one finds oneself (am I alone?) embroiled in a brain-straining struggle to master the proliferating and incommensurate mythologies that underwrite our spectacle lives. What sort of myth is Beuys? And Elvis? And Warhol? And what of their chance meeting on the paneled wall of this luxurious room?

What Goes On Here?

Lawler has visited her share of luxurious homes. Sometimes one gets the feeling Lawler wants us to linger over the inventory, to mutter back the litany of luxury, fingering, in our imaginations, each object in these high-hatted hoards. Lawler sucks us into the provenance porn, tweaks our scopic lust. *Who Are You Close To?* (1990) is frankly ravishing. The full-on complementaries—trading-stamp green against "Chinese red" walls, the supermarket graphic versus the patrician antiquity of the paneling. It's of course the old joke on the old bourgeois faux pas of privileging decor over art (you don't hang "major" art on a bright red wall!), but that is too easy by half. Lawler has cropped in on the hot spot, scuttled the context of

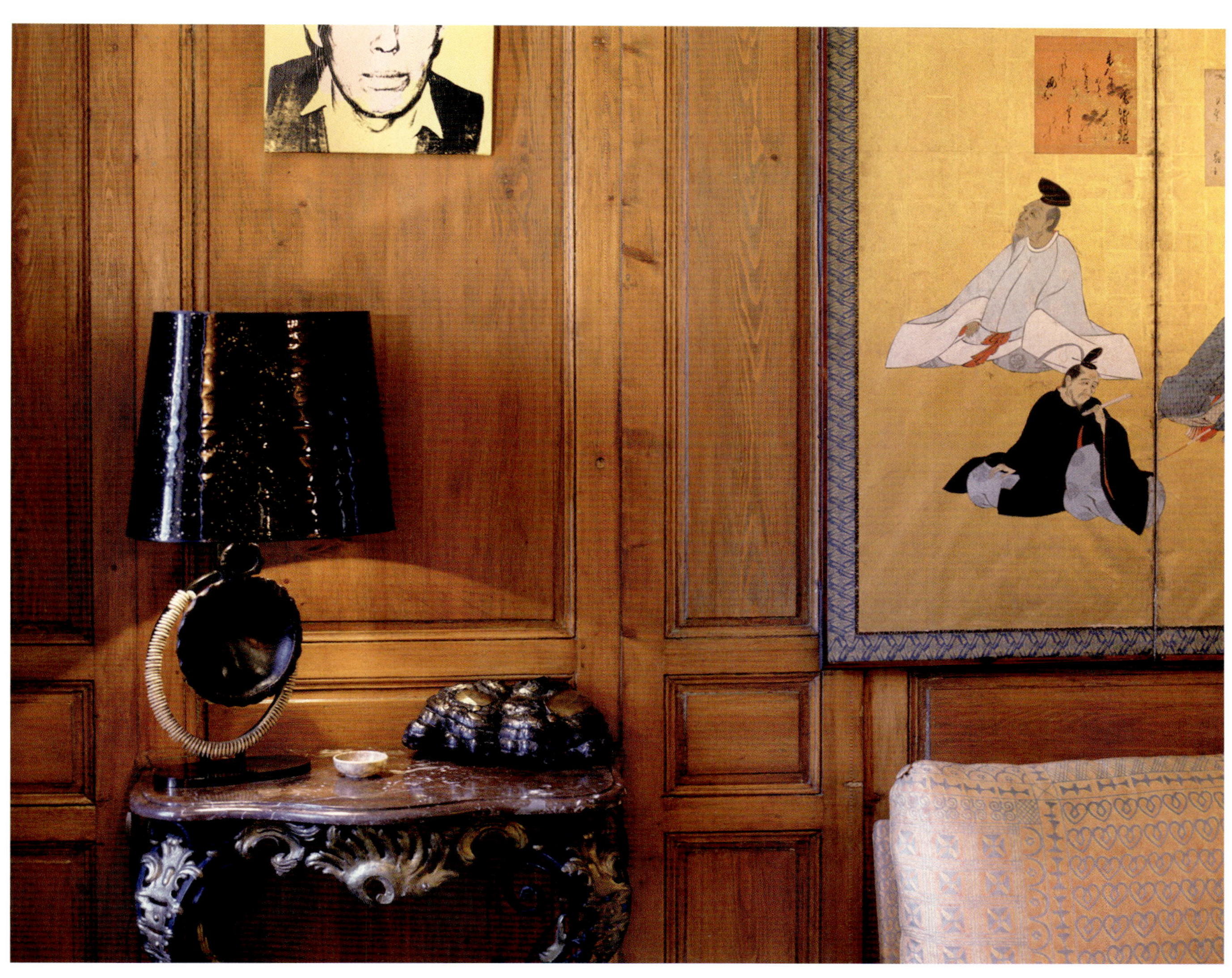

It Could Be Elvis, 1994
cibachrome, $29^{1/4}$ x $35^{1/8}$ inches

broader domestic and spatial detail, and in so doing pumped up the formal qualities to make of a shelter-magazine commonplace an icon as undeniable as Matisse's *The Red Studio*. And yet, by the time she shot the image, the high-style decor was already showing its age, just as the frisson of the This-Is-Tomorrow invasion of the well-heeled sitting room seems to us a memory, wistful even—a moment irrecoverably past, like an old photo of a Factory party we will never attend.

The mix of quizzical engagement and caught-in-the-act indictment that characterizes Lawler's regard registers perfectly in *What Goes On Here?* (1990), the first in a pair of views of the apartment of legendary art dealer Leo Castelli. The answers that come back from her art are never reducible to the platitudinous Eureka: "Ah yes, our every resistance subsumed in the maw of capital." They are, of course (subsumed in the maw of capital, that is), but Lawler's perplexity is always more multivalent. What of the strange orders that the collector creates and revises? What of the tales told with these trophies—and the ones these trophies tell about our own acculturation? And what of all this when the collector in question is Leo Castelli? *What Goes On Here?* boasts a blue Jackie, one "good" American pedestal table, an AbEx brushstroke by Roy Lichtenstein that happens to look a lot like a table, a sliver of Ellsworth Kelly peeking in from stage left, and, at the center of the action, Warhol's uncharacteristically butch 1964 self-portrait. Lawler's second shot of this setting, *Four Between Two Doors* (1993/1998), presents the same self-portrait but now moved to the background (to Jackie's old spot), with Johns's *4 Leo* (1970) assuming pride of place between the doors. Is it too much a strain to recall Andy's notorious recollection, that he was "too swish" for Bob and Jasper (thus explaining what he took to be their belated acceptance of him and his art), he the fey fashion illustrator, they with their still warm AbEx pedigree. Two 1960s queers and a couple of (closet?) doors; one turn in the psycho-subtle dance of canon formation, re-rehearsed in the foyer of the art dealer most becoming of a 1960s legend. Overreading is perhaps a danger here, but the domino effect of meanings is for me an absolutely predictable consequence of Lawler's intervention. She is susceptible to precisely this sort of associative logic, both with respect to her work generally and in terms of the rhythms of inclusion and exclusion endemic to canon-formation that, not least of all as a woman, are part of "her problem." Indeed Lawler engages the Warhol mythos as a microcosm of the culture he so amply figures, not by refusing that culture (as if we could somehow know our desire and ourselves outside our mass-mediated circumstance!), but by inhabiting it fully as a given that must be lived with and through. That Lawler may be seen to anticipate a turn in the Warhol literature, to provide a bridge, even, between the neo-Marxist apology, which remains the monument of Warhol studies, and the capacious revisions associated primarily with Wayne Koestenbaum is another story for another day. Suffice it to say that it is Lawler's manifest sensitivity to her own (necessary) complicity in the regimes she scrutinizes that accounts

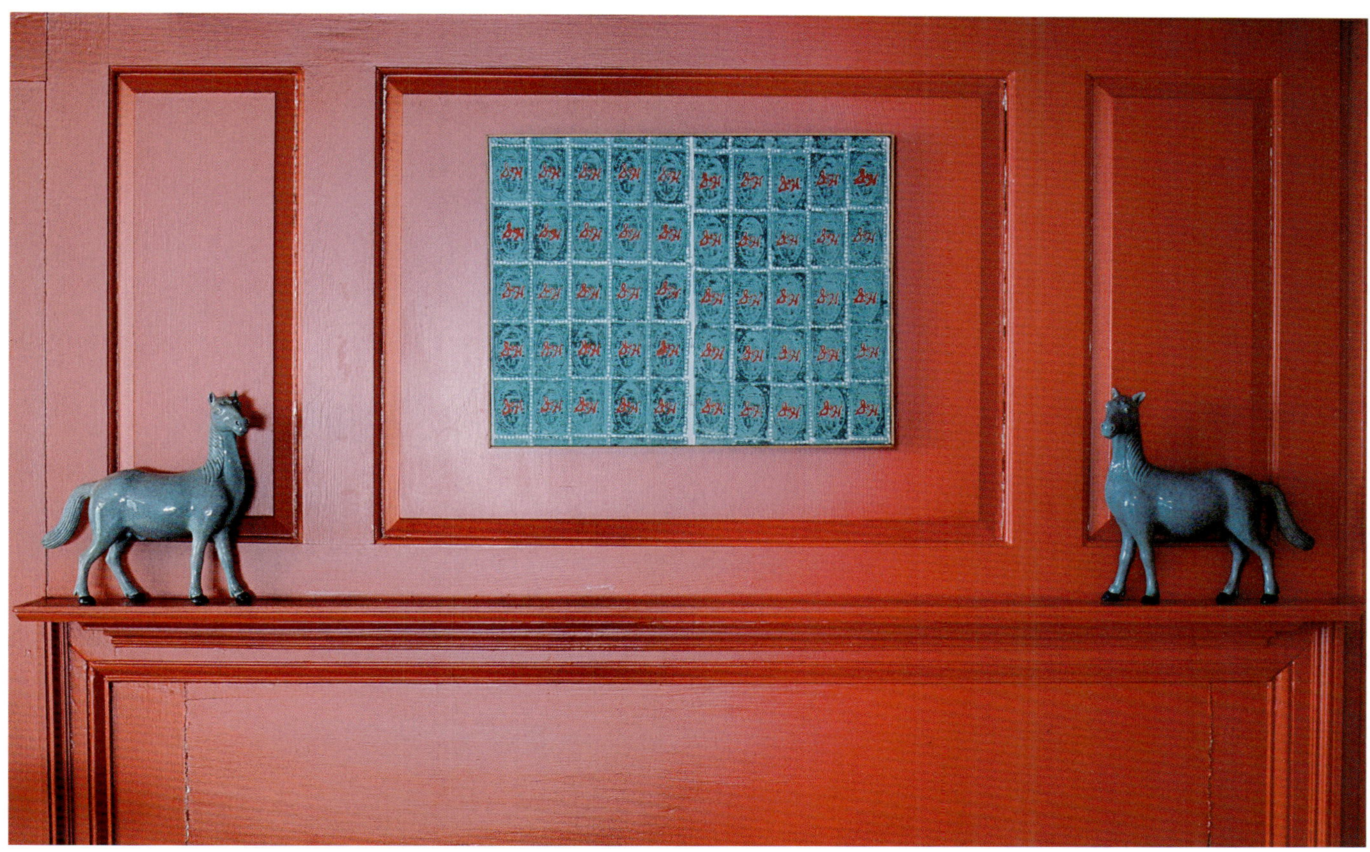

Who Are You Close To? (Red), 1990
cibachrome, 39 1/4 x 61 3/4 inches

for a certain "truth quotient" that does seem these days to set her apart from a number of her peers.

What is a Blank?

Whether by the pointed, formally ingenious, crop (*Who Are You Close To?*), the loaded nugget of language (*It Could Be Elvis*), or simply the apparently serendipitous drift of her viewfinder away from the putative site of action and toward the seemingly prosaic incident, Lawler's art is ever a matter of coaxing the unseen to visibility. Her gambit is a what-you-see-and-what-you-don't game: it could be Elvis—but it isn't. If one is to hazard a generalization as to how Lawler works her estranging effects, how she turns the frisson of the keyhole view of the collecting class's well-hung walls toward more capacious ruminations about, well, everything; if we ask how, in short, her works work when they are really working, the answer will hinge on the matter of syntax, of how she plays with and manipulates the way we make differences legible as meanings, catching us up and calling

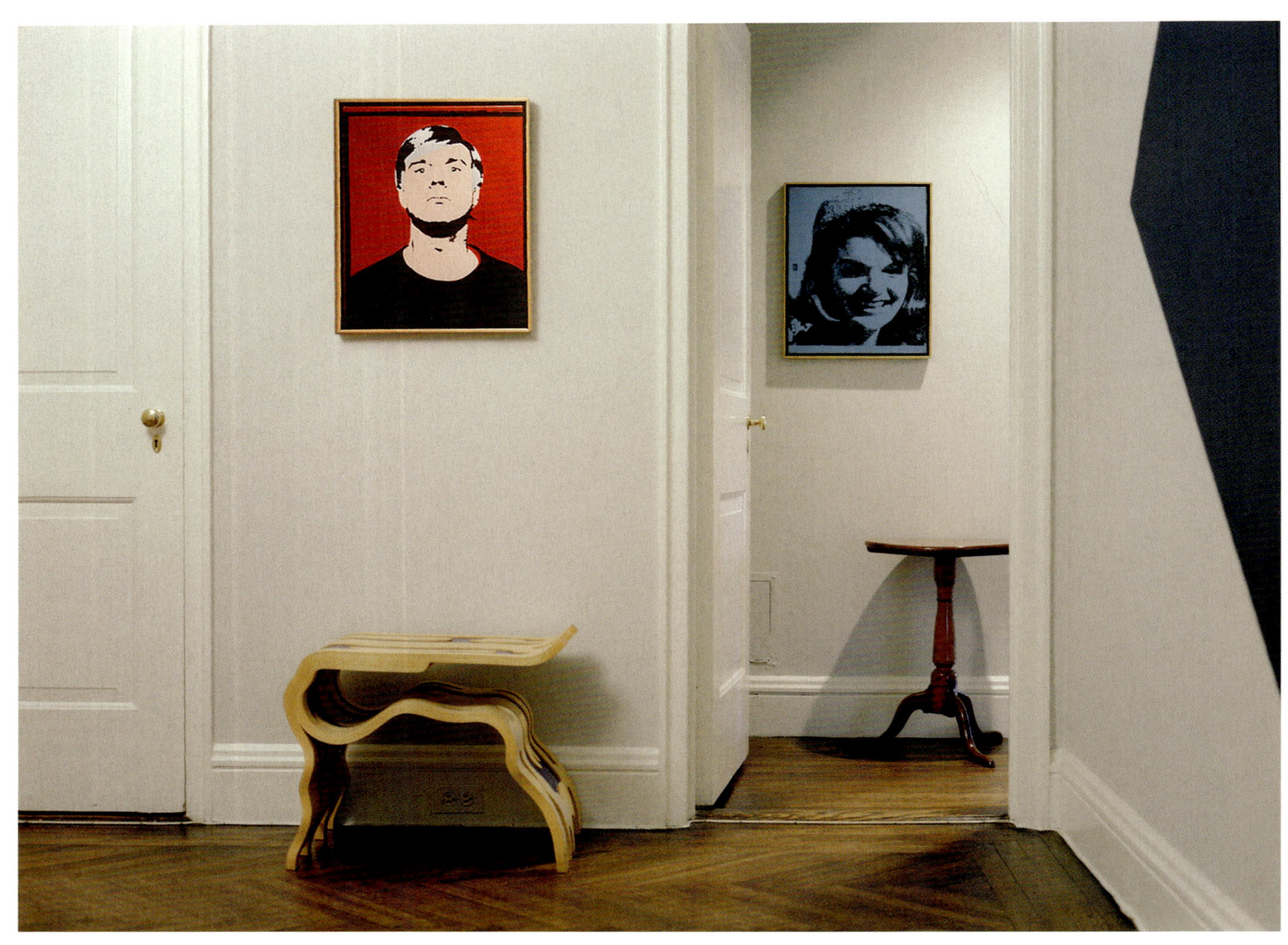

What Goes on Here, 1990
cibachrome, 40 x 54 inches

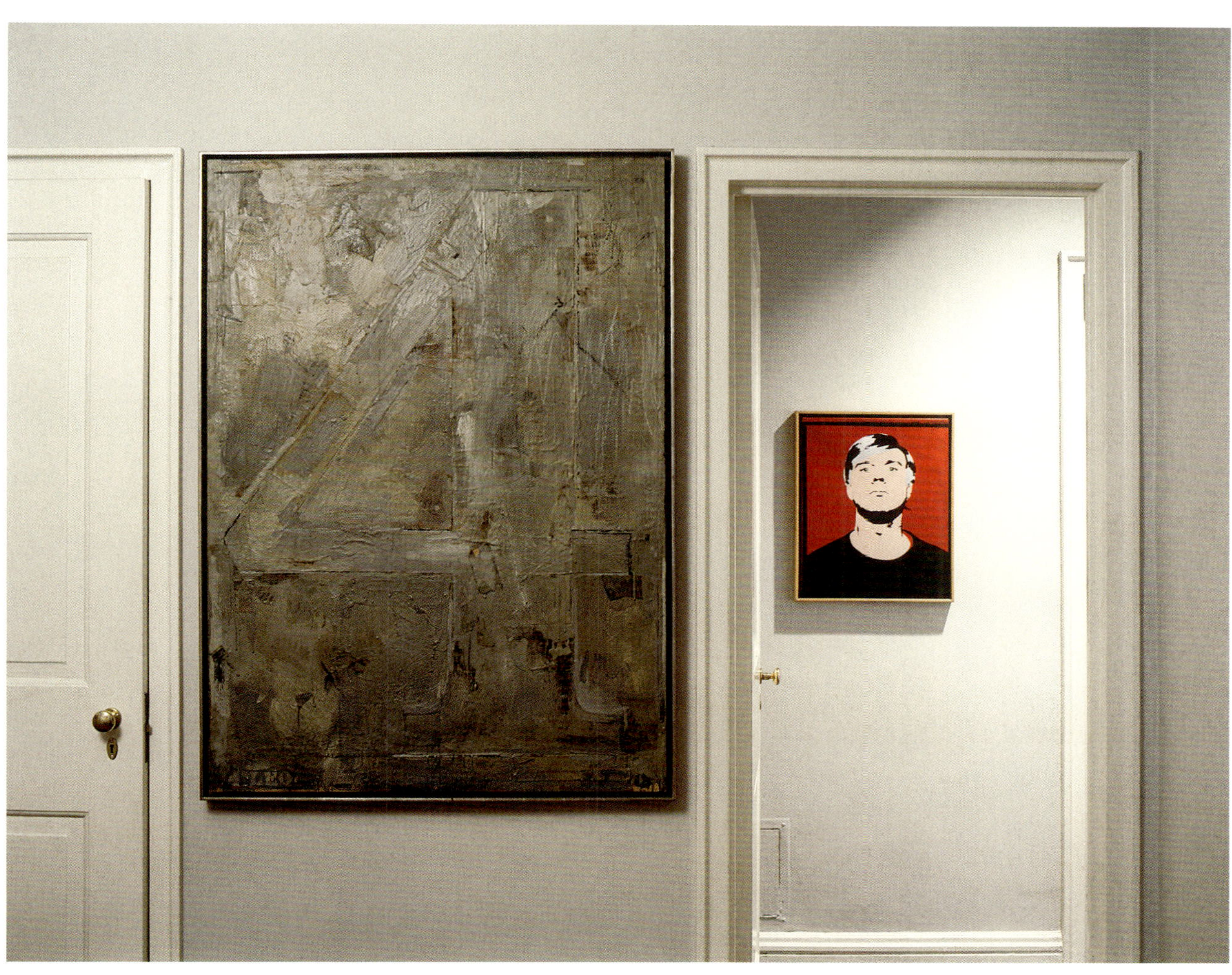

Four Between Two Doors, 1993/1998
cibachrome, 24 x 30 5/8 inches

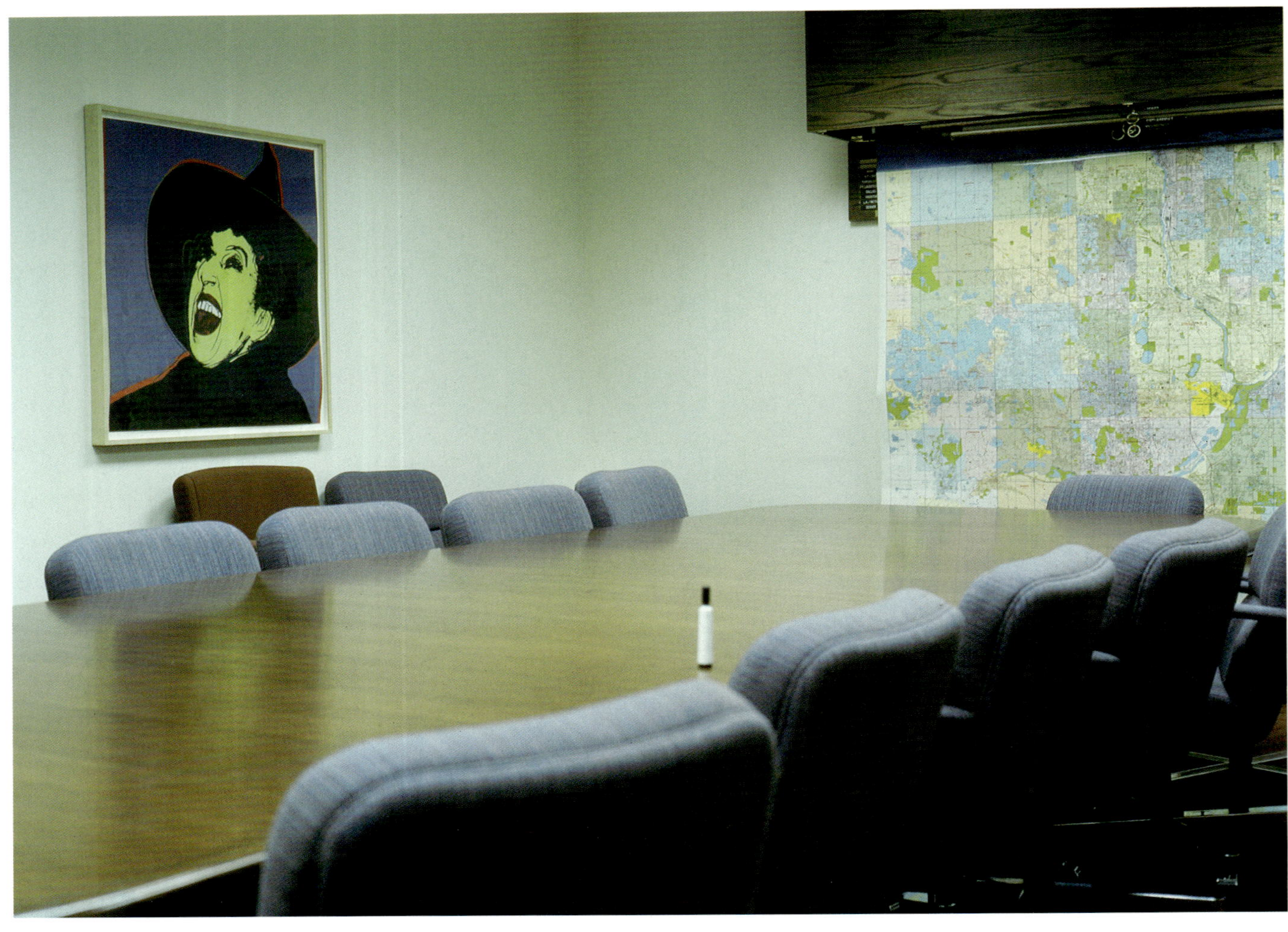

Who Says Who Shows Who Counts, 1989
cibachrome, $38^{1/4}$ x $50^{7/8}$ inches

attention to these often unexamined processes. If Lawler's gaming can at times verge on the quixotic, it is always, I will argue, alert making, in a way that tips it to the right side of the merely clever. I'm thinking of a work like *I-O* (1993/1998) that takes an ad-art incidental—the "i" and the "o" in the word "Brillo" on the famous carton happen to be highlighted in red—as the supposed nexus of meaning in, and thus the raison d'être for, her work. It is as if in scanning an image that shows fragments of a Frank Stella rug, a classic Eames lounge chair, and Warhol's celebrated icon, it would turn out to be the color red, the happenstantial affinity it proposes, that is the signifying unit by which we would parse and name what counts in this image. Funny-weird for sure, but Lawler's quirky gesture is also strangely effective as a way of getting us to question all of the other unspoken ways we bundle significance before this (or any) shot.

The artist reprised the color-over-content gambit a year later in *Pink* (1994/1995), a shot that brings a Warhol flower painting and a Gerhard Richter abstraction to equivalence on adjacent auction house walls, based again on a superficial tonal affinity. A Warhol next to a Richter, a painterly abstraction next to a screen-printed representation, a pink painting next to a pink painting: Forced into cohabitation, the juxtaposition asks us to rethink all that we think goes without saying about the couple and their relationship. For Warhol, the blank—his term for the monochrome panels he would juxtapose next to, say, an auto accident or an electric chair—was a kind of syntactical degree zero. A placeholder for nothing—and everything that might have filled the nothing with a something. In Lawler's *Every Other Picture* (1990) a behind-the-scenes peek into the storage rack at Boston's Museum of Fine Arts, Lawler muses on the voluble void, exposing it as an enabling trope in her own practice. Visible in Lawler's shot are portions of a typical Richter abstraction, Warhol's *Red Disaster* from 1963, and its matching blank. Among other things, Warhol talked about his blanks as an easy way to print money, so to speak—to increase the size of a given picture by adding a second panel and thus bring up its price.[2] Richter's abstractions, which are most often shown with his photo-realist scenes as a kind of counterpoint, have been often enough quipped about as Richter by-the-yard. Of course, one might also flip things around, consider them from the opposite vantage, as Lawler's purposeful juxtapositions inevitably encourage one to do. Now the photo-realist canvases are the blanks in Richter's oeuvre; the highly wrought and "densely individuated" abstractions the main event. Indeed, if we shuffle the deck yet one more time, we might ask of Lawler's shot: Is Warhol's monochrome-for-the-nth-time-around the blank to Richter's painterly opus or is Richter's AbEx cipher rather the blank to Warhol's loquacious void?

A work that remains more obdurate in the face of such art-about-art unpackings, *Who Says Who Shows Who Counts* (1989) offers up a myth of a very different cultural color. If Marilyn is the exalted blank, a kind of gold standard in both Warhol's oeuvre (and Lawler's reconstitution of it) against which the spectrum of celebrity types are charted, Margaret Hamilton embodies an outer point on that scale as the one-role demi-celebrity. The literal fifteen minutes. Indeed the single painting that adorns the boardroom setting (the Minneapolis First Bank in the 1980s heyday of the corporate collection) is one of Warhol's Myths, a print from the 1989 series of the Wicked Witch of the West. Head tilted back, laughing the mad laugh that annually curdled the blood of every *Wizard of Oz* watcher (of a certain vintage at least), the archetype of Technicolor evil is engaged here in a standoff across a polished conference table with a single Magic Marker, a midget missile in this cold war of meaning. In an oeuvre like Lawler's where packaging and its discontents is perhaps the most persistent theme, the fact that Hamilton was a victim of the vividness of her role (whoever she might become, she was always still the Wicked Witch) would not have gone unnoticed.

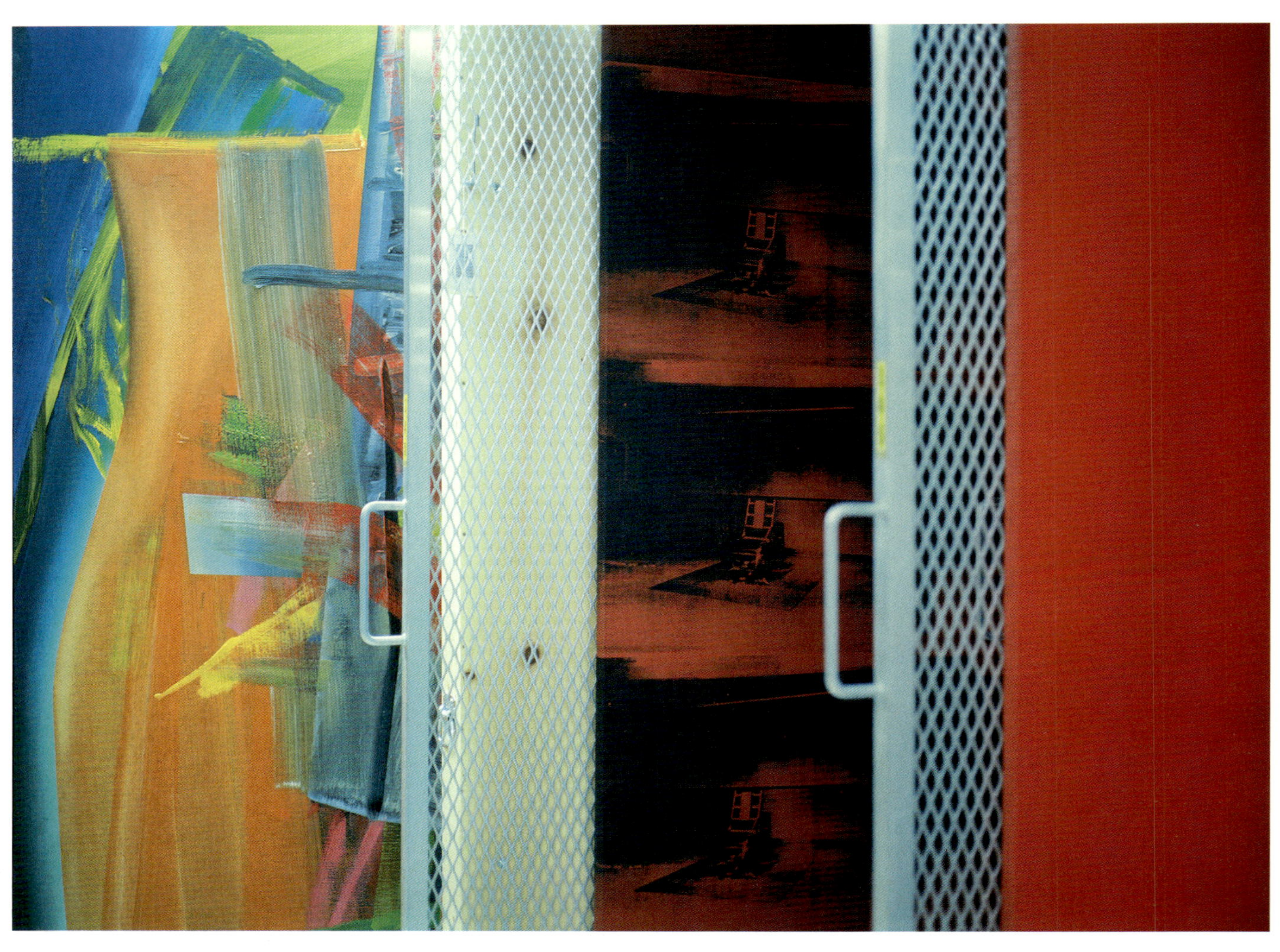

Every Other Picture, 1990
cibachrome with title as text on wall, 40 x 53 inches

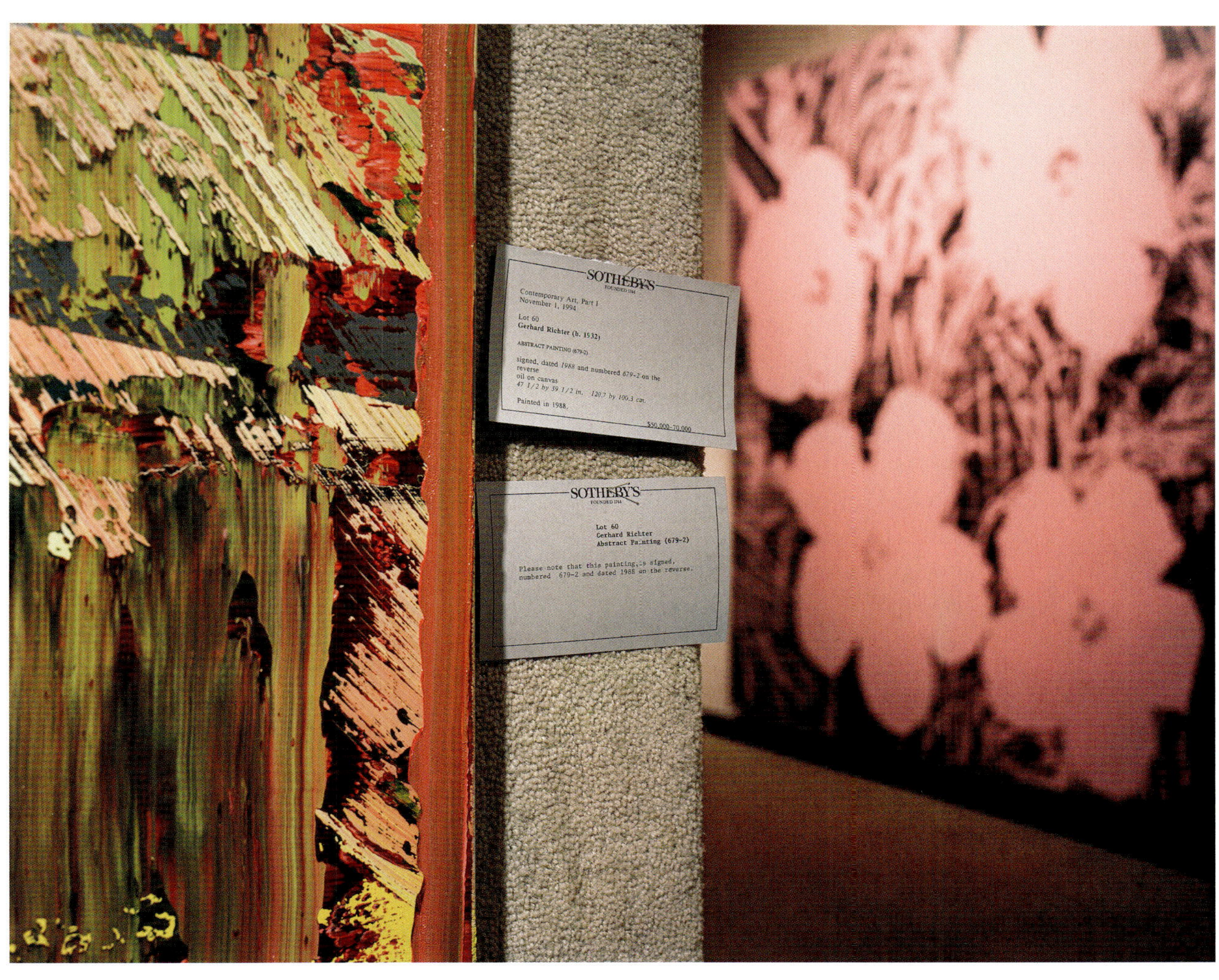

Pink, 1994/1995
cibachrome, 47 7/8 x 59 1/2 inches

Something About Time and Space But I'm Not Sure What It Is

In 1966, Andy let it be known that his forthcoming Leo Castelli show would be his last. He had already broached his intention to abandon "painting" on the occasion of his Sonnabend show the year before in Paris, and the months that intervened had seen his activities expand beyond the white walls of the studio—beyond even the silver ones of the Factory—to encompass his Exploding Plastic Inevitable, the legendary multimedia evenings that he presided over at the downtown club the Dom. His film "business" was thriving too, with *My Hustler* enjoying a modest, and for him first-time, box-office success. The show he delivered to Castelli comprised two halves, the cow wallpaper and the silver clouds, each of which would precipitate separate Lawler series,[3] the latter a multi-partite homage (the only work in an oeuvre of pictures of others artists' pictures I would describe as such). Titled *Something About Time And Space But I'm Not Sure What It Is*, and subtitled *(One)* and *(More)*, both 1998, the initial shot led to further variations (*Pleasure/More* and *Rise and Shine*, both 1998/1999, and simply *One*, 1998/2000). The images in the series are less matter-of-factly documentary than much of her work, less apparently deadpan in their regard. Compared to the period snaps of the installation—in which, the bobbing balloons suggest more cruddy conceit than replete spectacle—Lawler's images look souped up and seductive.[4]

For an artist as reticent as Lawler, an artist the critic Douglas Crimp once suggested seems to be "working against productivity," indeed for whom working against productivity "[makes] work possible,"[5] this obsessive-seeming reification cannot but count as an overdetermined remark. Or if not quite a remark—the word is *too* determined—then a nod of recognition, a sidelong glance even (if a largely celebratory regard can be so described), at the profoundly enabling dialectic in Warhol's practice that she must have appreciated in some way as her own: For Lawler, the moment when the white-walls career floats away like a bunch of glistening balloons seems to carry with it a utopian promise, but it is also a moment, as her work reminds us, that is bound to its dialectical counter-terms in self-packaging and promotion, naming and framing, a movement she symbolically reenacts with these wantonly ethereal confections. Poking fun at her fetishistic memorializing of Warhol's dematerial flourish, Lawler tints her images in a sour-candy spectrum, as if to honor the democracy—or inoculate against the industry?—of the proliferating multiple. But the affective temperature of her inquiry is far from rueful; in this series it is, once again, closer to wistful: Warhol (and here is his truth that animates Lawler's engaged ambivalence) is the only artist to deliver on the old vanguard promise of crossing the art-life divide as more than a purely symbolic feint, the only one to make us take his whole life, his whole business, as art—as business art. If Lawler were crying, this would surely be why.

Summer's Prettiest Paradox (I Don't Want No Retrospective)

Invited in 1968 by London's Institute of Contemporary Arts to survey his work to date, Andy responded with a blithely decimating hit on retrospective convention. In a breathtaking leveling of the artistic career to brand-name logo, he proposed that the thirty-two soup cans of his LA debut appear dispersed throughout the galleries to make up the entire show. Two years later, in answer to a second invitation to mount a retrospective, this time from the Whitney Museum, he answered with an apparently self-obliterating about-face. His intention: to show only wallpaper—and facedown! In both instances, Warhol's heretic inspirations were to give way to the greater good of curatorial convention; capitulation, for him, was the transcendent leitmotif.[6] For Lawler, his attentive reader, the dialectic that opens between the massive branding triumph and the dissipation of the art object in Andy's ceaseless rounds of gadflying that, ironically, the power of his logo enables, must resonate more vividly than ever as she contemplates the inevitable repackaging entailed in the mid-career retrospective. Lawler, of course, has picked up and performed Andy's thwarted indications in testing the conventions of display on numerous occasions. And indeed, an eleventh-hour source-checking visit to her studio found the artist predictably worrying her reluctant self's ascension to signature. In answering a query about her plans for the form and scope of the show, she fantasized the expansive, atrium-like front galleries of the Museum für Gegenwartskunst hung with massively scaled efforts—not her own, but those of other artists. Her place in these key halls, she mused, might comprise but the slimmest of physical interventions amid the customary fare.

On the eve of a show the artist has suggestively titled Louise Lawler and Others, it is perhaps less than surprising to discover that her exigent precursor should be whispering in both ears at once. Indeed, the vindicating bonus of my visit was a glimpse at Lawler's most recent photograph—a late-breaking addition to her Warhol corpus. Yet to find its final crop at that viewing, the shot in question featured the artist Cindy Sherman in the foreground, hovering forlorn but expectant at some anonymous hallway door—her *Untitled Film Still #4* (1977), a memorable early episode in her signature-making masquerade. Lawler's Pictures-generation peer and the woman artist who has enjoyed the most triumphal rise to stardom of that post-photography sorority, Sherman constitutes a new sighting in our constellation of art-star types. Who scripted her entry?, Lawler seems to muse. And what does it mean—and mean for me? Visible through a door in an adjacent gallery, Warhol's menacing red *Self-Portrait* (1986), the oft-repeated electrocuted-hair-day pose, here shed of camouflage to stand as the artist's most defiantly unembarrassed self-representation to date, sits in as plangent blank.

Notes

1. Benjamin H. D. Buchloh suggests various "dialectic pair[ings] of photographic convention" in Warhol's practice: mug shots and photo booth self-portraits, "glamorous stars with the most anonymous (and cruel) images of everyday life," etc. See Buchloh, "Andy Warhol's One-Dimensional Art: 1956–1966," in *Andy Warhol: A Retrospective*, ed. Kynaston McShine, exh. cat. The Museum of Modern Art (New York, 1989), 53.

2. Buchloh offers a quotation to this effect from a 1965 interview with Warhol in his suggestive discussion of the role of the monochrome in Warhol's ouevre. See Buchloh (see note 1), 46–48.

3. Victor Bockris, *Warhol: The Biography* (1989; expanded reprint Cambridge, 2003), 245–50.

4. Ibid., 249.

5. Douglas Crimp, "'Prominence Given, Authority Taken.' An Interview With Louise Lawler by Douglas Crimp," in Louise Lawler, *An Arrangement of Pictures* (New York, 2000), unpaginated.

6. Buchloh (see note 1), 54–56; Charles F. Stuckey, "Andy Warhol's Painted Faces," *Art in America*, no. 68 (May 1980): 102–11. Buchloh, relying on Stuckey's research, discusses the tension between Warhol's display conceits and the conventional exhibition protocols that often willed out.

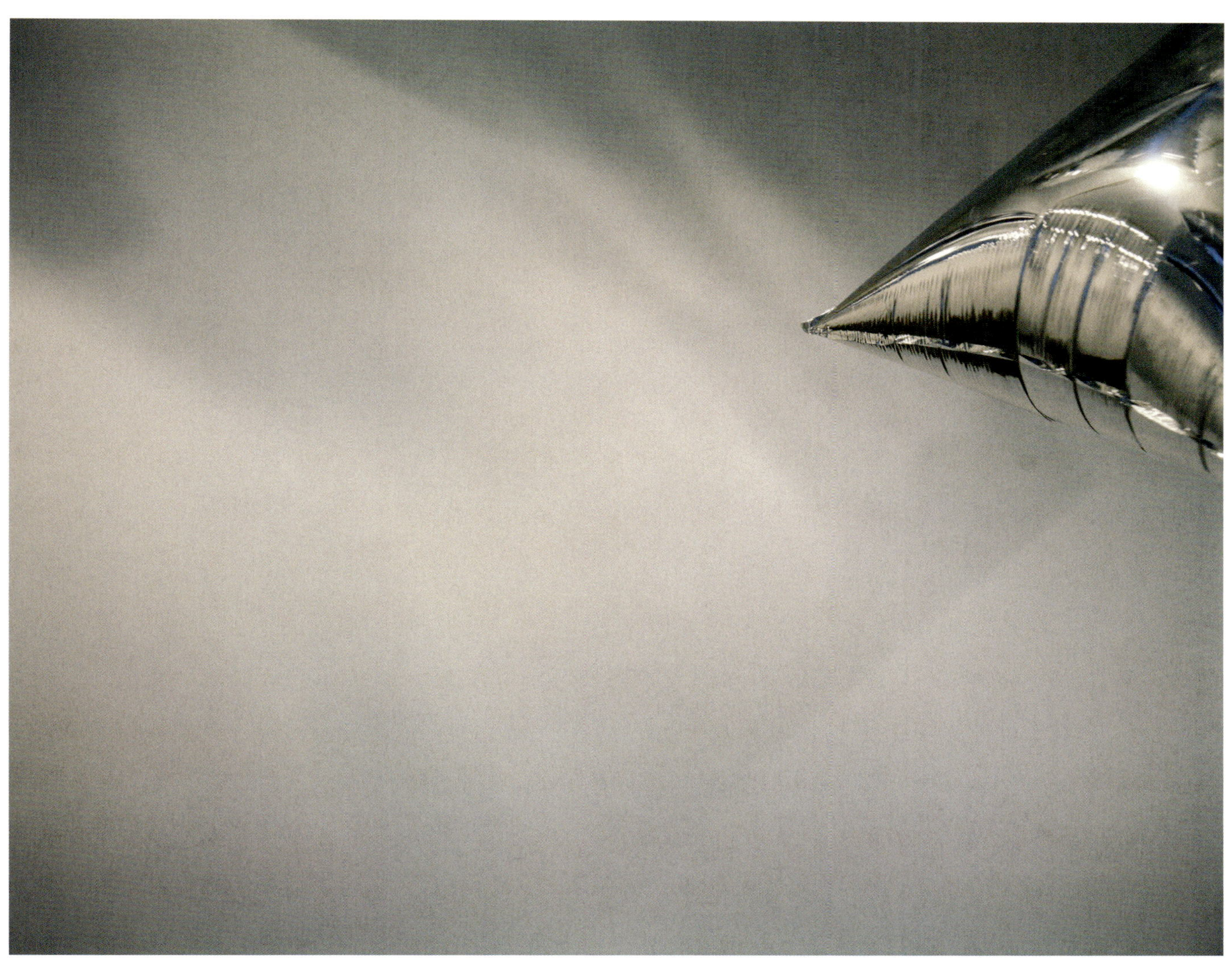

Something About Time and Space But I'm Not Sure What It Is (One) Natural, 1998
cibachrome, 24 x 29 1/2 inches

next page:
Something About Time and Space But I'm Not Sure What It Is, 2000
installation in More Pictures at Metro Pictures, New York

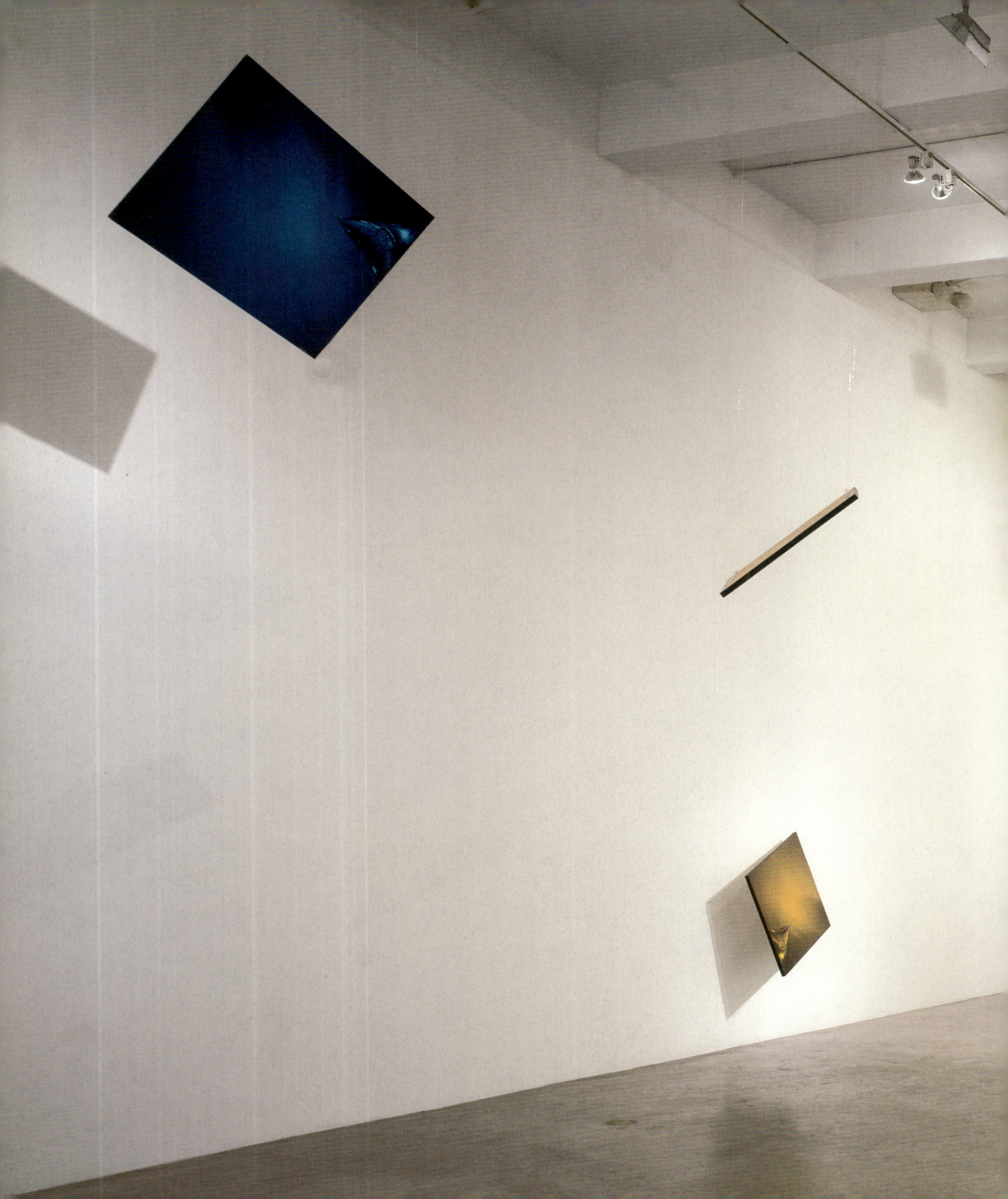

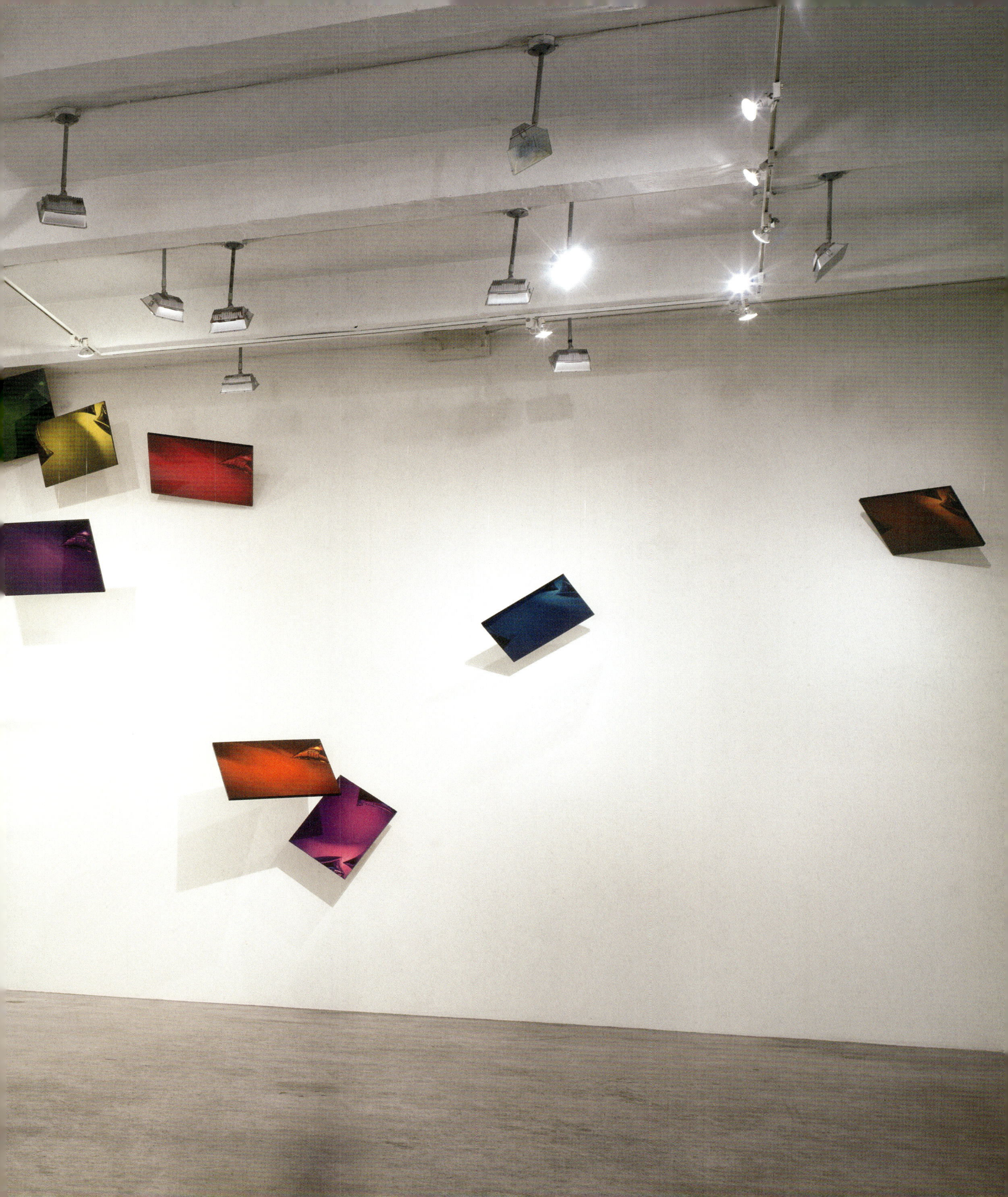

Pink and Yellow and Black II (Green Coca Cola Bottles) from **On a Wall, On a Cow, In a Book, In the Mail**, 1999
cibachrome, 27 x 27 inches

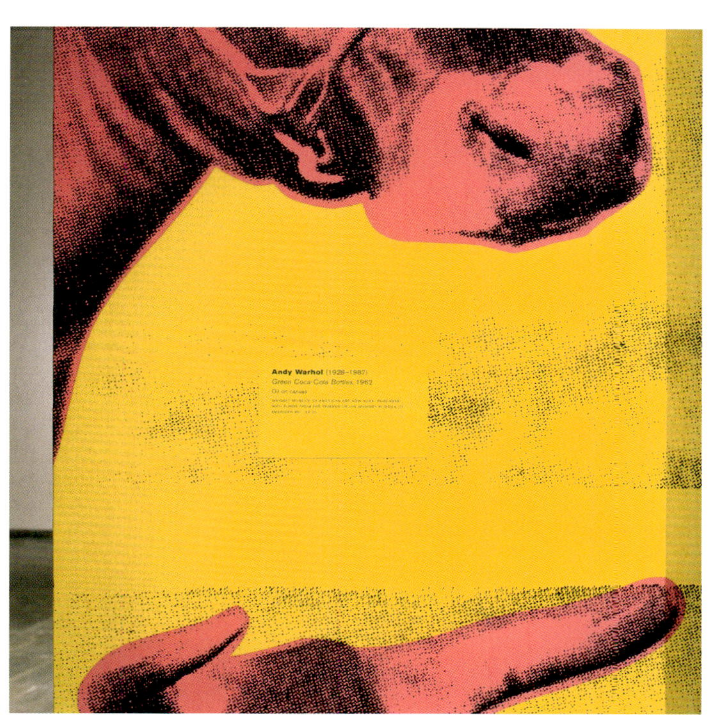
Andy Warhol (1928–1987)
Green Coca-Cola Bottles, 1962
Oil on canvas

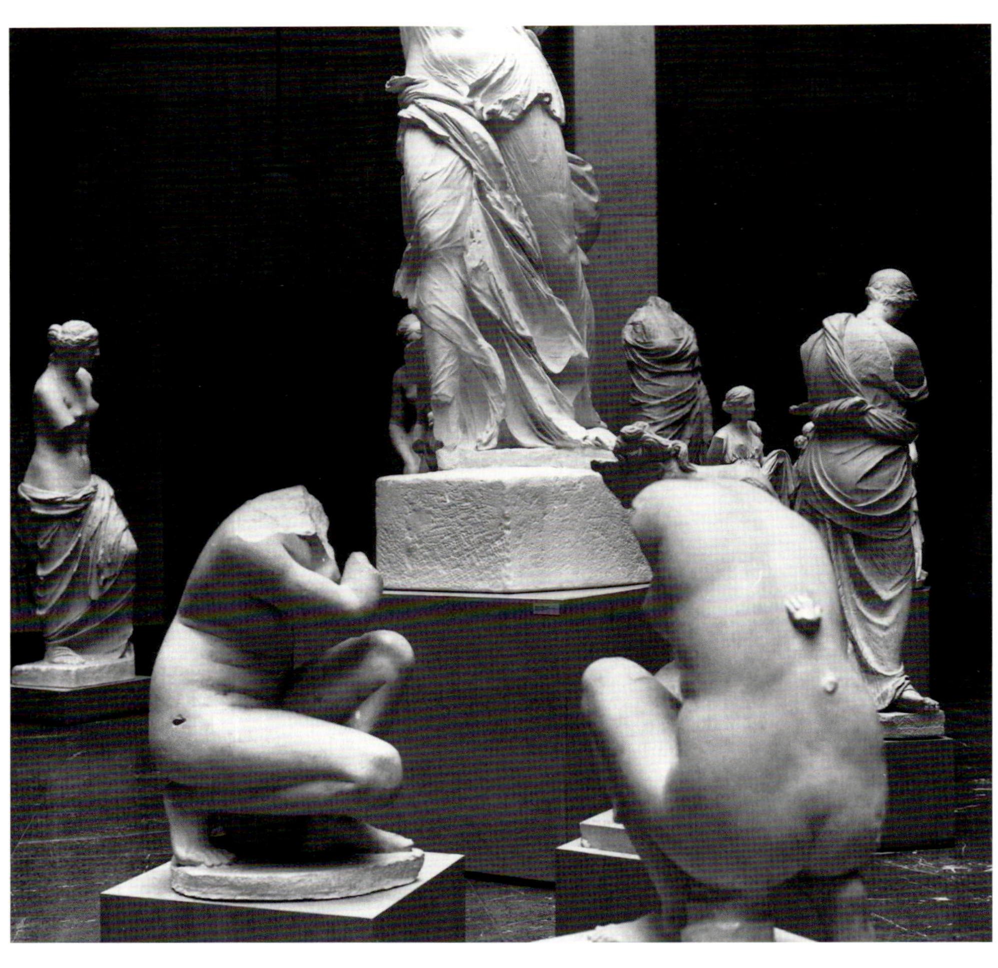

She Wasn't Always a Statue (A), 1996/1997
black and white photograph with mat, $17^{3/4}$ x $18^{1/2}$ inches (image)

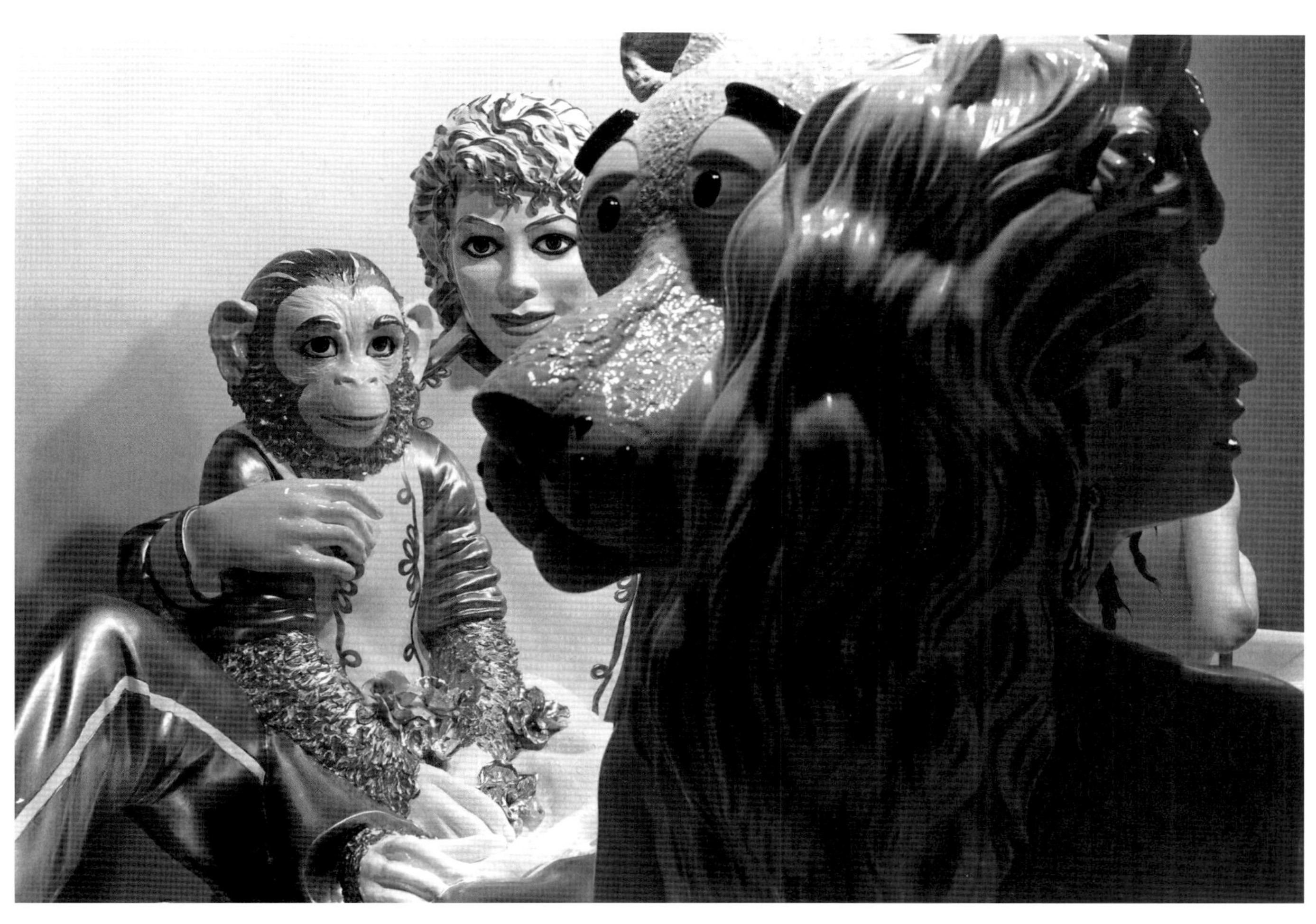

All Those Eyes, 1989
black and white photograph with title as text on mat, $27^{1/2}$ x 31 inches (image)

Michael, 2001
cibachrome, 59 3/4 x 46 inches

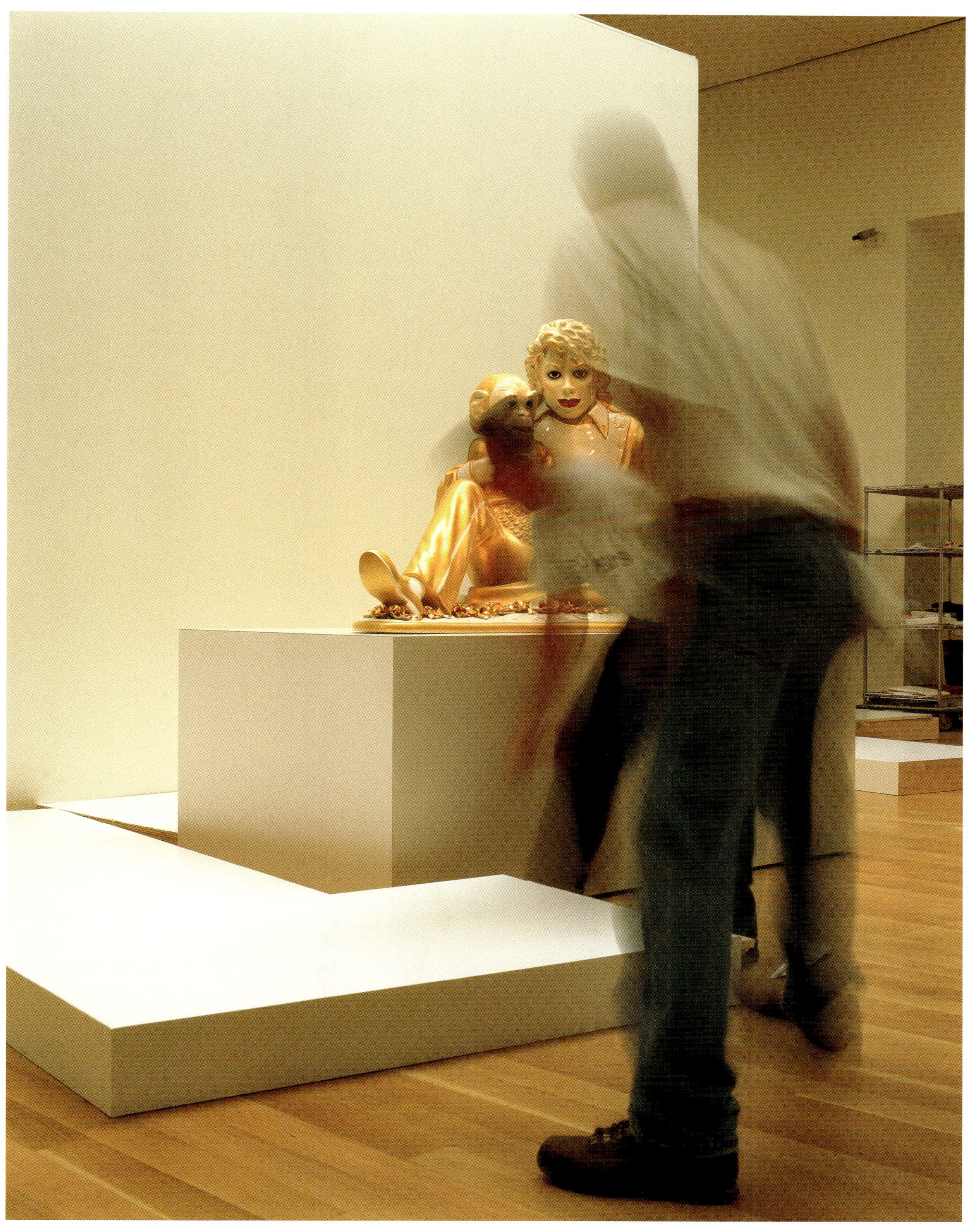

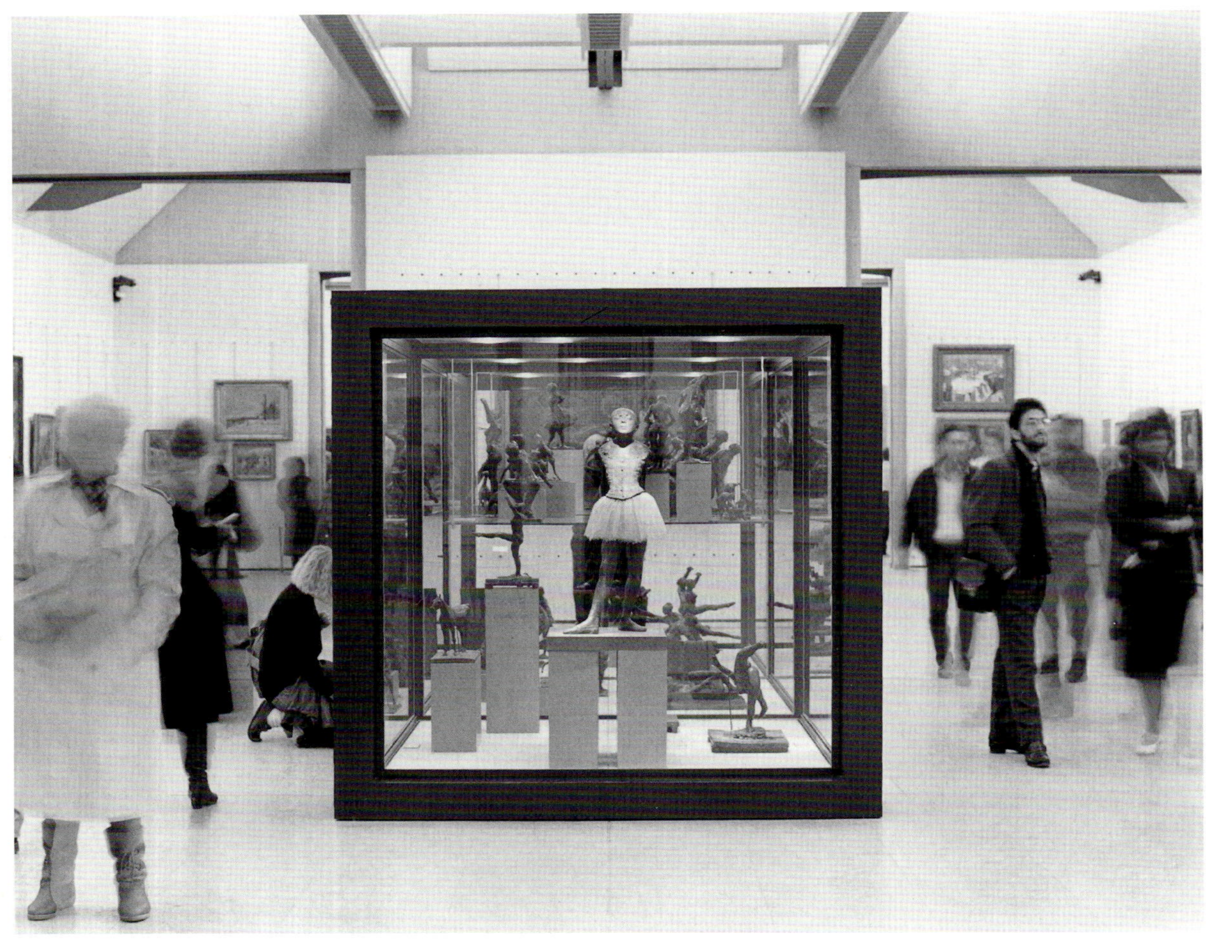

The following year her glass "cage" remained empty for the first two weeks of the exhibition. When finally exposed she was likened by one critic to an "expelled foetus" which if smaller "one would be tempted to pickle in a jar of alcohol."

Glass Cage, 1991/1993 (panel 1)
black and white photograph with text on mat, 12 x 15 inches (image)

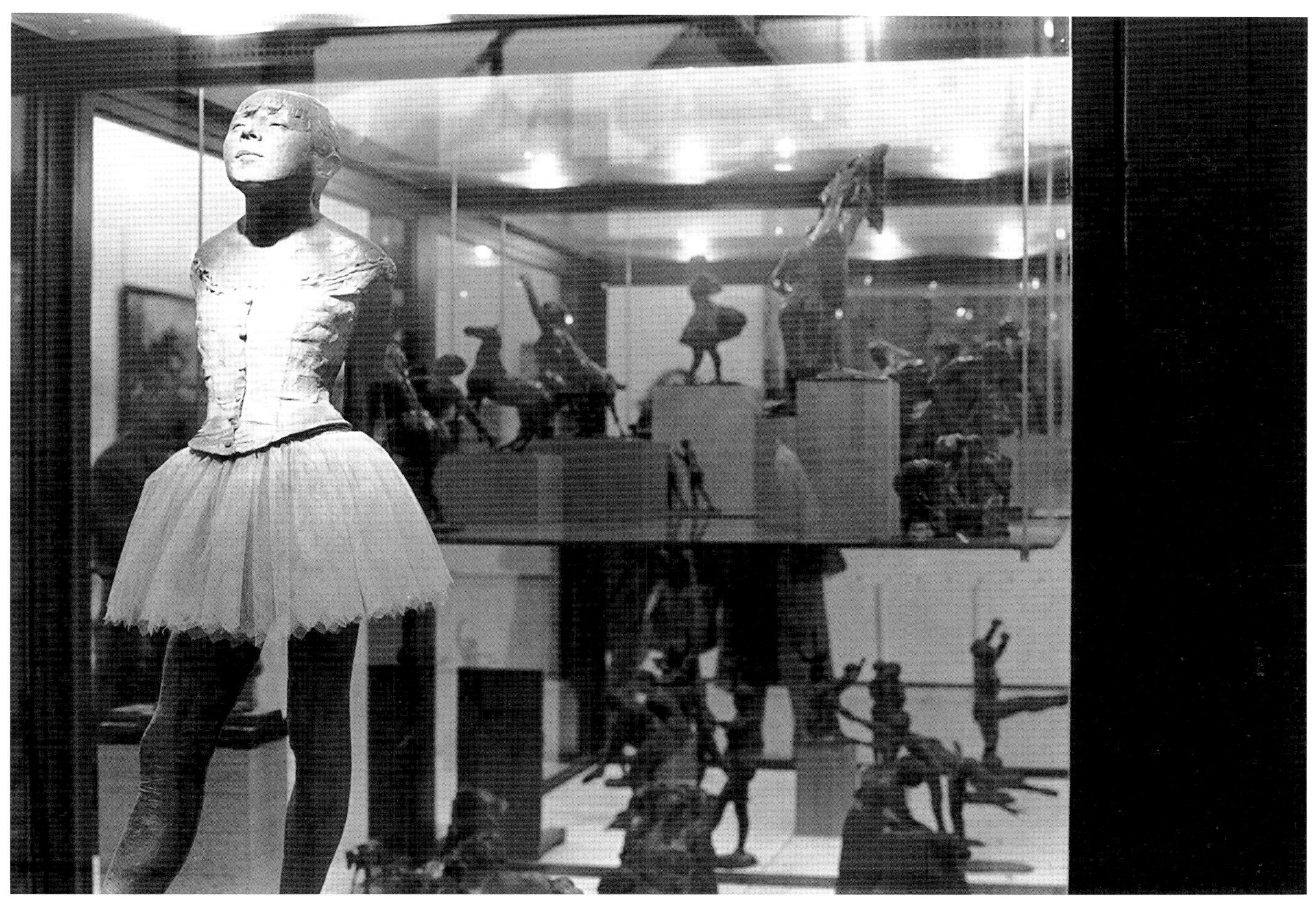

PARIS

Glass Cage, 1991/1993 (panel 2)
black and white photograph with text on mat, 15 x 21 1/4 inches (image)

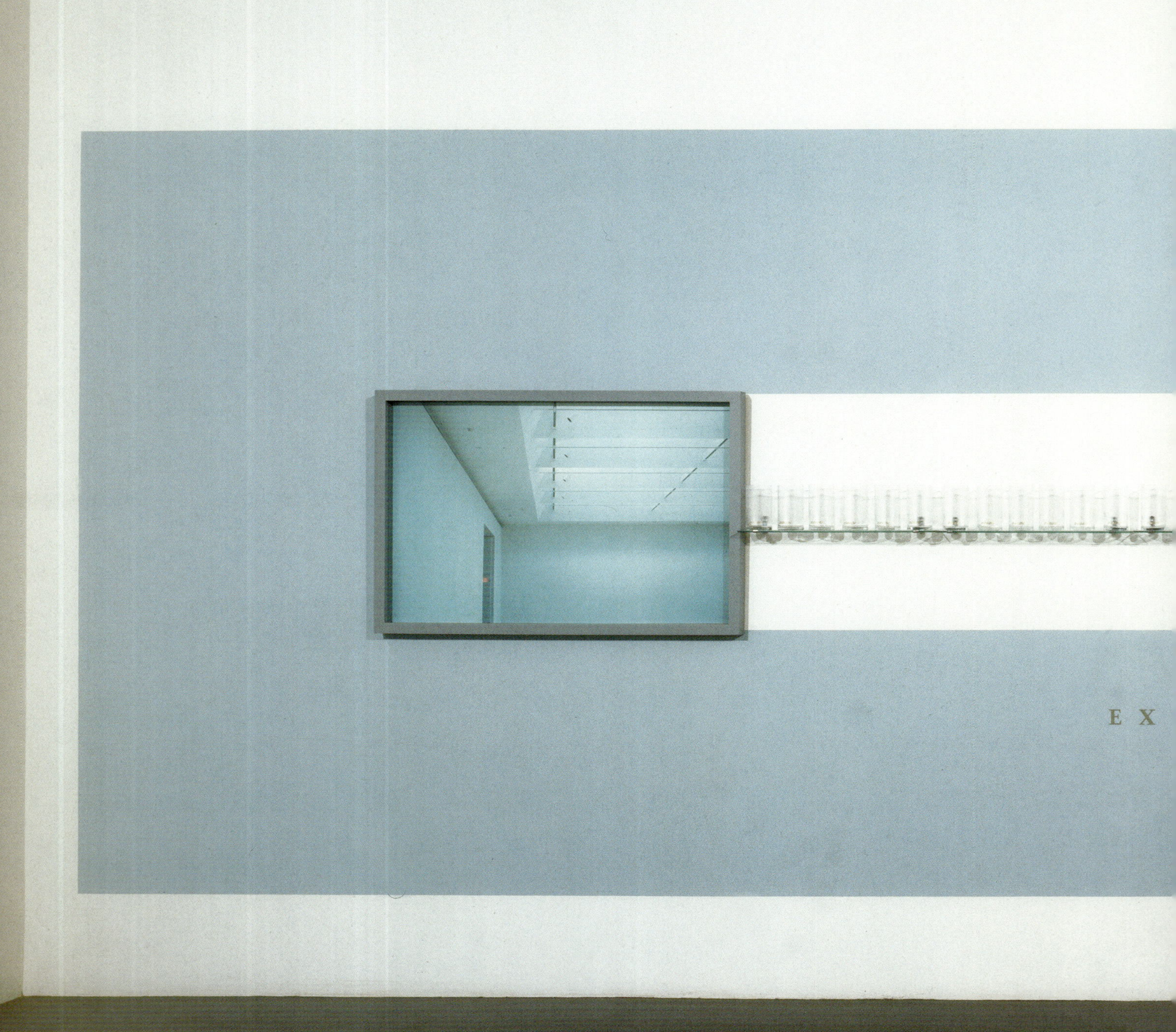

E X

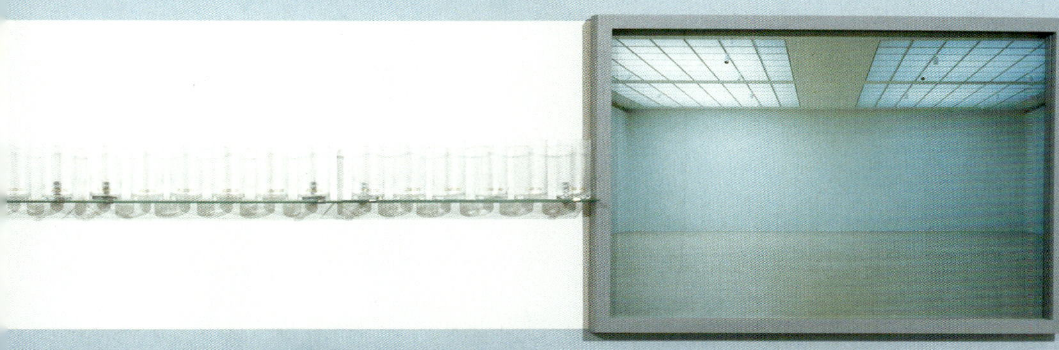

TION

7

artscribe

THE INTERNATIONAL MAGAZINE OF NEW ART

MAY 1990 £3.00/$5.50

RECOGNITION MAYBE, MAY NOT BE USEFUL

Louise Lawler

Jörg Immendorff
Painting and Politics

Art and Evolution
Darwin or Jabberwocky?

Anish Kapoor
at the Venice Biennale

Thom Puckey
Alchemy in Amsterdam

+ SATELLITE NEWS SUPPLEMENT

DISPLACEMENT AND CONDENSATION: A CONVERSATION ON THE WORK OF LOUISE LAWLER

George Baker and Andrea Fraser

Friday, December 12, 2003
178 East 2nd Street, New York

George Baker: Here is my favorite recorded statement by Louise Lawler. It spells out why I think of her as one of the key artists to emerge in the 1970s and early 1980s: "It is no longer a matter of trying to subvert or intrude. Those strategies are now recognized and invited. Now it is a matter of finessing, which is certainly not enough."[1] This statement seems to herald a recognition that her own artistic project, while critical, is also critical of previous avant-garde strategies and positions—that maybe it is even predicated upon their foreclosure.

Andrea Fraser: Subvert and intrude? Versus finessing?

Baker: It is a strange use of language, rather tortured and wonderful. "Now it is a matter of finessing, which is certainly not enough." She seems to be announcing the closure of avant-garde opposition and transgression. Do you agree?

Fraser: I wonder when she developed that perspective. Is that quote from the 1990s? Is it a perspective that she would already have held in the late 1970s? We need to think about how Louise's strategies developed and changed from the late 1970s to the present. Would you read it again?

Baker: "It is no longer a matter of trying to subvert or intrude. . . . Now it is a matter of finessing."

Fraser: Actually, I think Louise's work is all about subversion and intrusion. But those operations may be performed less in her substantive "works"—her objects and images—than in her work as an artist, in her practice. What she's constantly subverting is her own position as an artist, or more generally, the role of the artist in relationship to the frame, to the art apparatus.

Baker: You're right, this is a retrospective statement, made later on in Lawler's artistic career. But I'm wondering if one way of rethinking even her earlier work in the 1970s and early 1980s is to realize how she is *not* continuing the project of institutional critique as that project was defined in the late 1960s and early 1970s. She is *not* continuing the neo-avant-garde or the avant-garde project. She is somehow attempting to invent ways of working that can still be described as critical, but they are no longer oppositional, and they are no longer in fact subverting

previous pages:
Exhibition, 1987

Installation:
MOCA, 1987
cibachrome, 26 x 39 inches
You Could Hear A Rat Piss On Cotton – Charlie Parker, 1987
cibachrome, 26 1/4 x 39 inches

Text on glasses "You Could Hear A Rat Piss On Cotton" – Charlie Parker, shelves, painted wall, transfer type, overall size 90 x 260 inches

opposite page:
Artscribe cover, May 1990

anything. Questioning the role and position of the artist may not be to subvert it. It may be to entrench it, to transvalue it.

Fraser: I may be taking her words a bit more literally than you are. You're jumping from her statement to an interpretation of her project in relation to avant-garde traditions. But if one takes the words literally, "subvert and intrude" are precisely what Louise does in her work.

Baker: How so?

Fraser: To subvert means to reverse, to turn around, to upend. I don't know how else to describe the way Louise has repositioned herself in so much of her work, presenting and representing art, galleries and museums, in her images, installations, and interventions; accomplishing what I've called a "reversal of positions of presentation"[2] by presenting, rather than simply being presented by, the structures and relations that define the frames and the sites of art. And she accomplishes that reversal by intruding in those structures. She intrudes with oddly inappropriate matchbooks, with unofficial or redesigned invitations and letterhead, with wall texts and captions, words and language that don't belong. Her work is *very* intrusive. Which is not to say that it isn't also defined by extraordinary finesse.

Baker: The matchbooks are a good example of a portion of her work that utilizes supplementary insertions into situations, lectures, or exhibitions. This is surely a strategy that derives from Conceptual art as it was active in a variety of locales. I think of Cildo Meireles's *Insertions in Ideological Circuits* in Brazil. Like those previous examples, Lawler's insertions are not sanctioned, invited, or legitimate. Lawler is the great example of an artist who often creates works for exhibitions to which she is not invited, as for example, her letterhead project for documenta 7 back in the early 1980s.

Fraser: The invitation she sent out to a Lincoln Center performance of *Swan Lake* (a performance she had nothing to do with presenting) is another great example. If that's not an intrusion, I don't know what is.

Baker: But on another level, maybe Lawler's statement points to the fact that no matter whether or not an artist chooses to follow certain avant-garde tactics, these strategies are already recuperated. They are already somehow a kind of working plan for how one becomes an artist by the moment of the late 1970s or early 1980s. So that they are not truly in any sense a subversion, or even an intrusion. One is called upon to make these kinds of gestures. Quite precisely "recognized and invited." We can't be naive about that anymore.

Fraser: But one of the differences I see between Louise's interventions and earlier avant-garde models is that many, if not most, of her interventions were quite explicitly sanctioned. While I still see her work as subversive and intrusive, I do agree that she rejected the posture of oppositionality, the pose of the outsider. However, I'm not sure this implies that she saw subversion as "already recuperated." That's a perspective that led to a lot of cynical art in the 1980s. What I think Louise's work did begin to recognize is that the process of recuperation is more deeply rooted in the structural ambivalence of a field of which artists and their subversions are a fundamental part. I would even say that relations of collaboration and complicity between artists and art institutions is one of Louise's central subjects.

My other question about what you are saying has to do with the tendency to see a kind of historical unfolding of practices sequentially, say, from avant-garde models to their rejection or being surpassed. In fact, it may have been only in the 1980s that "institutional critique" as an avant-garde strategy was being recognized and constituted, retrospectively.

Baker: Understood for the first time.

Fraser: Yes, and at the very same time that it was seen as being surpassed. My own essay about Louise's work from 1985, "In and Out of Place," may have been part of that process. The first generation of "institutional critics"—Marcel Broodthaers, Hans Haacke, Daniel Buren, Michael Asher—had been active since the late 1960s. But it was only in the early 1980s, with essays by critics like Benjamin Buchloh, Douglas Crimp, and Craig Owens, that those practices began to be identified as "institutional critique." My generation, as students of those critics, were taking their ideas up, almost at the same time as the critics were publishing them, but as

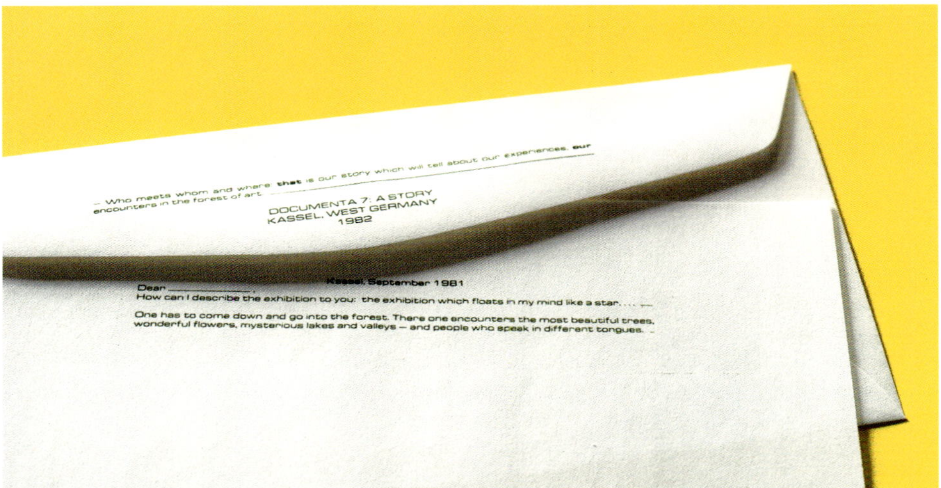

documenta stationery, 1982

Two sheets of stationery and one envelope with excerpts from a letter to the participating artists from the director of documenta 7, Rudi Fuchs

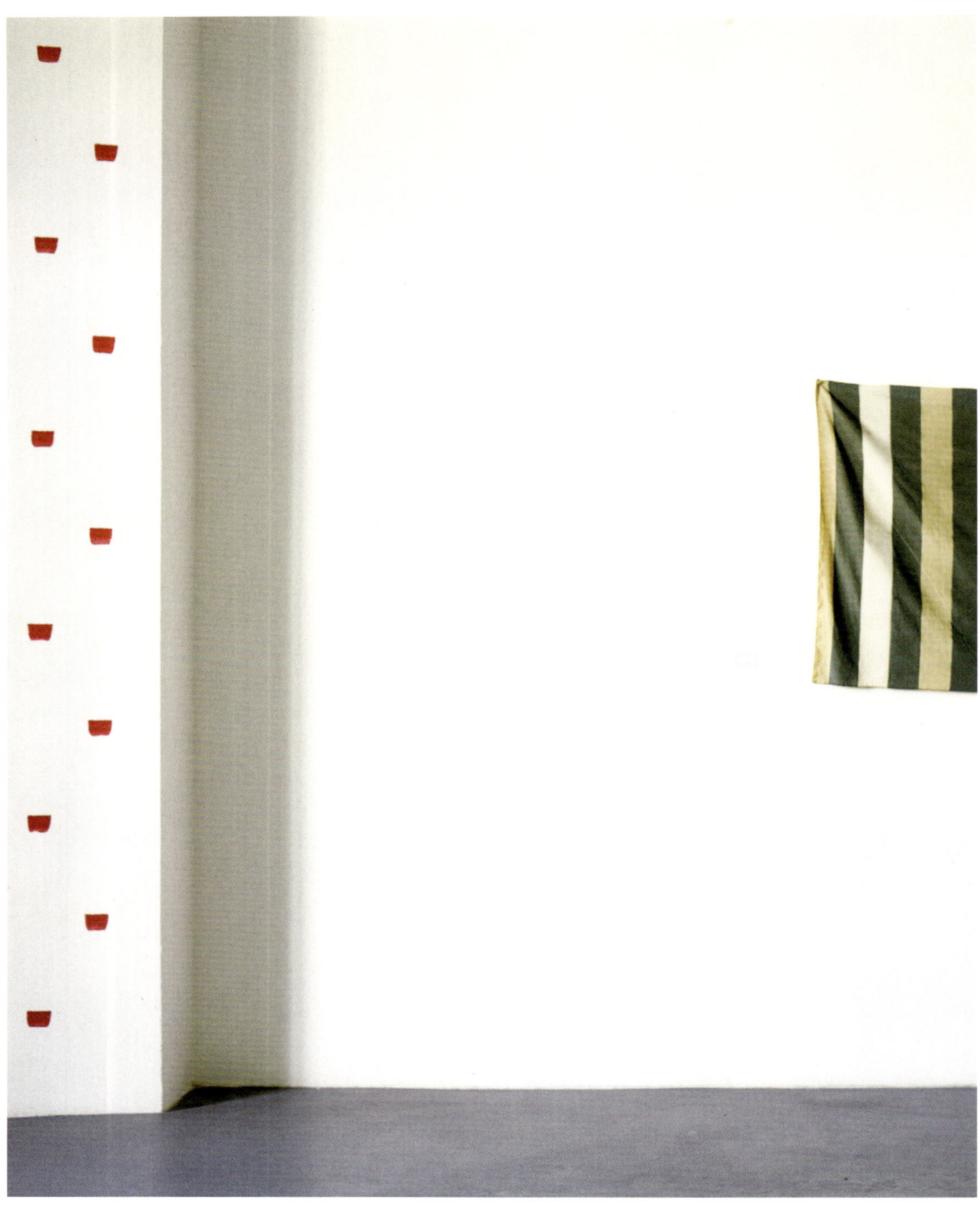

Work by Niele Toroni and Daniel Buren installed in Collection d'artistes at Collection Lambert, Avignon, 2001

already codified. So, by 1985, when I wrote about Louise's work, I could distinguish her work from a framework that I saw as historical but which actually was only coming into being at that moment.

Baker: Right, but if you follow the old adage that "the owl of Minerva only flies at dusk," then just at the moment that history can finally be recognized and written it is also in some sense already over. I would like to suggest that Lawler may have been one of the first artists to realize this for the art practices of her own time. She realizes the necessity of inventing a new set of artistic strategies that while connected to Conceptual art and institutional critique, are set in a new cultural formation and act and react in new ways. I think a recognition of this shift is in fact present too in your essay on Lawler from 1985. Can we discuss how and why you came to write this essay?

Fraser: I was a student in the Whitney Museum Independent Study Program, sitting in on Craig Owens's art criticism class at the School of the Visual Arts. I had met Louise through Allan McCollum, who I met through Thomas Lawson, who also taught at SVA, and I proposed to Craig that I write something about Louise for his class. He said, well, why don't you develop something serious and I'll try to get it into *Art in America*. He was an editor there at the time. He was a big fan of Louise's work. Very little had been written about her at that time. I was nineteen.

Baker: It is hard to imagine that moment: when nothing really had yet been written about Lawler, and when a nineteen-year-old would take up the challenge. I think it is very telling that one of the best essays on Lawler's work was written by a fellow artist.

Fraser: There still isn't much written on Louise's work, and much of what has been written strikes me as problematic. I was involved in identifying her work with institutional critique. Since then, that framework seems to have been laid out in an increasingly literal and reductive way, as if her strategies developed as a programmatic, even instrumental response to a particular agenda. I don't think that's the case at all. However, in retrospect, it may be that I played a central role in the formation of that programmatic reading.

Baker: We should identify what this "programmatic" reading has been. I would say, however, that your "In and Out of Place" now, almost twenty years later—when a certain programmatic reading of Lawler's work has become more common—is a somewhat disruptive essay to read. For example, its title seems to refer more to a spatial or sculptural practice than to a photographic, image-based, representational practice. That aspect of Lawler's work that was built around installations, text-based projects, and sculpture has continued to this day, but often has been seen by critics as an unresolved or unresolvable aspect of her work. It has thus often been ignored. Lawler is received now basically as a photographer. It is the understanding of her work that is codified in her recent book *An Arrangement of Pictures*.[3] In your essay of twenty years ago, you hardly even mention photography.

Fraser: In 1985, she had never really exhibited her photographs. She had published photographs in *October*[4] and elsewhere, but actually, I would still say that Louise doesn't "exhibit photographs."

Baker: What do you mean by that?

Fraser: Well, she shows photographs, but they are always framed. She *installs* photographs. She produces photographs that she *presents* in various ways: with texts, with different mats and frames, in specific juxtapositions and arrangements, on color walls, as paperweights. For me, however, the title "In and Out of Place" doesn't refer to sculpture or installation. I was trying to read Louise's *practice* as a practice. It's actually about performance.

Baker: What? How, in 1985, can you see Louise Lawler's work as performance? As performance art? That is rather your practice.

Fraser: I wouldn't call her work "performance art"—"performative" maybe, but in 1985 that term was not yet part of the critical lexicon. Yes, performance may be my practice, but you have to understand that Louise's work and the view of it I developed in that essay inaugurated my own work as an artist. In the context of a postmodern discourse centered on the appropriation of images, objects, and texts, Louise *also* began appropriating positions and functions in a fundamentally performative way. That's what distinguished her work from all that other "appropriation" art of the moment. In the context of a postmodern discourse centered on the displacement of images and objects, she displaced herself, particularly within positions of presentation. For me, it was a pretty short step from there to performing museum tours.

Baker: But I still don't understand why you are calling this a performance. What strategies by Lawler are "performative"?

Fraser: *Arranging* pictures, *producing* matchbooks, *issuing* gift certificates, *sending out* invitations, *presenting* art and institutions through those activities . . .

Baker: So what was more important to you was less the actual arrangement of pictures that Lawler would exhibit, than the activity of arranging itself? Lawler's act-

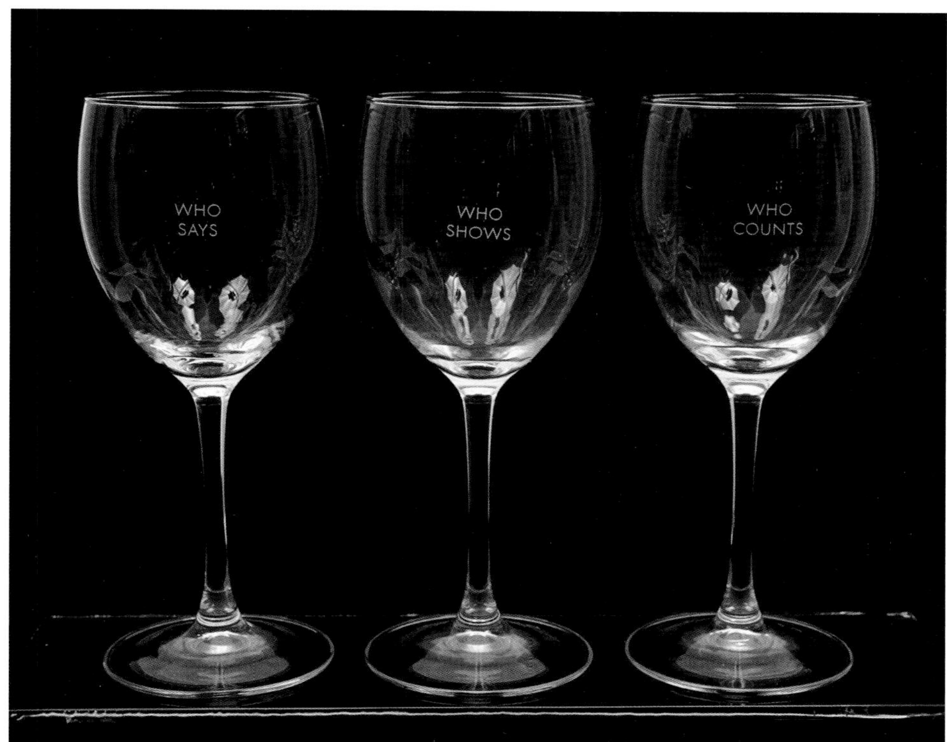

Who Says, Who Shows, Who Counts, 1990

Three etched wine glasses on glass shelf, nickel plated brackets, edition of 50, produced for the benefit of Artists Space

ing as a "curator" or as an "art consultant"? Meaning that you prioritize less the work produced than Lawler's mode of production, even what we might call her labor? She occupied the position of a worker. This runs through her entire project. And Allan McCollum's quite different project too, we could say. It is this that is performative for you. Actually, it is a foregrounding of labor, a linking of artist and worker. I'm still having trouble with seeing this as a performance though, or as performative.

Fraser: I took up the question of artistic labor quite directly in an essay I wrote about Allan McCollum's work in 1986.[5] But in 1985, I wasn't thinking about Louise's work in terms of labor. I still don't think I would today. I was thinking of practice, position, and function in terms that were influenced by Marxist cultural theory, but also by psychoanalytical film theory, by the Baudrillard of essays like "Gesture and Signature," and by Foucault—that was the mid-1980s mix! It was through that matrix that I tried to differentiate Louise's strategies from those of Asher, Buren, Haacke, and Broodthaers. Listen to this: "Rather than situate institutional power in a centralized building (such as a museum) or a powerful elite which can be named, she locates it instead in a systematized set of presentational procedures which name, situate, centralize."[6] It does sound rather Foucaultian, doesn't it?

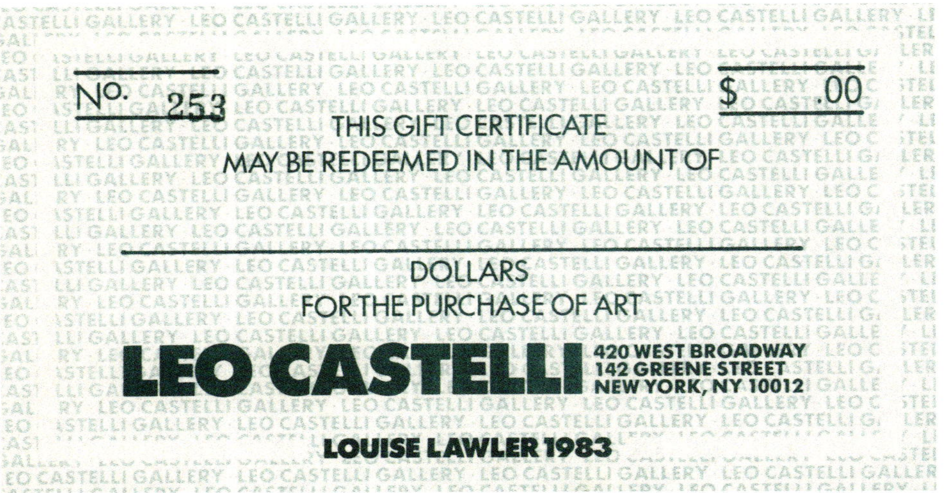
No. 253

$ .00

THIS GIFT CERTIFICATE
MAY BE REDEEMED IN THE AMOUNT OF

DOLLARS
FOR THE PURCHASE OF ART

LEO CASTELLI
420 WEST BROADWAY
142 GREENE STREET
NEW YORK, NY 10012

LOUISE LAWLER 1983

Leo Castelli Gift Certificate, 1983

Produced for and installed in Drawings/Photographs, Leo Castelli Gallery, New York, 1983. They were available for purchase until the downtown gallery closed.

A gift certificate was also produced for the Margo Leavin Gallery for inclusion in the exhibition Nothing Sacred, 1987.

Baker: Yes, it is actually a theoretical intensification of what looking to a frame or to art's context might mean as a critical strategy. So performative here does mean—since you have now brought up the name of Foucault—something rather different than "performance art." You are using the term as theorists today such as Judith Butler do when she describes what is called "performativity." It signals an attentiveness to the way certain discursive formations actually instantiate the objects they might otherwise be understood as merely describing.

Fraser: Perhaps, but what I see as Foucaultian here has more to do with where institutional power lies and how it functions: not in architecture, or in the museum as a building, or even in an elite class, but in a set of structures and systems that are discursive and also relational. I see Louise's work as part of a step from a substantive to a relational understanding of institutions as well as of critical practice.

Baker: Now we might finally be able to understand the citation from Lawler with which we started. If it is no longer a matter of "subversion" or "intrusion," if it is no longer a matter of avant-garde strategies we might otherwise describe as oppositional, it is now a matter of finessing. Which would mean: working within structures, within discourse, immanent to the way power operates and in some sense alongside it. Displacing it, redirecting it perhaps, but not opposing it.

Let's return to your notion of Lawler's practice as the performative occupation of positions within an institutional system. What are the positions that we can identify? If I remember your essay correctly, there are three.

Fraser: I included the position of an artist who exhibits in galleries and museums, that of a publicist/museum worker who produces material that supplements cultural objects and events, and that of an art consultant or curator who arranges works by other artists.

Baker: You are missing something: Lawler has come to be known as an artist whose work approximates the labor and appropriates the forms of a very specific type of gallery work, namely, the labor of an installation photographer, documenting works of art for the gallery, museum catalogue, or auction house.

Fraser: But it isn't really very precise, is it, to list these "positions"?

Baker: Then evidently we need to continue to unpack this notion of what you understood as a "position" and Lawler's performance of such positions. It seems that one of the ramifications of this idea is a kind of relational intensification, by which I mean that Lawler begins to occupy *more* than one position in the institutional apparatus of the art world. The combination of disparate positions, their interpenetration, could itself be a critical activity—a relational one, not a substantive one, as you have put it. To occupy the position not just of an artist, but of an artist and a critic at the same time, an artist and a curator at the same time, to undo what Craig Owens once called the division of labor in the art world: this would itself be the way a critical activity would operate. So in fact this critical activity is still about labor. It's also about collectivity, about collective labor.

Fraser: But I would still be careful about thinking of Louise's work in terms of labor. According to Marx, it's the confines of commodity production that reduce human activity into labor—the alienated labor congealed in alienable objects. But I see commodity production as one of the central things that Louise has managed with "finesse." A great example of this is her gift certificate for Leo Castelli Gallery from 1983. If an artist today made a gift certificate for an art gallery, it could only represent a cynical admission of the reduction of the art object to the most abstract of commodities—that is, currency. But Louise managed to engage and even intervene in the economic conditions of the work of art on a material and functional level, and to do so without functionalizing herself as labor.

One of the things that separates Louise and other artists of her generation such as Allan McCollum from the conceptualists who came before them and from my generation after them is their effort to keep instrumentalization at a certain distance. This is what I would like to read into the quote with which we began. The first generation of Conceptual artists and "institutional critics" may have pursued a kind of self-instrumentalization as a transgressive gesture in the context of a critique of artistic autonomy. Many artists of my generation, on the other hand, have taken up that self-instrumentalization in the context of what increasingly looks like the historical dissipation of artistic autonomy, pursuing a literal functionalization rather than a strategic one. One way of understanding Louise's project, is that

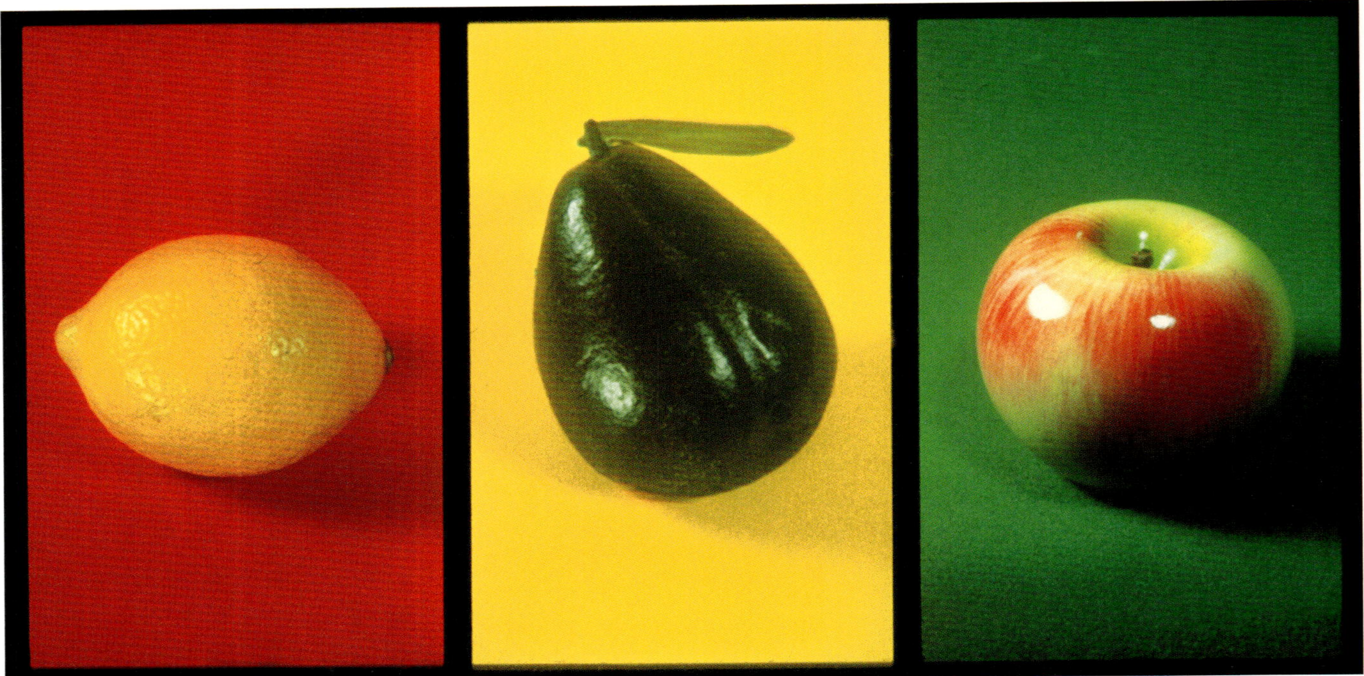

Slides By Night: Now That We Have Your Attention What Are We Going To Say, 1985

An automated slide piece was installed to be seen through the windows at Metro Pictures, January 5–26, 1985, Tuesday–Saturday, 5–10pm only

she's tried to chart a course between these options, maintaining a *performance* of functions with an extraordinarily sharp eye for the pitfalls of false resolutions—or the false revolutions of the avant-garde imagination. I would call that finesse.

Baker: It is clear that the younger generation of critical artists who follow the generation of Lawler, Barbara Kruger, McCollum, and Sherrie Levine, surely reacted to the commercialization of most of those practices in their embracing of the gallery system, in their strategy of working with and within it. This younger generation surely hasn't followed the golden path that leads to a gallery career at Mary Boone, Paula Cooper, Marian Goodman, or Metro Pictures. Maybe Lawler once again is somewhat of an exception. She didn't turn out to be a Barbara Kruger; she didn't turn out to be a Cindy Sherman. But surely a younger generation returns to "instrumental" or even what I would call specific neo-avant-garde practices such as those of Conceptual art on this basis alone, as a protest against the failure of an attempt to invent post-avant-garde or postmodern critical strategies, strategies that were perceived as simply collapsing into affirmation.

Fraser: Yes, that may be true. But one can also see that, rather than resisting Louise's work, a range of younger artists have broken it down into parts, taking up some particular aspect of it. With artists like Thomas Struth, for example, the photograph of the museum installation has been turned into a grand genre of photography in itself.

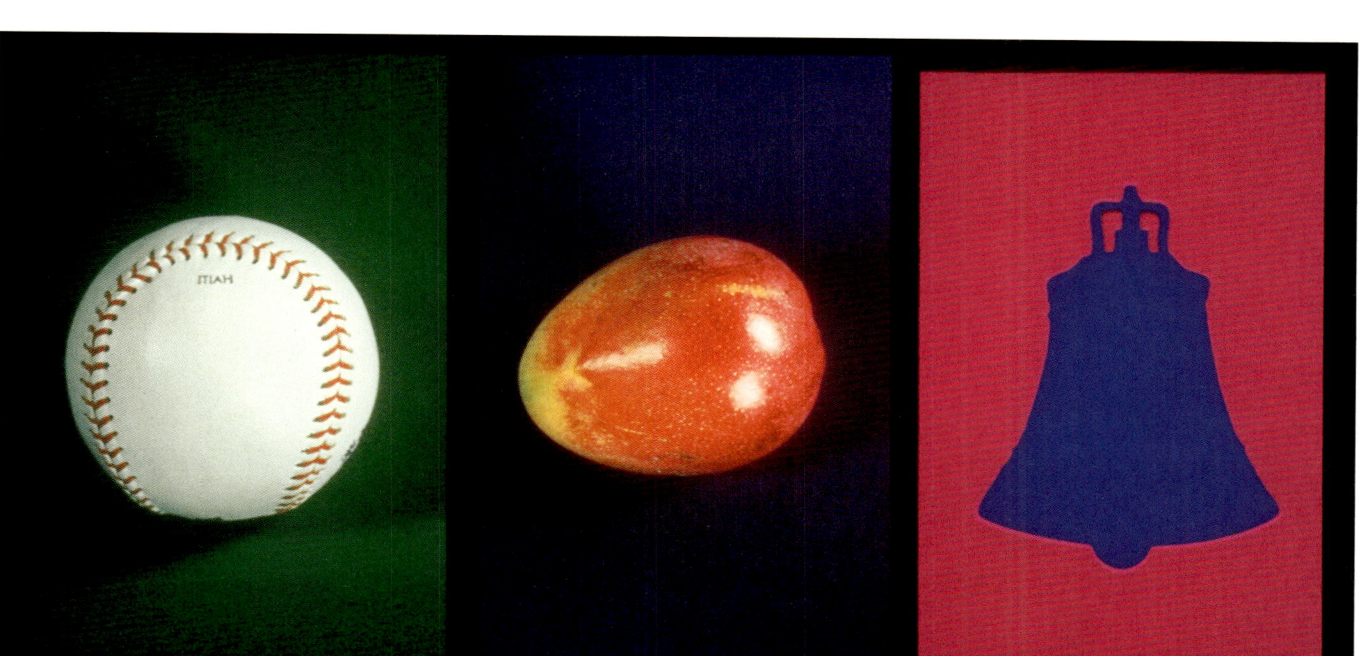

Baker: There are other photographers who haven't monumentalized Lawler's strategies, but hook into overlooked dimensions of Lawler's work to transform photographic practice: Andrea Robbins and Max Becher, for example, and their use of those high-intensity, almost kitsch colors that Lawler has often employed, on their frames and as image borders. Despite your refusal to recognize her as a photographer, many contemporary photographers have obviously seen her work as revitalizing.

Fraser: Louise's use of colors, particularly in painting gallery walls, has often been seen as an intervention in the frame. Here again, however, one finds artists and also curators who have taken up her strategies only to fall into one of those pitfalls of false resolution we mentioned earlier. In this case, they get turned into a positive program of "institutional reform" by artists and curators who seem to believe that by painting walls a surprising color, or using a different kind of wall label, one can render the frame less transparent. But what one usually ends up with is just a more blatant form of visual manipulation.

Baker: In fact, the kind of work you are referring to has signaled a more aestheticized relation to the institution: salon-style installations, arrangements of art that are somehow pre-modernist, reaching back into the history of institutions beyond the white cube/autonomy approach.

Fraser: And now we have the curator-as-producer-of-spectacle and the artist-as-institutional-stylist.

Baker: Do you want to name names?

Fraser: I'm not sure it's necessary. What we're talking about here has become one of the dominant modes of exhibition-making, for curators as well as artists.

Baker: But are you also implying that the aspect of working in tandem with and amplifying institutional aspirations—as opposed to critiquing them—is already folded into Lawler's project?

Fraser: Perhaps. And perhaps Louise foresaw that potential. If so, I would say that she has tried to guard against it in her own work by continually shifting and displacing the strategies that she brings into play. That may be one way of resisting the condition of being "already recuperated" that we discussed earlier. But it's also why, I imagine, exhibitions and catalogues such as this one here in Basle, or her recent book, *An Arrangement of Pictures*, may pose particular difficulties for her.

Baker: What do you see as these "difficulties"? You just did a big retrospective book yourself.

Fraser: The totalizing demands of these kinds of frames, which are not only frames for works of art but for artistic practices, allow very little room for finesse. They demand adherence on a very immediate, intimate, subjective level.

Baker: I'm not sure that I agree. Actually, I think there is a major difference between Lawler's recent book and yours that points not only to a split between yourself and Lawler as artists, but perhaps as well to a wider generational difference. To do a book of photographs like Lawler's *An Arrangement of Pictures* is a very different project than a retrospective catalogue, for example. Your book is in fact an encapsulation of projects, very much retrospective. But I see *An Arrangement of Pictures* as much less of a retrospective statement with the kind of claim to totality that a retrospective catalogue makes. In fact, Lawler admits in one of her published interviews to having thought about writing down a series of descriptions of all of her projects, many of which were ephemeral and site-specific installations whose context we can no longer access as they don't exist as documentary images. But she can't do it. She hasn't done it. She cannot provide an "authoritative" reading of her own work, a set of statements of artistic intentions. And you seem to have no problem providing such descriptions of all your work, in painstaking detail. Somehow it is anathema to Lawler to pin her work down, to provide an explanation of her own practice sanctioned by the figure of the artist. That is the space that she needs and that the work needs to continue to claim. In some sense, it is still an aesthetic space, a claim that there is a place for interpretation and reception, and that the artist should do nothing and in fact must do nothing to interfere with this because it would betray the autonomy of the work.

Fraser: But aren't you interfering, pinning the work down, betraying its autonomy, in ascribing such needs and intentions? In supposing to know what she is and is not able to do? I think you're overlooking the deeply ambivalent and contradictory character of her practice.

Baker: How is it contradictory?

Fraser: Because all the work is about how *everything* interferes with the kind of unfettered reception that you just described!

Baker: I don't think you are confronting my point. You *embrace* instrumentalization of yourself as an artist, but this also extends to your own work. To write descriptions of all of your works and projects for your catalogue, as you have just done—returning in fact to the example of Michael Asher and the format of the well-known catalogue that he did in collaboration with Benjamin Buchloh—this is a strategy that Lawler has rejected. Maybe this will change, but Lawler has not seemed able to encompass that kind of relationship to her own work. This seems to suggest what I would almost call a kind of faith, a belief that the work cannot be pinned down by the artist, and should not be pinned down by the creator of the work. It can only be understood in its reception, it can only be understood in its cultural emplacement, and this process is collective. Do you find such a strategy coy? Or heartfelt?

Fraser: Neither. I find it to be, precisely, a *strategy*—which is not to say that it's necessarily instrumental or programmatic. I may agree with you that it's a strategy born of need, of what one is or not able to tolerate as an artist. But I don't think that has anything do to with faith in the process of reception. Rather, I see it as an extremely fraught and exacting effort to resist that process, as it exists, or better, to evade it. Is that another way of understanding "finessing"? I see it as a profoundly ambivalent strategy that emerged in response to the profoundly contradictory condition not only of art and its reception, but of being an artist. And this is what I think is so profoundly difficult about Louise's work—for Louise herself, perhaps, as well as for critics to understand.

Baker: What exactly is so hard to understand?

Fraser: Its particular—extreme—integrity with respect to the condition of being an artist. I mean, that one cannot simply "produce," that one cannot simply settle into an artistic identity: that one cannot simply occupy the position of "artist" in relation, not only to the apparatus, but to one's own practice, which, as a constructed mode of production, is also a product of that apparatus, but which is nevertheless the identity in which one must live out one's professional life. So that, in each instance and each moment and each context in which one is called upon to occupy that identity, to be oneself as an artist, or simply to be an artist, to produce, one must engage that demand and the mechanisms of positioning and framing through which it produces you as an artist. This goes back to my point about performance. Louise's work is not only about the objects: it's about the practice, the position, the function, the person . . .

Baker: I think Lawler would *strongly* object to the reading you've just laid out. Her work is precisely not about herself personally, it is not about her identity.

Fraser: No, her work is not about *her* identity, but it is about artistic identity. Another one of my favorite works by Louise is her response to an invitation to be on the cover of *Artscribe* magazine in 1990, when *Artscribe* was running portraits of artists on their covers. She submitted a publicity photo of Meryl Streep instead! Across the image, Louise had the text "Recognition Maybe, May Not Be Useful" printed with her name under it. She recently used an image of that cover on an unofficial "bookmark" to the book *An Arrangement of Pictures* which also contained "errata"—a great example of how she reframes her own projects. But the original cover is itself a great example of the precision with which Louise approaches invitations and the attention she pays to the minute details of framing and presentation. And that precision has had definite consequences for her production. It may be why she waited so long to do a book like *An Arrangement of Pictures*, or a survey exhibition like the one this catalogue has been produced for. People have been asking Louise to do surveys for years. The demand Louise makes on herself—to confront each situation in which she is asked to work by making an intervention—is extraordinarily exacting. It's a demand that causes her to reject quite a few invitations. This is the aspect of Louise's practice that became an ideal for me in the mid-1980s, a standard that I hoped to live up to. However, to go back to your question about the differences between her practice and mine, there may be a way in which I and other artists of my generation took refuge from that demand in a kind of critical didacticism. It may be that our efforts to find a "true" resolution to the contradictions and ambivalence that confront us as artists have sprung as much from fatigue in the face of that demand as from critical commitment.

Baker: That is a very beautiful way of putting the dilemmas of Lawler's practice. I could take up your words and use them to confront what seems to be the problem of criticism, too, when faced with Lawler's work. Her work has been massively misunderstood, I think, and this because of a need to resolve the work's very

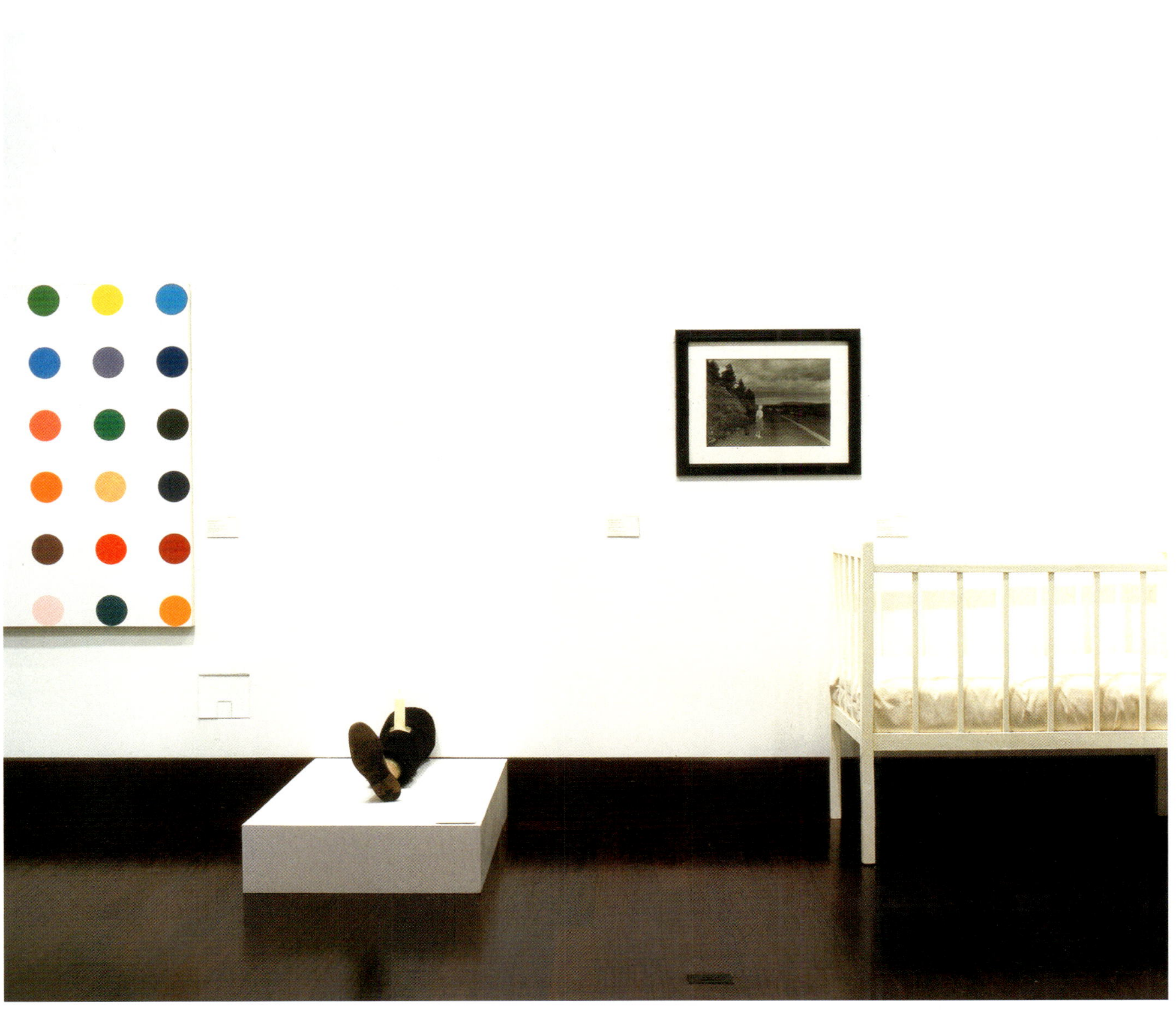

Sentimental, 1999/2000
cibachrome, 41 x 49 1/4 inches

fraught ambivalence, its multiplicity of meanings. Perhaps this situation is finally beginning to change.

Fraser: I hope so. I think there's been a truncated understanding of Louise's work, one that fails to encompass the full range of displacements that she's performed, even upon her own work. But we can also see that failure as evidence of the success of her strategies. Her practice doesn't constitute a stable object that a critic can simply contemplate. I would say that the most challenging of her displacements are not spatial or even functional, but temporal, in the way she continually reframes her own work. Here's another example of "finesse": the way she takes the historical conditions of her own reception into account. Daniel Buren allowed us to understand the spatial displacement of art—its movement from the studio to the museum, gallery, or private home—as a condition of its institutionalization. One of the truncated understandings of Louise's work is that she's "documenting" that same process. But much more central to Louise's work is the temporality of those displacements, a temporality in which she intervenes by constantly re-presenting and re-framing her own work. The *Artscribe* cover is a very direct intervention in the way artists are called upon to represent themselves. However, its contextual, performative, subversive character is lost in its retrospective apprehension as representative of a certain artist's strategy. But then she reproduces it as a bookmark with "errata"! She brings it back to life as an intervention in the context of a new moment of self-presentation: a coffee-table book. She's doing that constantly.

Baker: By arranging her images in different groupings . . . ?

Fraser: Placing them in subsequent slide shows . . .

Baker: Recaptioning them, changing titles . . . ?

Fraser: Including photographs in different publications with new juxtapositions, using them in paperweights . . .

Baker: You have put your finger on perhaps the essence of Lawler's work. It is a project of continual re-presentation—not representation—but the openness of the artistic object to be re-presented, to be presented again, and to become different in that re-presentation.

Fraser: That's a great way of putting it. And I think the key to that strategy lies in its temporality.

Baker: I'm not sure I understand how you are using that word, but temporality is often linked to discussions of photography. So maybe this provides us a way into

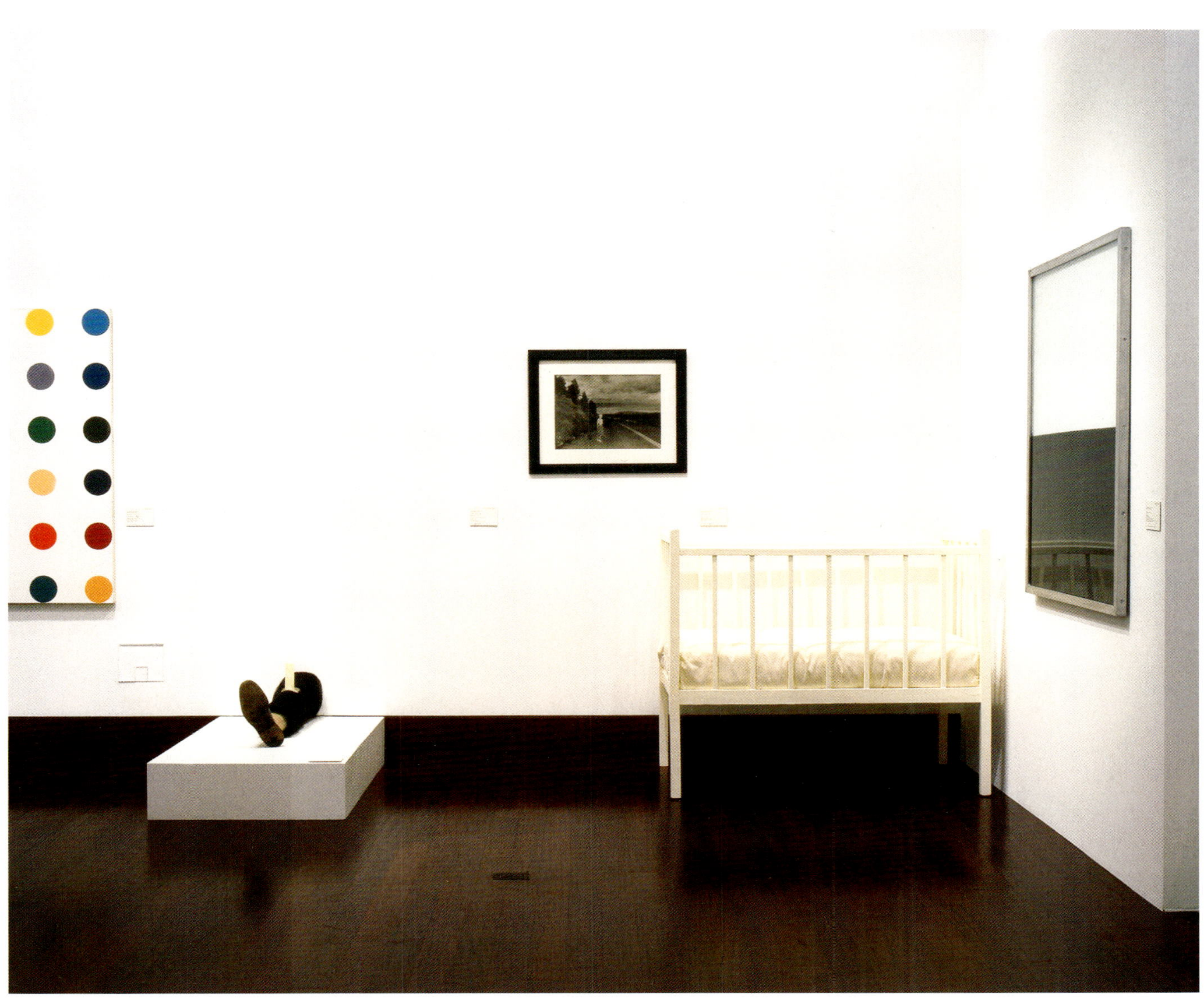

Unsentimental, 1999/2000
cibachrome, $47^{1/2}$ x 57 inches

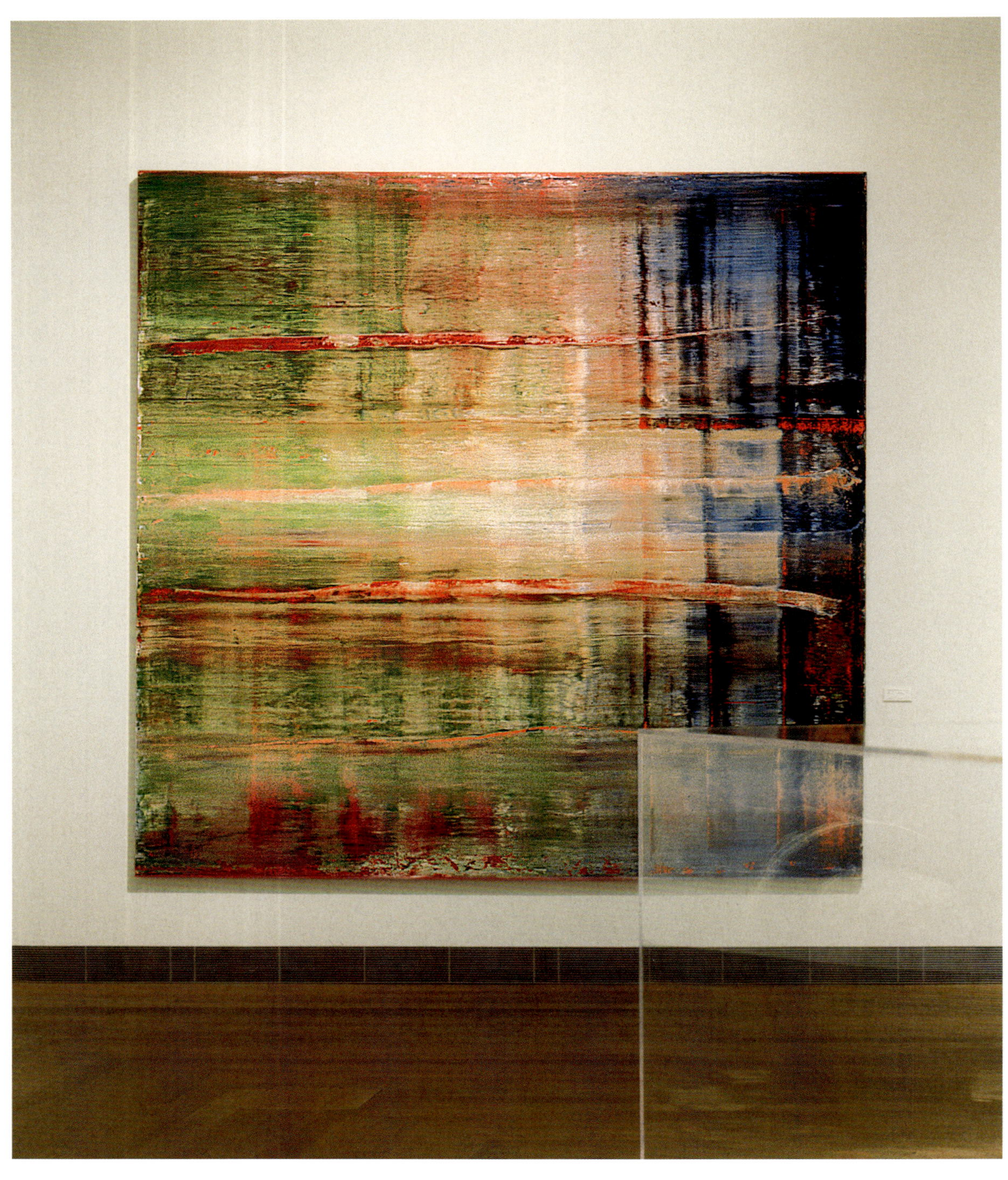

Painting and Sculpture, 1998/1999
cibachrome, 2 parts, 47 3/4 x 41 inches (each)

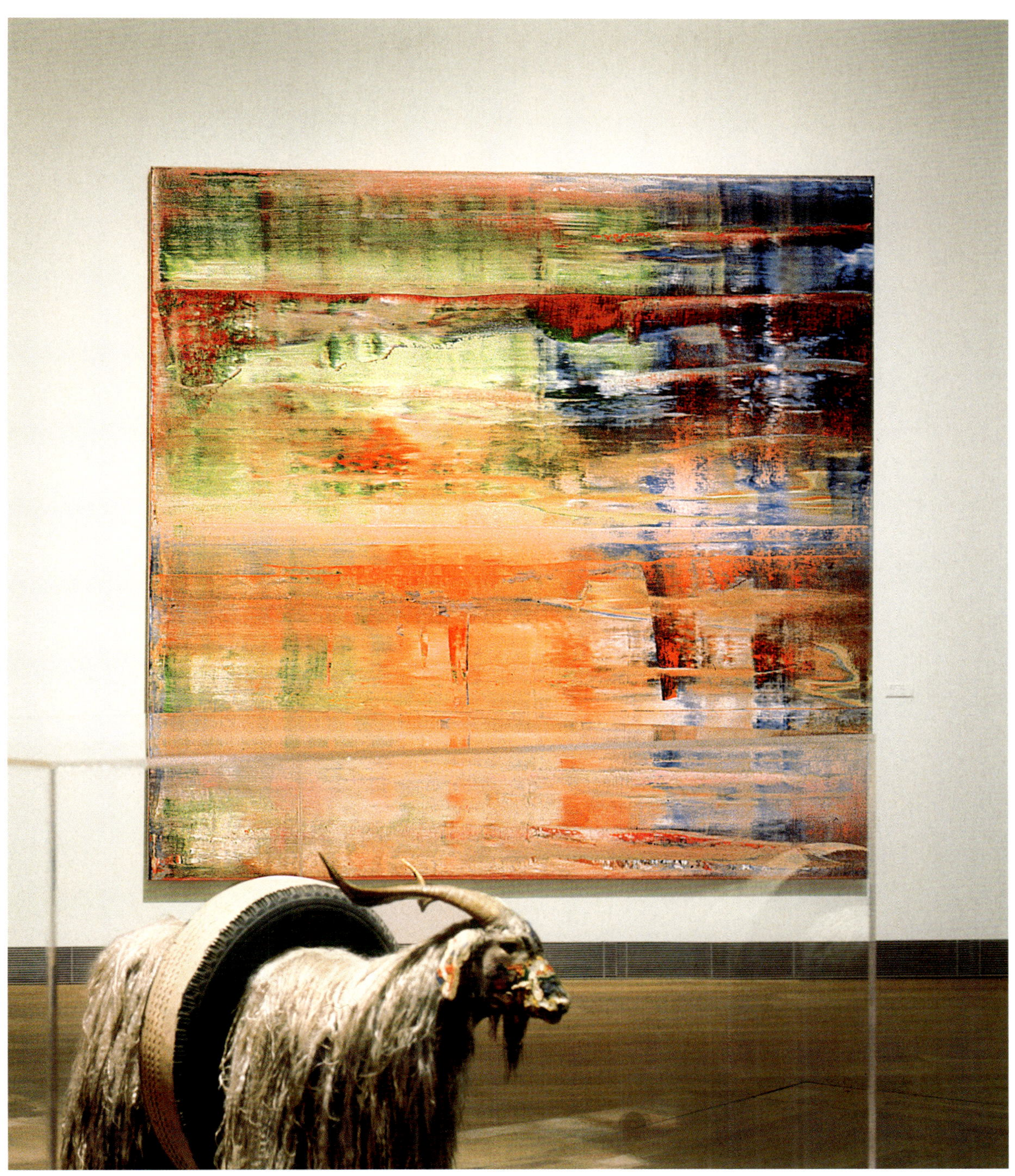

discussing her photography more specifically. We need to understand the links between her strategies of *re*-presentation and the photographic *representations* that she creates.

Fraser: You can see a kind of temporality at work quite explicitly in some of the image sequences in *An Arrangement of Pictures*. I'm looking now at the photographs *Unsentimental* (1999/2000), and *Sentimental* (1999/2000). They are two different installation shots of the same exhibition. You have a sense of the temporality of walking through an exhibition space and the shifts created by that movement, which, in the context of a book, become the shift from one page to the next. And then there is another kind of displacement that takes place in the two linked but different titles. You find this everywhere in Louise's work.

Baker: It is hard to think of installation photographs as being either "sentimental" or "unsentimental."

Fraser: Here are two others: *Painting and Sculpture*. Two cibachromes. In fact, they are two different Gerhard Richters . . .

Baker: . . . set off by the transparent display case around *Monogram* by Robert Rauschenberg . . .

Fraser: And look, after that . . . this is hilarious. It's a photograph, called *Monogram*, of a monogram on a sheet on a bed, below *White Flag* by Jasper Johns!

Baker: That's a great chain, the Rauschenberg *Monogram*, to a real-life monogram, to the Johns "sign." And then ending, on the next page, with Jackson Pollock . . .

Fraser: *Pollock and Tureen*.

Baker: This makes me think of the last sentence of your essay on Lawler: "Whatever position she may happen to occupy, she is always somewhere/something else." You could say the same thing specifically about her photographs. They are installation photographs—a supposedly "low" language even more anti-aesthetic and banal than a Duchampian readymade—but they have a double life. They occupy more than one position. They speak more than one language. And they begin to insert an expanded notion of the art object into a practice that on the surface seems to be nothing more than a project of re-photography, appropriating and re-photographing previous objects of art. Her photographs in fact expand, open, and extend the very definition of what a work of art can be. One of my favorite photographs in fact seems to acknowledge this. It is entitled *Open*.

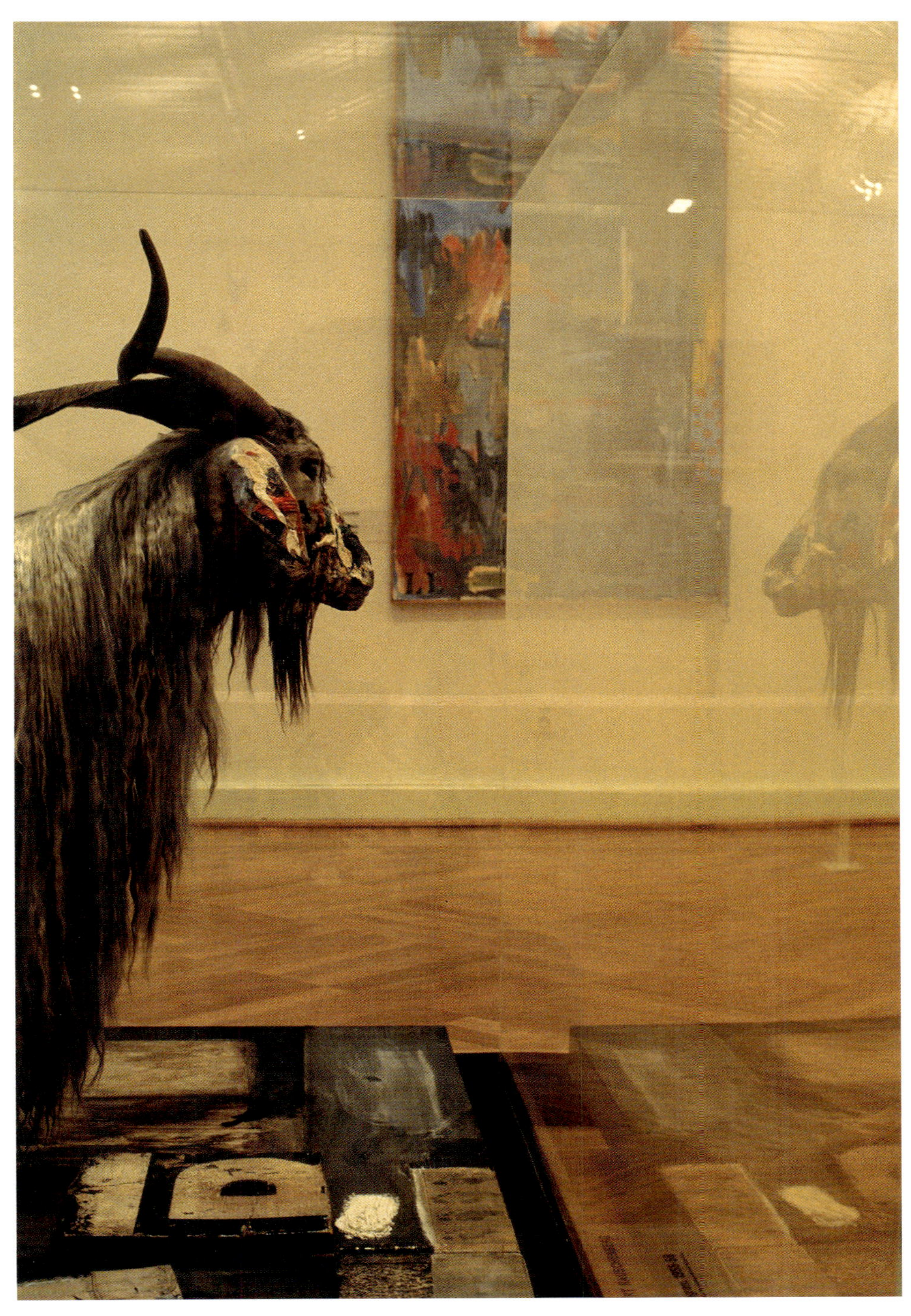

Untitled, 1987
cibachrome, $39^{1/4}$ x $27^{3/4}$ inches

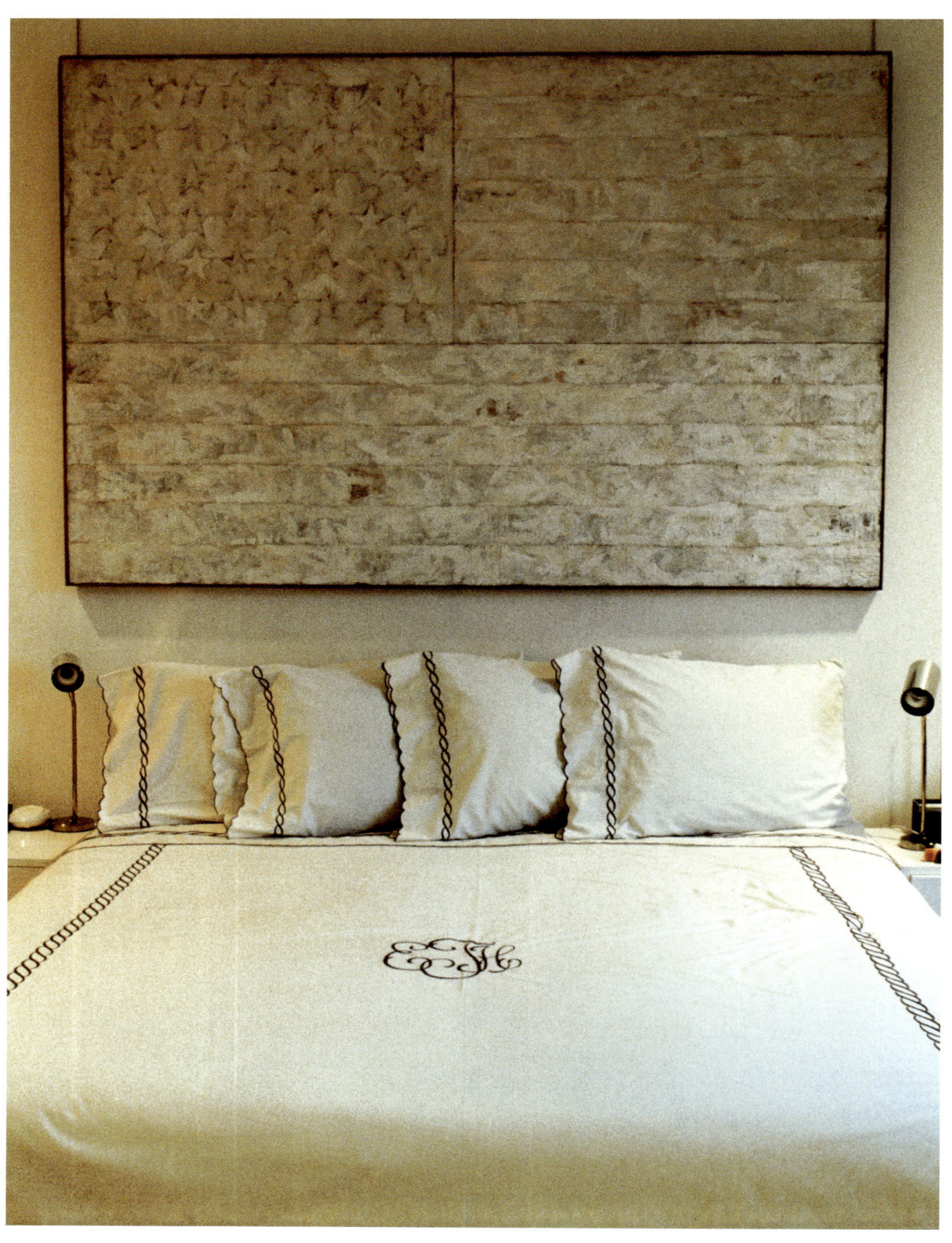

Monogram, 1984
cibachrome, $39^{1/2}$ x 28 inches

Fraser: In the mid-1980s, one of the ways I experienced the demand posed by Louise's practice was as the demand never to produce a work of art.

Baker: I find that hard to follow.

Fraser: What I mean is, by always working on the margins and with supplements, Louise has managed to skirt the central space, as an artist as well as with the art objects she produces. She makes objects that look and "act" like works of art, but they are always pulled out of that central space by a supplement—something that is also part of the "act," but that performs the work of de-centering: the title or caption, the way a wall is painted, the mat, the text on the mat, and then the text on a glass, on a matchbook, the image as a paperweight. Or look—a picture of a parrot!

Baker: I've never understood the photograph of the parrot. Is it an art object? Arte Povera? A reference to Manet's *Woman with a Parrot*? What is that photograph?

Fraser: I don't know if I understand it either. It's a parrot. Does it have a relationship to her *Bird Calls piece*?

Baker: Is it the logo to *Bird Calls*?[7]

Fraser: My recollection is that it's just a photograph of a bird. On a red background. It has some relationship to her own representations of works of art on colored backgrounds. I have no idea where I'm going with this.

Baker: The parrot photograph is a problem!

Fraser: Yes, I guess that is how I understand the parrot picture: as a problem! I see it as one of Louise's interventions in her own practice. What her work has represented for me is the notion that the "work" of the work of art is not the objects produced, not the photographs, but the whole continual process of production and presentation, the practice of displacement in the continual negotiation of framing and locating and identifying and naming and constituting. That's what the "work" of art—of art making—is. And I still believe that. And I still think that Louise doesn't make art objects. Of course, she makes matchbooks and texts and photographs. But Louise's work is not those objects. It's the process in which those objects or images are put into play and continuously renegotiated and resituated.

Baker: I agree with you but I think that is just part of what we confront in Lawler's project, and this is part of why her practice is very paradoxical. I think that one of the things that she has shown us, and that is just beginning to enter the reception of her work—I'm thinking of Douglas Crimp's recent interview with her, published in *An*

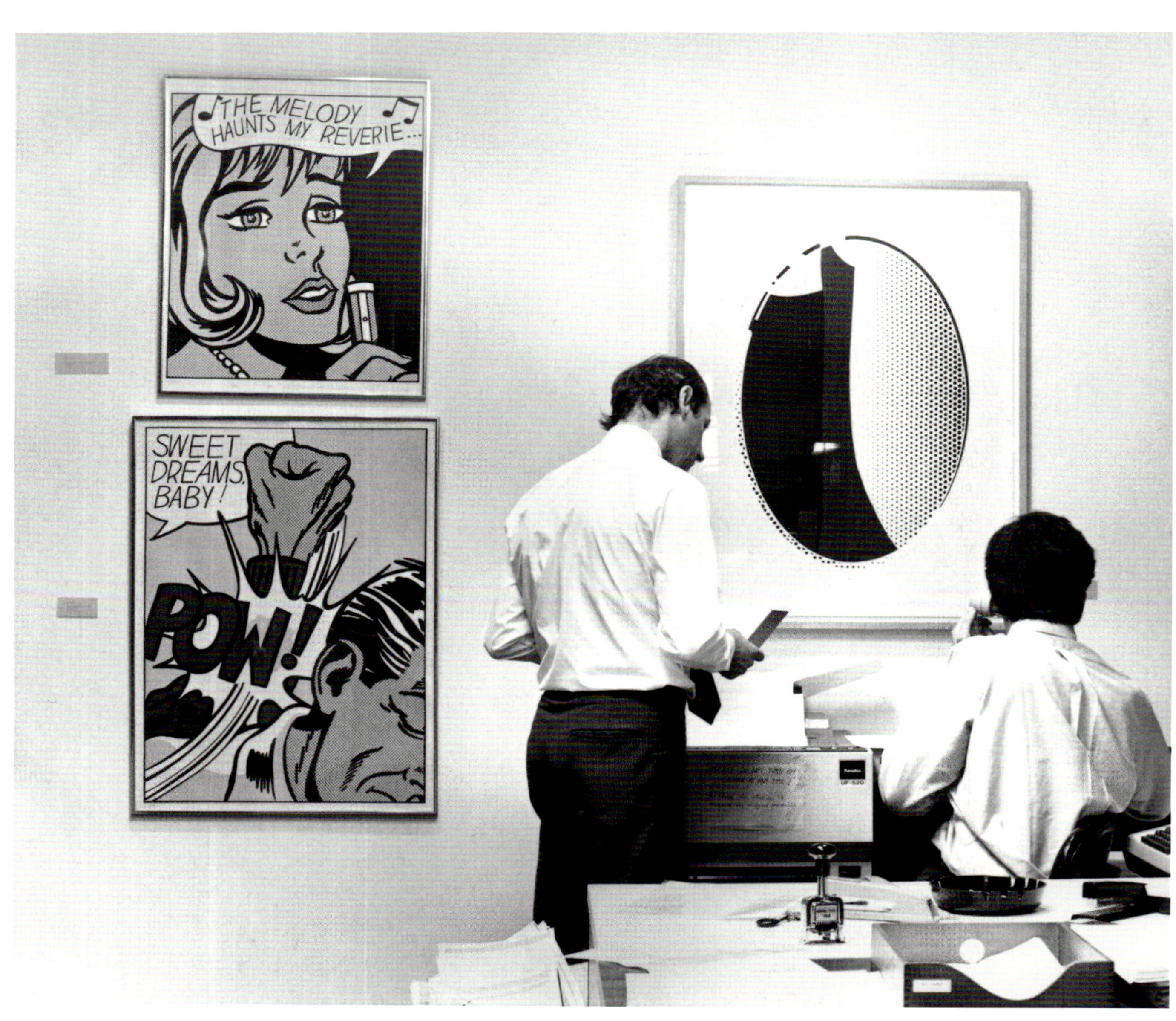

Arranged by Donald Marron, Susan Brundage, Cheryl Bishop at Paine Webber, 1982
black and white photograph, 19 1/2 x 21 3/4 inches

Arrangement of Pictures, as perhaps the first acknowledgment—is that a certain generation of discourse around postmodernism was so bent on displacing autonomous aesthetics and displacing modernism that the kinds of aesthetic experiences that modernism once was thought to hold out to the viewer were somehow anathema. And to turn to the frame, to turn to context, to turn to displacement strategies, to turn to rethinking one's position within presentational strategies, this was an aspect of Lawler's work that was seen in a manner that was one-dimensional. This is the programmatic reading to which we have been referring. I think one of the things that she shows us is that to turn to those displacements themselves opens up a new form of aesthetic experience that we need to rename. We can't call this experience the same thing that we used to call it, in the moment of modernism, say. We need to invent language for it. But it is crucial to the work.

To be more precise: We need to see not only the *displacements*, but the *connections* that Lawler's work establishes. I think there is a way in which the photographs by Lawler that "work" for me—she uses that word, she talks about the work "working" in it's process of reception—well, the works that work for me are the ones that in displacing away from thinking of art as an autonomous object, create what we might call new condensations. In displacing our former beliefs about art, they create new connections and new relations that the work of art was never before thought to be able to sustain.

Fraser: Can you explain what you mean by "new condensations"?

Baker: It is my understanding that when Lawler is working, she takes a lot of photographs. That is her process. They obviously don't all make it into her oeuvre, they don't all become works.

Fraser: I think very few of them do.

Baker: So I wonder: Why do the ones that make it into her work make it there? I think that what you see in the best photographs by Lawler, the ones that "work," is that the works of art depicted therein are now being related to objects that it might previously have been inconceivable to bring into connection with historical works of art. This is thus not a reductive but an expansive project, not one that tracks only the dissipation of the life of aesthetic objects but their affective expansion as well. An example: the image called *Longo, Stella, Hunt at Paine Webber*, which shows the security guard in the lobby of an office building hung with art.[8] It is a demonstration of alienated labor but also of a body newly connected to the frozen figure in a work by Robert Longo. The connection of a living while alienated human body to the Robert Longo image is one that has always struck me as intense. Crimp and Lawler discuss the "poignancy" of her work in their recent interview. For me, that poignancy lies in these connections. In these strange condensations—of art and other objects and beings.

Or another image, again from the *Paine Weber* series: the Roy Lichtenstein works hung on the wall next to the copy machine, being used by workers. In this relationship, the work of art finds its destiny, in a way. I mean, the connection is not entirely arbitrary. It "works" because the condensation here is almost fate. Such a photograph isn't just a demonstration of the alienation of the work of art in the corporate collection. It is also somehow an image of a new life for the work of art, one somehow internal to it that we haven't been able to see before. It is not only a melancholic image.

Fraser: I sometimes feel that my mind doesn't work in ways that are subtle enough to engage Louise's photographs. But I love this image: *Salon Hodler*.

Baker: Why do you love that work?

Fraser: Because it's an image of the bourgeois unconscious, or rather the unconscious of the bourgeois salon. It has a very literal title, one of Louise's most literal titles, that just says what it is: *Salon Hodler*. In the lower half of the image you have tables and chairs that imply human interaction but seem frozen in the repressive propriety of their arrangement. But floating above them, like in a daydream, are paintings of bodies intertwined in the sensuous contact that the tables and chairs would never admit.

Baker: And again, we witness strange condensations in that collision: the seriality of the chairs echoed in the repetition of the lovers' bodies.

Fraser: But then you have this telephone right in the middle of the picture, this old-fashioned telephone! [Laughs.] What is it doing there? It disrupts this opposition and the reading it seems to demand. It is neither here nor there, neither fantasy nor repression. It's just something . . .

Baker: . . . that is there.

Fraser: Something banal, functional. You could say that it evokes an impending interruption of the interplay between elements of decor. Imagine a person called to the phone, walking into the room with a purpose, unseeing, the room instrumentalized, our own aesthetic looking displaced. Is it another moment of repression? Or is it another kind of connection? There's a resistance to interpretation.

Baker: So there is what Roland Barthes calls the "punctum" in Lawler's photographs.

Fraser: Look at this one: *It Could Be Elvis*. [Laughter.] It's hilarious!

Baker: That image is a great example of the dynamic you've just isolated. It is hard to know what we are looking at. It's Joseph Beuys . . . by Andy Warhol.

Fraser: "Condensation and displacement," "resistance to interpretation"—we're in psychoanalytic territory here. But again I would suggest that a psychoanalytical reading of Louise's work is best performed not on her representations, as specific signifiers, the "latent content" of which we can decode, but rather on the structures of associations in her work. That's where the resistance to interpretation might best be located. Think about the rubric for Louise's early collaborative works with Sherrie Levine: *A Picture is No Substitute for Anything*. There is a kind of desire that is produced in that displacement.

Baker: And in that interdiction.

Fraser: But what does that phrase mean? *A Picture is No Substitute for Anything*. What does that mean? The reading of that phrase in the 1980s would have been that a picture is no substitute for anything because there is no original to begin with. Right? But what does it really mean?

Baker: They took the phrase from a line in the Hollis Frampton–Carl Andre dialogues. In a flat-footed understanding, it also could mean that a picture is in fact *unsatisfying* on a certain level: A picture is no substitute for a real experience, and art is no substitute for real desires.

Fraser: I like that reading—although it probably would have been anathema to the postmodernist thinking of the 1980s. OK, so a picture is no substitute, it's unsatisfying. What are we left with? We are left with these endless substitutions, endless displacements. That's the poignancy in Louise's work for me. It's a question of what's behind that surface of displacement. Maybe it's nothing . . .

Baker: I'm reminded a lot of Andy Warhol as you say these words. I'm reminded of that famous line: "If you want to know all about Andy Warhol, just look at the surface of my paintings and films and me, and there I am. There's nothing behind it."[9] I love Lawler's works about Warhol, like the photograph of the Marilyn Monroe painting given two different captions, both extremely affective: *Does Marilyn Monroe Make You Cry*? and *Does Andy Warhol Make You Cry*? Warhol has represented for art history the epitome of a type of affect-less, depersonalized production, and yet it is increasingly evident that no artist's work has been in fact as replete with affect as the project of Andy Warhol. The affiliation of Lawler's work to Warhol's is now perhaps clear to everyone, but that problematic of a deep affect emerging from that which superficially seems depersonalized now extends to her work as well. You have just put your finger on one potential reason why these Lawler images—so flat-footed, so potentially banal and instrumentalized—why these images that follow the work of art into its own full debasement at the hands of the auction house, at the hands of the collector or the gallery, why these images in fact affect us so intensely. Their debasement opens up this other, "poignant" dimension.

There is a sub-genre of Lawler's practice that we haven't yet discussed, and that shares in this dynamic. Lawler has consistently documented the transformation of her own institutional frames; here, quite literally, I am referring to her reactions to the three different spaces that her gallery, Metro Pictures, has occupied, each one grander than the last (and perhaps we can place Lawler's early exhibition at Artists Space in this sub-genre as well, as that show was linked to her eventually showing at Metro Pictures). Every time Metro Pictures has moved, her first show has been some kind of investigation of the transformation of the new space: the arrangement of works by gallery artists in the first space; a slide show at the second Soho Metro Pictures, responding to its new scale and its transparency from the level of the street; and then the first show at the new Chelsea space that documented the renovation of the decrepit garage space into the pristine white gallery.

Fraser: There's something shocking to me about the photographs of the Chelsea renovation. When you come across them in the *An Arrangement of Pictures* book they feel almost violent. Brutal.

Baker: Well, I see them as her photographic inversion of Michael Asher's physical denuding of the gallery space at the Galleria Toselli, which could seem violent.

Fraser: I'm thinking of the way in which they break through the delicacy of the other images in the book.

Baker: I think they are shocking in the way that they now really and completely abdicate the creation of the artistic object to the commercial realm, to the gallery, to the institution. Now even the renovation of this space into a larger, grander, and purer temple of commodification—the big white gallery in Chelsea—becomes that which produces images that look like Gabriel Orozco photographs (a decayed red wall awaiting replastering, *Red (Rectangle)*, 1996), or sculptures that look like works by Donald Judd (the ventilation system units strewn across the floor, *HVAC*, 1996). There is a correspondence here between the mechanisms of the gallery space as a space of commerce, and the forms of contemporary art. She shows us the strange identity between them; it's almost a tautology. And this happens throughout Lawler's practice: for example, when she makes her series about the auction houses Sotheby's and Christie's (published in her book *Louise Lawler: For Sale*), the images

Sappho and Patriarch, 1984
cibachrome, $39^{3/4}$ x $27^{1/2}$ inches

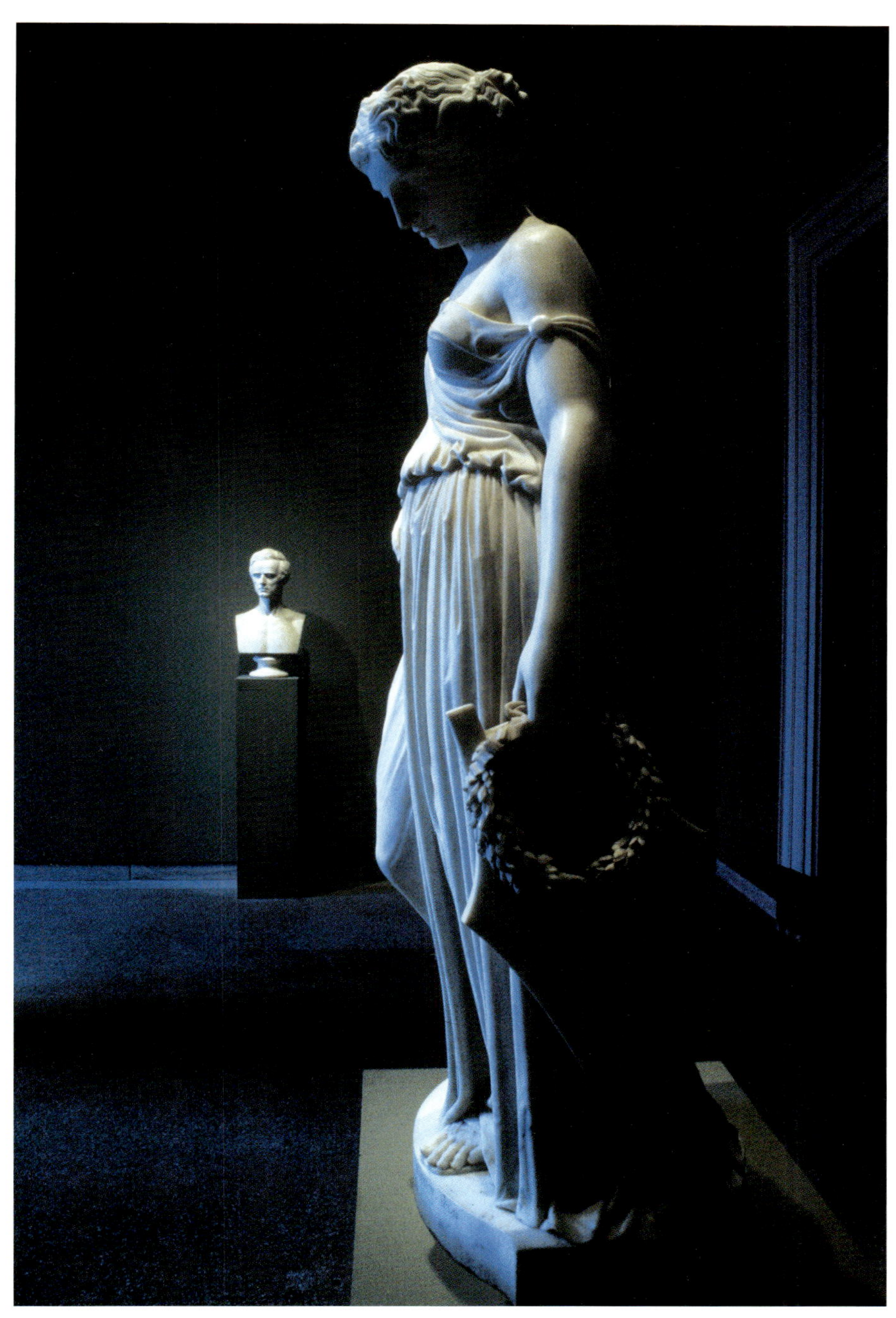

Is it the work, the location or the stereotype that is the institution?

of the auction houses' spaces and the architecture and accoutrements therein are presented as if they were avant-garde sculpture installations. When you see the empty auction room at Sotheby's—the unused easels, the walls and barriers and blank display surfaces—they all combine to look like an installation photograph of an exhibition of modernist sculpture circa 1960. You are shown a line of "client phones," but it makes you think of the seriality of minimalist sculpture, or the commodity aesthetic of an artist in the 1980s like Haim Steinbach. To abdicate the production of avant-garde form to the commercial apparatus: here is the collapse of oppositionality with which we began this conversation.

Fraser: I want to understand the sequence of the Metro Pictures renovation images in *An Arrangement of Pictures*. They follow *Sappho and Patriarch*, a much earlier image, which has an important text caption: "Is it the work, the location or the stereotype that is the institution?" In that photograph you see two sculptures, but you are made to pay attention to the lighting and the pedestals. That perhaps is how it connects to the next image, *HVAC*, in which you focus on the shape of the aluminum air-conditioning units, which glimmer in the light and seem to be approximating the shape of pedestals. Then there's *Red (Rectangle)* and after that you have a photograph of a Warhol Brillo Box next to a red carpet. The text here relates to what you were just saying—I guess you would have read it as an answer the previous caption's question: "It's location, location, location!"

Baker: No. The answer is: it's the stereotype. *Red (Rectangle)* is a cliché: the aesthetic power of the photograph now seems hardly disguised, but it emerges from a collapse of photographic documentary into the old topos of urban spaces of decay and the down-and-out. Just as this aesthetic "power"—the play of colors and forms—is a found power and an inauthentic one, the photographs are also a lie. These spaces aren't down and out at all. Not anymore at least. It's a stereotype, not truth, and the same can be said for the traditional topoi from which documentary photography draws its powers of aestheticization. Martha Rosler deconstructed the connection of documentary images to urban decay more than thirty years ago now.

Fraser: Issues of authenticity were seen as central to all art that emerged during the theorization of postmodernism in the 1980s, and the strategies of appropriation and rephotographing that took hold during that period were read as forms of a critique of authenticity, originality, and of the unique, auratic object. It recently occurred to me, however, that such strategies of quoting and appropriating—by virtue of their very self-conscious, strategic, willful in-authenticity—are actually reaching toward another kind of authenticity, a more authentic authenticity, as the other, the negative, the beyond, of the false authenticity they self-consciously refuse. That's what I had in mind when I wondered what was behind, or beyond, the surface of Louise's displacements.

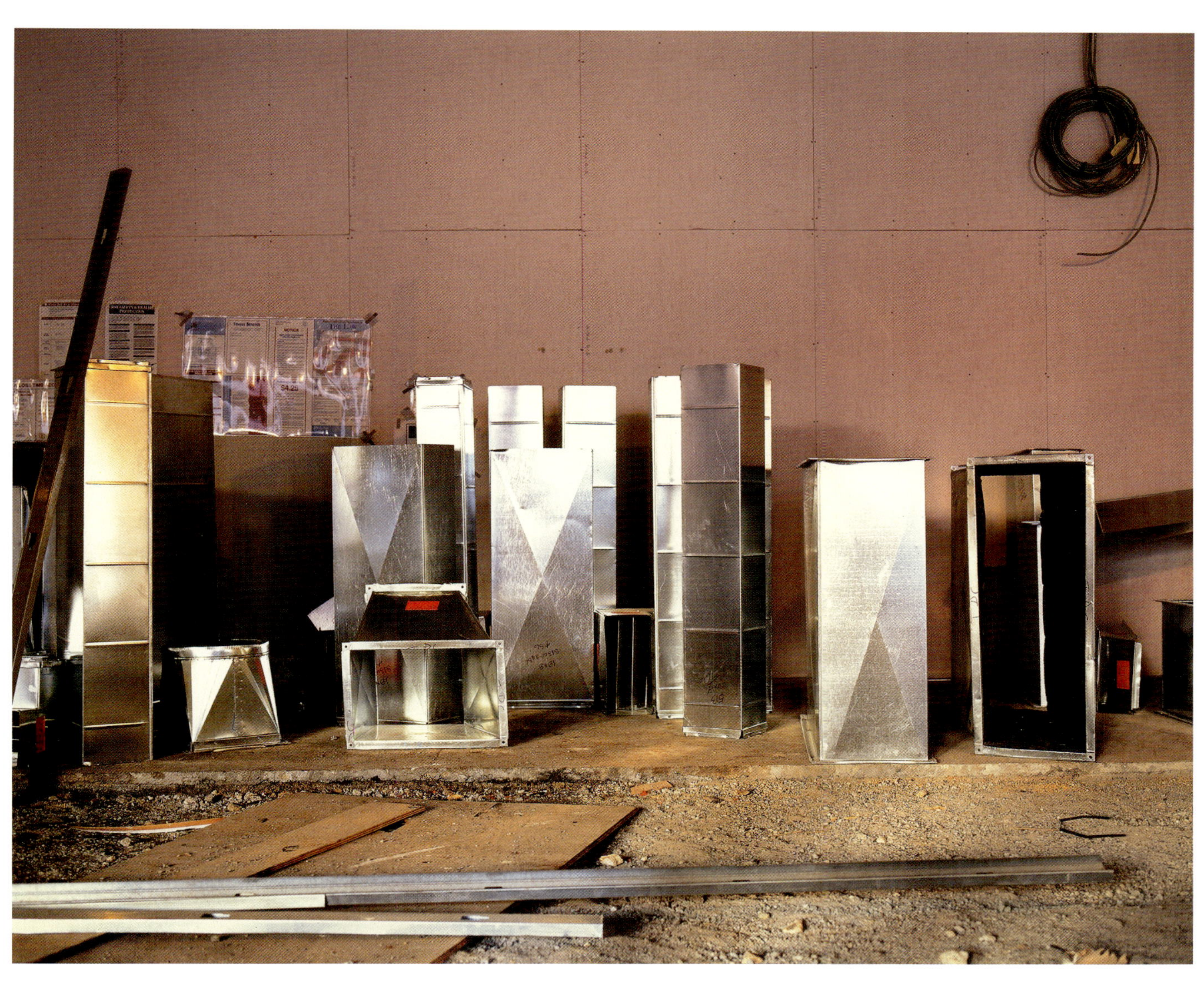

HVAC, 1996
cibachrome, 47$^{7/8}$ x 61$^{3/4}$ inches

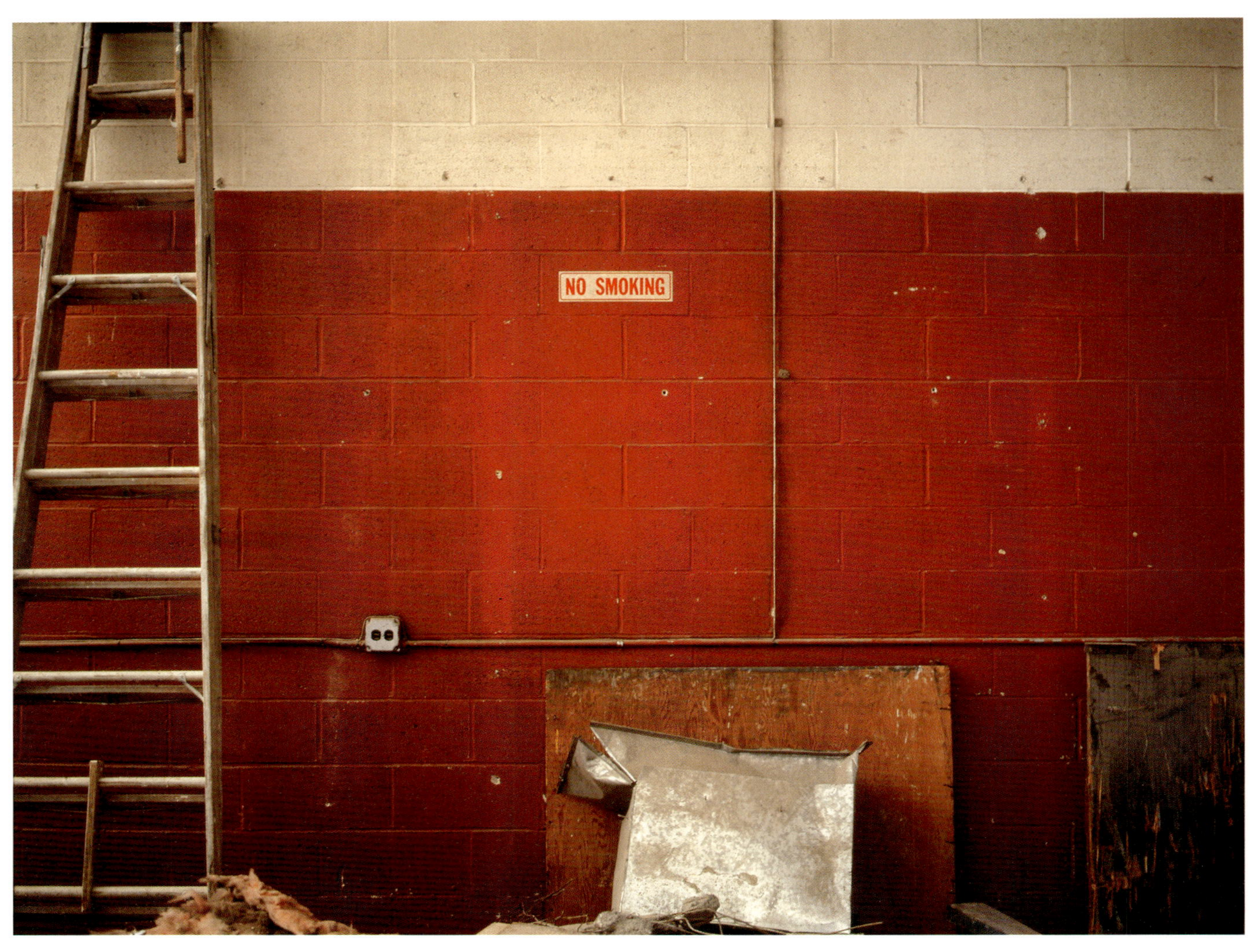

Red (Rectangle), 1996
cibachrome, 48 x 62 1/4 inches

Baker: Is what you are saying like what happens in Allan McCollum's project, where by producing "surrogate" works of art, he theatricalized the gallery (that was his word for it), producing in a sense a "surrogate" or false gallery as well? One that is almost more authentic than a real gallery by being inverted in this way? I'm actually fascinated by such theatricalizations. They are quite different from what critics have called minimalism's "theatricality." In McCollum, it is a literal engagement with theater and acting, with theatricality as fiction and the inauthentic double of an object. I was unaware until recently that Lawler wanted to do precisely the same thing to the gallery. She planned a work entitled *Matinee: Leo Castelli Gallery* where she would replace the gallery staff with actors, and Diane Keaton had agreed to sit at the front desk.

Fraser: I think she was trying to get Woody Allen to play Castelli.[10]

Baker: Well this idea doesn't get realized, but something like it does happen eventually without the celebrities in your work *May I Help You?* (1991), which you produced in cooperation with McCollum. You did in fact replace the gallery staff at American Fine Arts with actors.

Fraser: I never thought of it in relationship to Louise's earlier *Matinee* project, but maybe there is a relationship. She had told me about that project. I also collaborated with Louise in 1988, on a video called *The Public Life of Art: The Museum*, which was shot in the Museum of Modern Art and Metropolitan Museum in New York. I wrote a script for a kind of tour, which I performed, while she acted as an art director, framing shots, framing me as well as the two institutions.

Baker: So in these theatricalizations, the movie-plex, the cinema dream factory, comes literally to displace and replace the gallery. Just as, in other works, the rigor of avant-garde negation will enter the movie house, as when Lawler proposed her work *A Movie Will Be Shown Without the Picture*.

Fraser: Art has long been considered an arena of fantasy, but recently I've been thinking that art institutions don't simply exhibit scenes of fantasy to us. They *are* themselves fantasies in the sense that they are scenes of satisfaction.

Baker: And the fantasy is always: I wish I was satisfied. I want to be satisfied.

Fraser: They are replete not only with objects of satisfaction, surrogates subject to continuous substitution, but also with the narratives in which satisfaction is temporalized, in which desire is put into play and kept in play.

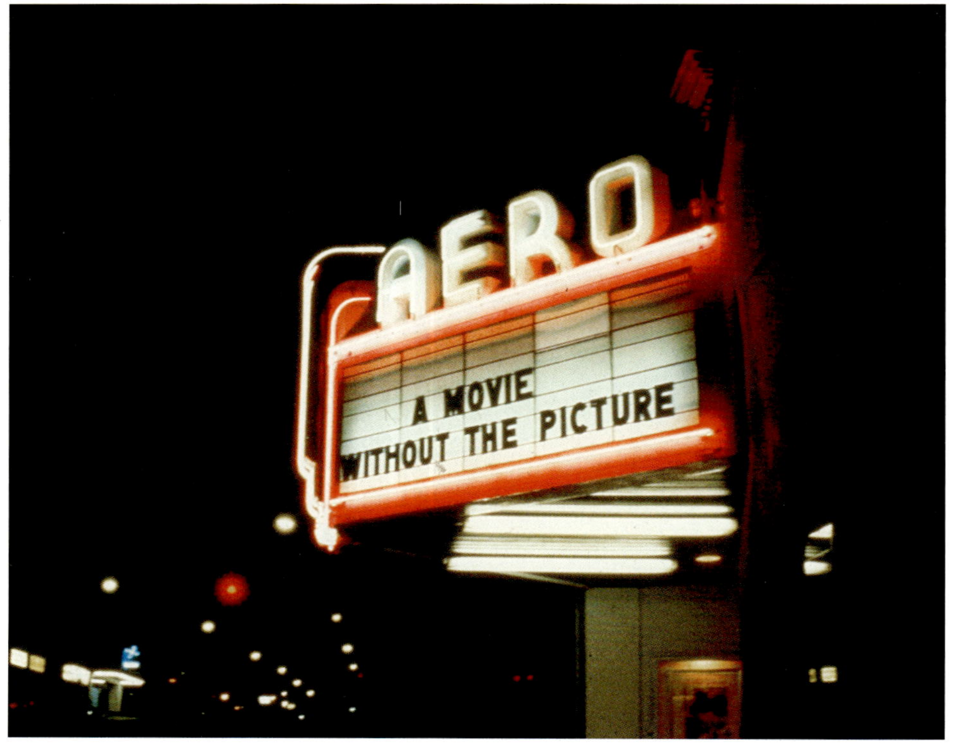

A Movie Will Be Shown Without the Picture, 1979

Aero Theater, Santa Monica, California

The marquee, poster, and announcement read "A Movie Will Be Shown Without the Picture." The house lights went down, the curtain went up, but the audience was faced with a dark screen as they listened to the soundtrack of *The Misfits*.

Baker: This is perhaps linked to your disorienting idea of Lawler as a performance artist. Is that a way of estranging her work from authenticity? To perform one's own work is somehow to make a work in quotation marks, in the same way that an actor acts? That is somehow scripted, produced *for* you in fact rather than produced *by* you?

Fraser: I didn't say that she's a performance artist, only that her work is about how we perform our positions and functions within our field.

Baker: I still want to know what is "poignant" in the work of Louise Lawler. I still want to discuss this. I think I know.

Fraser: OK, you start.

Baker: I think it's something very different than any kind of critical impulse that we have imagined in the work up to now. It has to do with creating relations—as you have been mentioning throughout this conversation—but relations that we haven't really recognized as legitimate up until this point. Relations perhaps so radical that we still have a hard time admitting in fact that they *are* relations. Like creating relations between a Léger and a group of chairs in the photograph *Three*

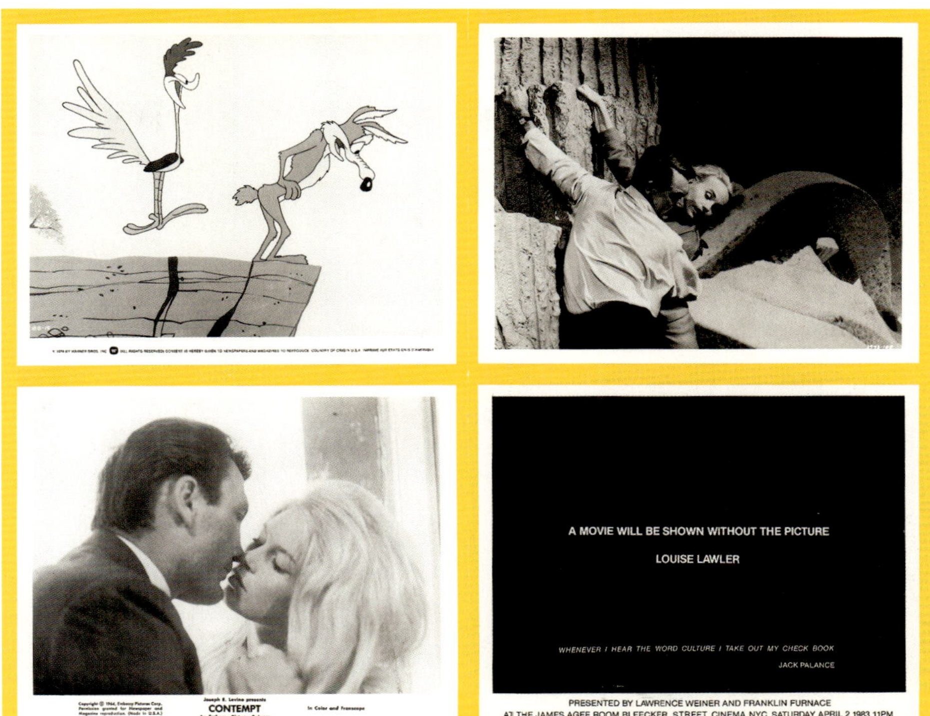

Poster produced to announce **A Movie Will Be Shown Without the Picture**

As participation in In Other Words: Artists' Use of Language, Part 2, Franklin Furnace, New York, 1983. *What's Opera, Doc?* (a cartoon) and *The Hustler* were "shown" with the projector lightbulb removed at the Bleecker Cinema.

Women, Three Chairs. Or creating relations between a security guard and a Robert Longo. It is not just a deflation of the Léger to be hung above the dining-room chairs. Yes, there is a traditional critical impulse here, as the comparisons perhaps bring out the failure of the functional desires at the heart of Léger's machine aesthetic, or highlight the comfort with which the image appropriation in the Longo becomes "private" property, ensconced behind a guard. But the affinities created surpass even these critical illuminations. Lawler's project is not just to string together art world positions, to create relations between the functions of artist, critic, curator, and gallery worker, for example. She is involved in revealing relations that inhere between disparate objects in the world, and these relations are close to and attached to the living desires that we embed in works of art. Her documentary practice begins to capture the strangeness of the life of art objects, but they are objects that we as human beings invest with so much emotion and desire. Actually, in these strange correspondences and affinities, the desire that we invest in art objects is shown in Lawler's images to be much more strange than we ever imagined. You look incredulous . . .

Fraser: No, but I think you're a bit too literal—or maybe not literal enough. You're talking about relations, but in a substantive rather than a relational way. And that may also be where you're missing the performative. Louise does not just represent

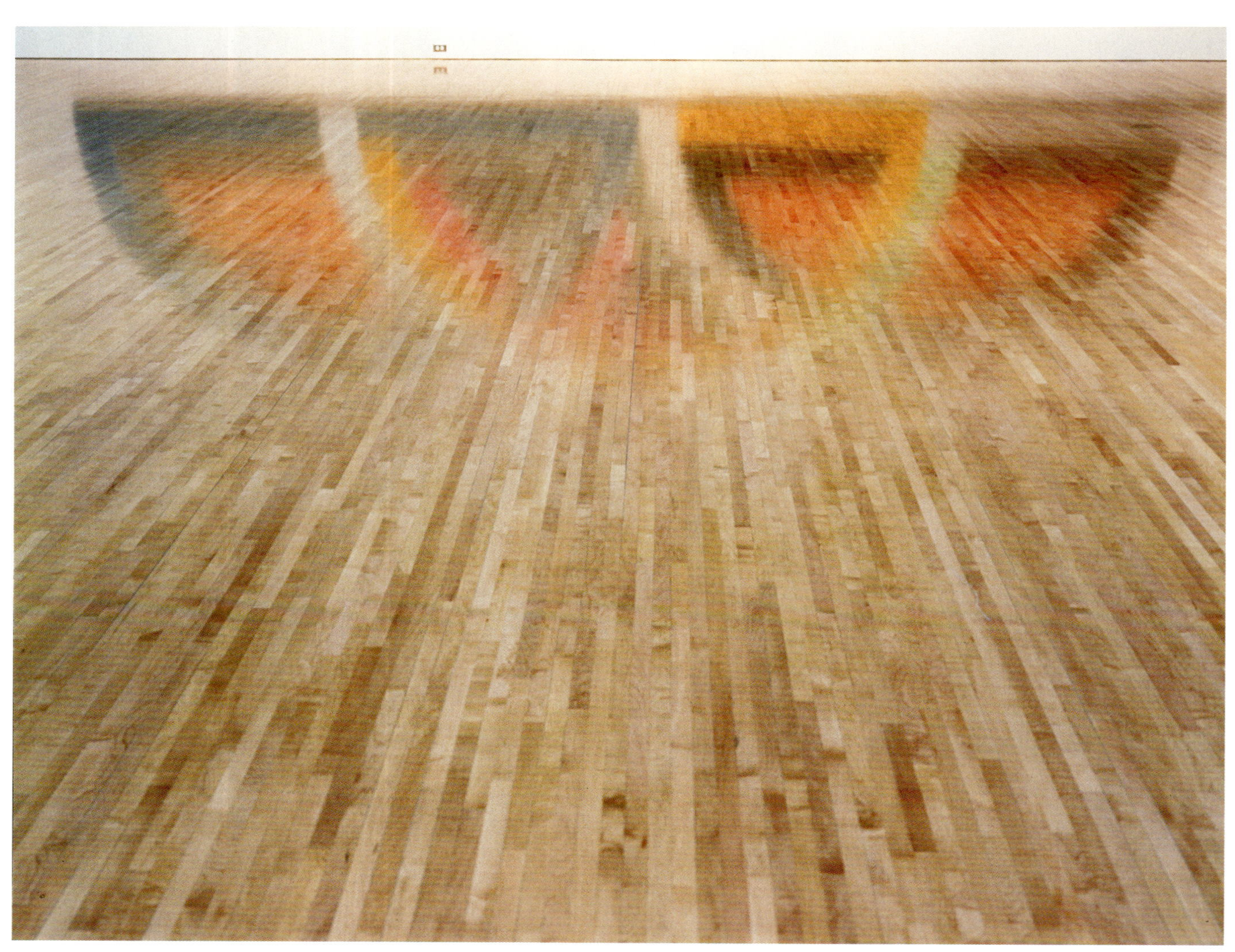

How Many Pictures, 1989
cibachrome, 48 1/16 x 61 7/8 inches

relationships in her work, she produces them through her work. Encountering a work by Louise is never simply seeing it. One is addressed by her work, interpellated by it. And it is *you* as a viewer who is being addressed, *you* who is being looked at, looked back at. They look at you: think of how many of her photographs include the gazes of other works of art. When there aren't gazes, there are reflections or bright lights. They call out to you: there is a text. Hey! *It Could Be Elvis*!, *This Drawing is For Sale*! They question you: *Does Andy Warhol Make You Cry?*, *Did You Get What You Deserved?*

Baker: *Did You See Your Parent of the Opposite Sex Naked?*

Fraser: *What Else Could I Do?* They are asking you what you want. They are questioning you on the level of your desire and your interest in looking. There are objects that are "kind": they are looking out for you. There are other objects pictured that are mute or oblivious. We see remainders or fragments of people's lives. Did she take this photograph because there's art above the fireplace or because there's a branch of mistletoe hanging from the ceiling? The text caption reads: "Once there was a little boy and everything turned out fine. The End."

Baker: That is the best caption in all her work. It is from her mother, right? She says somewhere that her mother found that written on a wall.

Fraser: Louise's early rubric was *A Picture is No Substitute for Anything*. But you could say that her work is all about substitution, it's about what Allan McCollum has called the "surrogate." It's about the lives of art objects, and the way that our own lives and desires are invested and projected into the lives of objects that *interact*—on the page, on the wall, in specific spaces—in our stead. That is why they are calling out to us and looking out at us.

Baker: We are implicated in the life of these objects that Lawler depicts. I was trying to say that a moment ago. It is at the basis of this project of condensations, correspondences, affinities.

Fraser: And everything is slightly askew. Here's a photograph of a Stella painting reflected in the floorboards. The caption is: *How Many Pictures*. No question mark this time.

Baker: How do you understand that caption?

Fraser: I'm not sure. It addresses me, but in a way that's askew. There's no one looking out at us from this picture, but the gaze is always manifest in reflections. There is a mirroring. The painting is reflecting itself. Reflecting on itself? Isn't that a defining act of subjectivity? Is that what we project onto paintings that reflect on themselves—an act that actually excludes us in its self-enclosure? The caption also excludes us, with its missing question mark.

Baker: I think of "how many pictures" have been reflected in those floorboards. If the institution's architecture were like a photograph, if it had a memory, all of those pictures would exist together. It's overwhelming.

Fraser: But what's most important about this photograph is the electrical outlet down here at the bottom of the wall.

Baker: [Laughs.] OK. Is that poignant for you? Another punctum?

Fraser: What's most important is what desire is being produced or sustained, hidden, or protected in a photograph like this.

Baker: Do you have an answer?

Fraser: An outlet? An opening? Art? The aesthetic?

Baker: So it's about redemption. And it's her fate too as an artist that she is concerned with. It's her objects too that she re-imagines and wants to redeem . . .

Fraser: . . . that she wants to keep afloat.

Baker: There is one thing that I've never had the privilege to see, and that is what a Louise Lawler photograph itself looks like in a private collection. I would like to see that someday.

Fraser: I wonder if she would do that? To rephotograph her own work in a collection. I wonder what it would mean?

Baker: I wonder what it would look like.

Notes

1. Martha Buskirk, "Interview with Louise Lawler [May 20, 1994]," *October*, no. 70 (Fall 1994): 106.

2. Andrea Fraser, "In and Out of Place," *Art in America* (June 1985): 123.

3. Louise Lawler, *An Arrangement of Pictures* (New York, 2000).

4. See Louise Lawler, "An Arrangement of Pictures," *October*, no. 26 (Fall 1983): 3–17.

5. Andrea Fraser, *Allan McCollum*, Investigations 18, ed. The Institute of Contemporary Art (Philadelphia, 1986).

6. Andrea Fraser, "In and Out of Place," (see note 2), 124.

7. The authors have since been informed that the photograph of the parrot was originally intended to be produced as the album cover of Lawler's 1983 recording of artists' names as bird calls, but was later presented independently as a photograph.

8. Again, the authors have since been informed that while this photograph was used "journalistically"—as an illustration for other authors' texts—it was not in fact ever made into an independent photographic "work."

9. See Gretchen Berg, "Andy: My True Story," *Los Angeles Free Press* (March 17, 1963): 3.

10. The artist has offered the following correction: it was Leo Castelli who originally suggested casting Woody Allen to play the former's role. Lawler had contacted both Dustin Hoffman and David Bowie.

They Have Always Wanted Me to Do This, 1995
cibachrome, $23^{5/8}$ x $18^{1/2}$ inches

Auction II, 1989/1990, was installed by Louise Lawler in her exhibition A Spot on the Wall, Neue Galerie, Graz, 1995, above the reception desk and photographed to produce the work *They Have Always Wanted Me to Do This*.

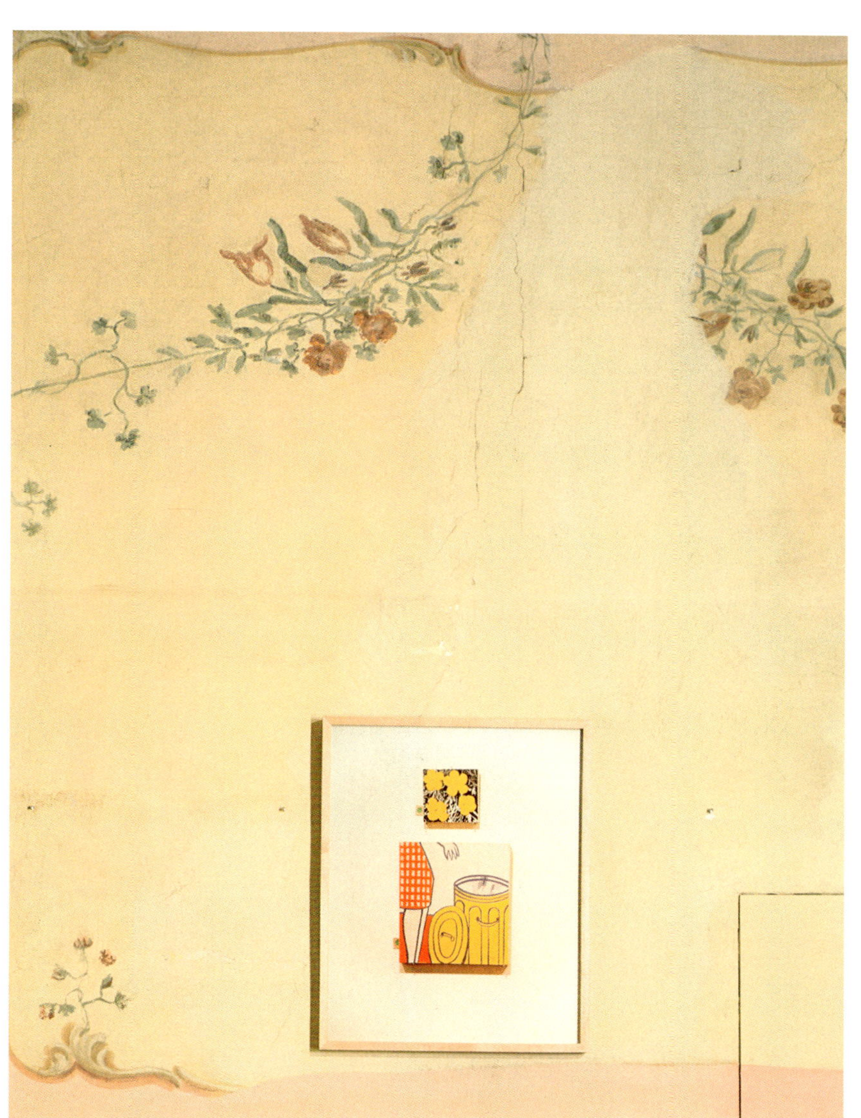

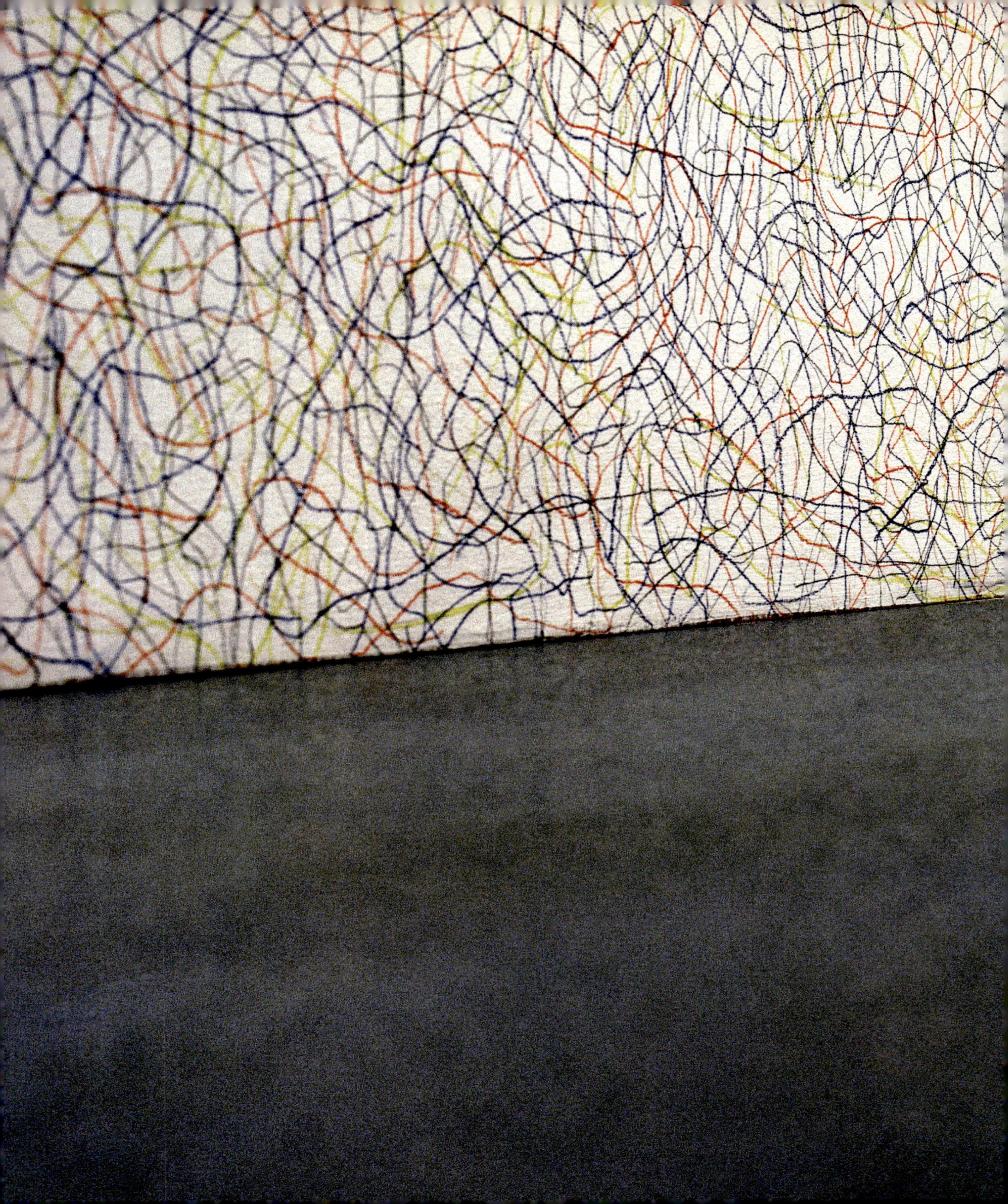

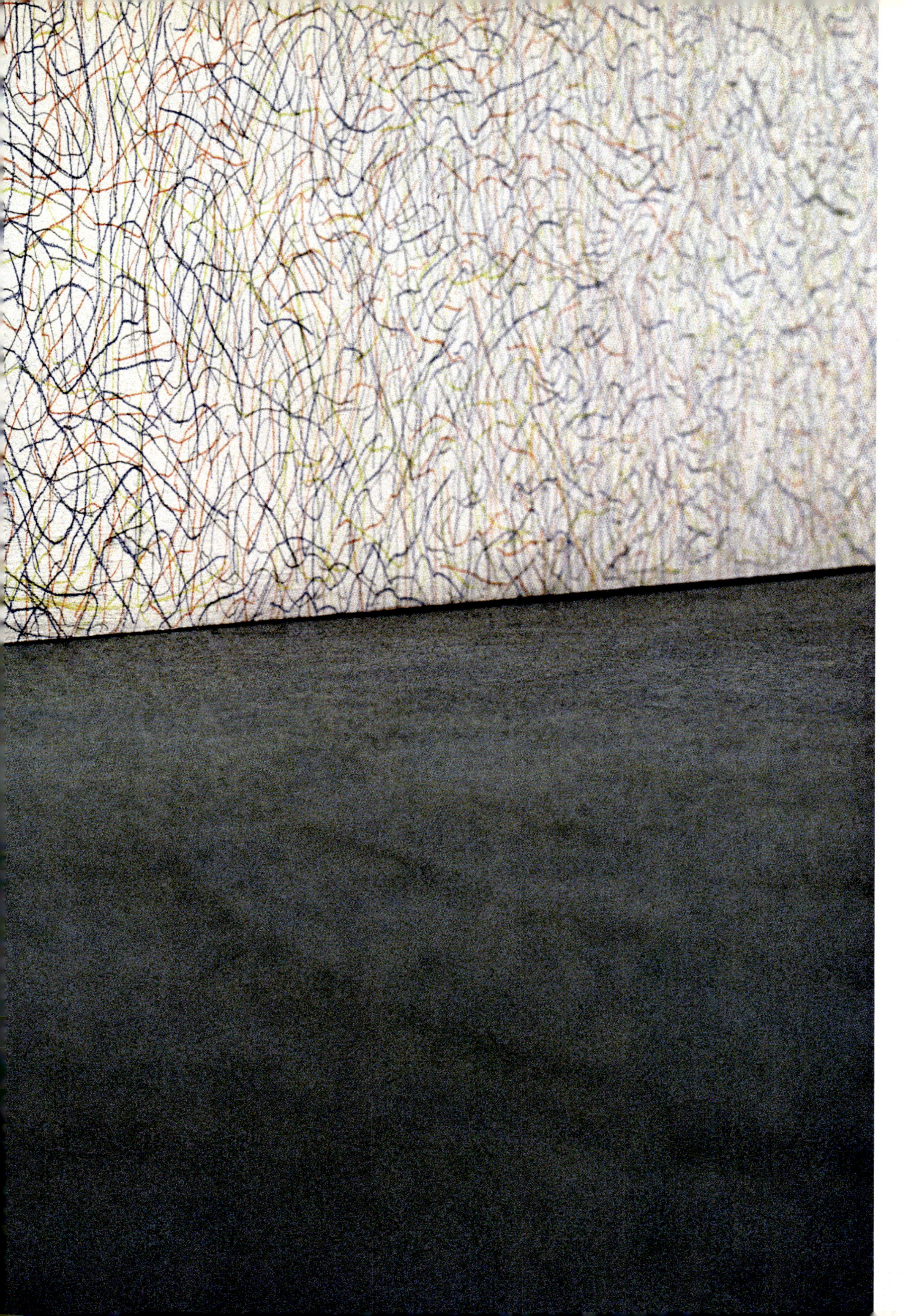

previous page:
Drop Bush Not Bombs, 2001/2003
digitally produced cibachrome, 48 x 72 inches

This Way I Can't Fight, 2002
cibachrome, $40^{3/8}$ x $49^{3/4}$ inches

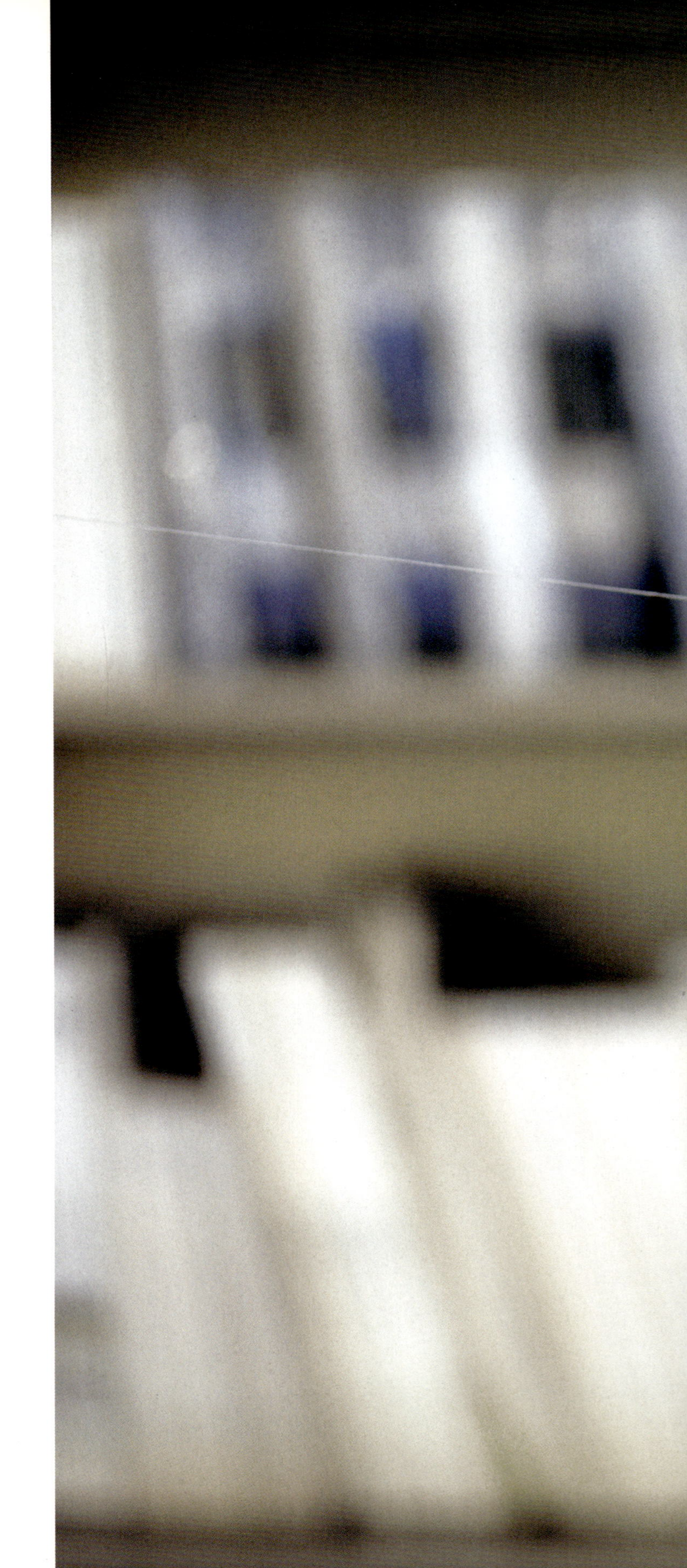

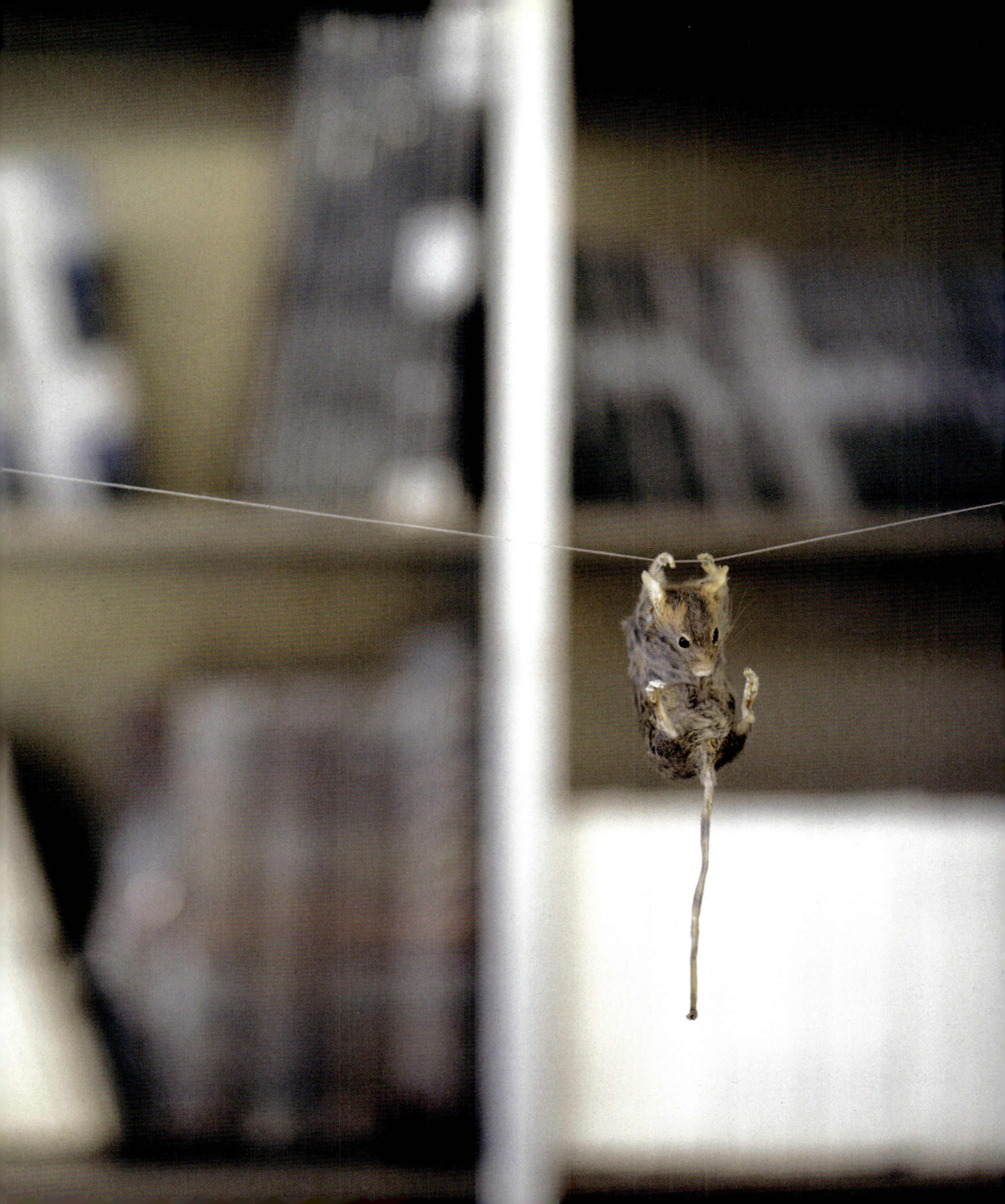

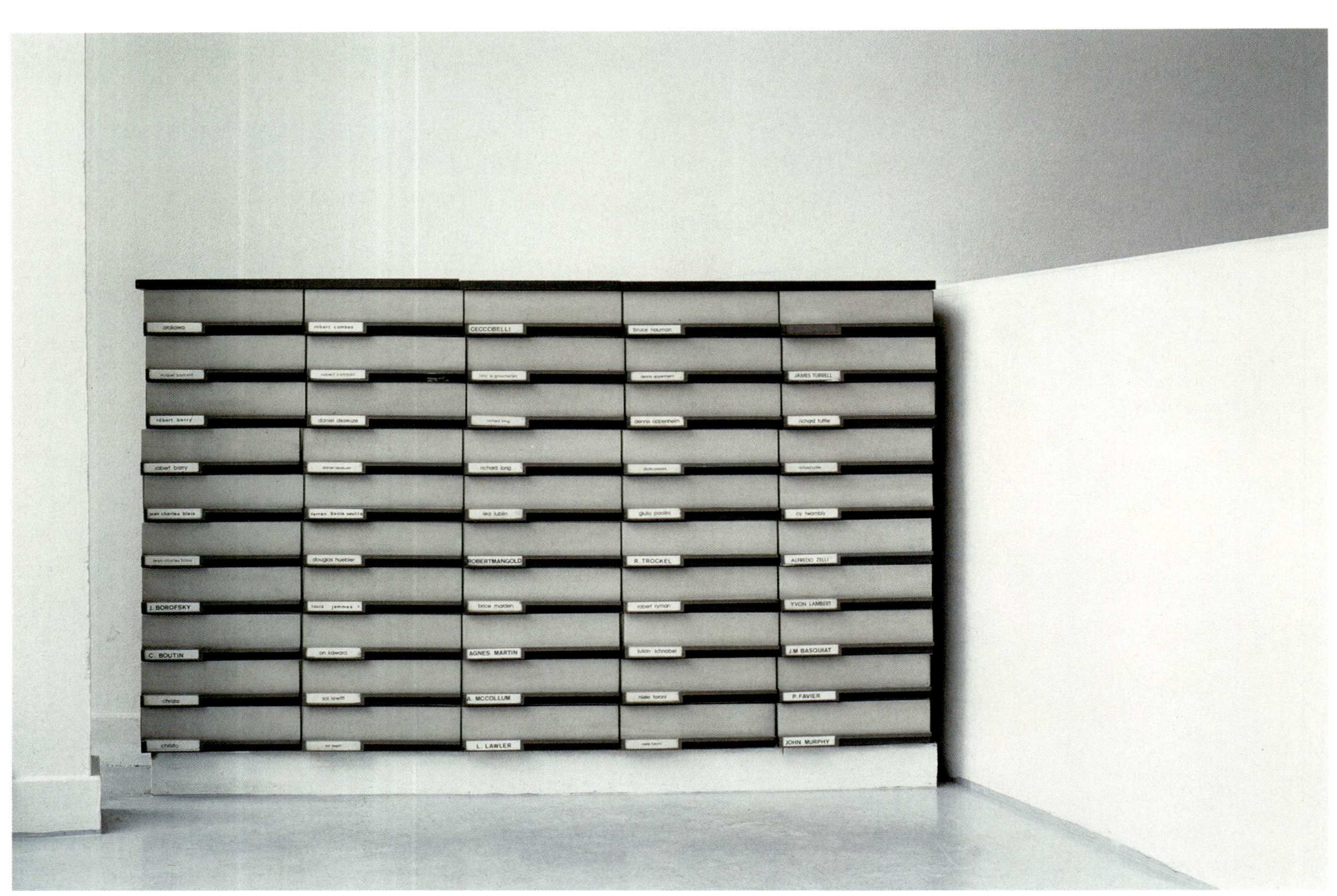

Les Coordonnées, 1988
cibachrome, 26 x 38 3/4 inches

Louise Lawler

Born 1947 in Bronxville, New York. Lives in New York
Attended Cornell University, Ithaca (BFA 1969)

Selected Solo Exhibitions

1979
"A Movie Will Be Shown Without the Picture." Aero Theater, Santa Monica.
1981
"Jancar/Kuhlenschmidt." Jancar/Kuhlenschmidt Gallery, Los Angeles.
1982
"An Arrangement of Pictures." Metro Pictures, New York.
1984
"Home/Museum: Arranged for Living and Viewing." Matrix, The Wadsworth Atheneum, Hartford.
1985
"Interesting." Nature Morte, New York.
1987
"Enough" (Projects: Louise Lawler). The Museum of Modern Art, New York (brochure).
Metro Pictures, New York (and 1989, 1991, 1994, 1997, 2000).
1989
"The Show Isn't Over." Photographic Resource Center, Boston.
1990
"The Enlargement of Attention: No One Between the Ages of 21 and 35 Is Allowed" (Connections: Louise Lawler). Museum of Fine Arts, Boston.
1994
"Press-papiers, cartes postales, images et cannibalisme." Centre d'Art Contemporain, Geneva.
1995
"A Spot on the Wall." Kunstverein München, Munich; Neue Galerie am Landesmuseum Joanneum, Graz; De Appel, Amsterdam (exh. cat.).
1997
"Monochrome." Hirshhorn Museum and Sculpture Garden, Washington (brochure).
2000
"More Pictures." Neugerriemschneider, Berlin.
"Paint, Wood, Plaster, Fabric, Glass and Other Pictures." Richard Telles Fine Art, Los Angeles.
2001
"Controlled Temperature." Art & Public, Geneva.
"Dunn-Rite and Other Pictures." Studio Guenzani, Milan.
"More Pictures and Other Pictures." Galerie Meert Rihoux, Brussels.
2003
"New Walls." Galerie Yvon Lambert, Paris.
"Probably Not in the Show." Portikus, Frankfurt/Main.
"Add To It." Portikus, Frankfurt/Main.

Selected Group Exhibitions

1978
"_______, Louise Lawler, Adrian Piper & Cindy Sherman Have Agreed to Participate in an Exhibition Organized by Janelle Reiring at Artists Space, September 23 through October 28, 1978." Artists Space, New York (exh. cat.).
1980
"Amalgam." Castelli Graphics, New York.
1984
"Ideal Settings." With Allan McCollum. Diane Brown Gallery, New York.
"New York, ailleurs et autrement." Musée d'Art Moderne de la Ville de Paris.
1985
"The Art of Memory: The Loss of History." New Museum of Contemporary Art, New York.
1986
"Art and Its Double: A New York Perspective." Fundació Caixa de Pensions, Barcelona; La Caixa de Pensions, Madrid (exh. cat.).
"Damaged Goods." New Museum of Contemporary Art, New York.
"L'œuvre et son accrochage." Centre Georges Pompidou, Paris.
1987
Maison de la Culture et de la Communication de Saint-Etienne. With John Knight (exh. cat.).
1988
"Work by Louise Lawler and Allan McCollum and Fixed Intervals as Matter of Agreement." With Allan McCollum. Le Consortium, Dijon.
1989
"A Forest of Signs: Art in the Crisis of Representation." The Museum of Contemporary Art, Los Angeles (exh. cat.).
1991
"Hugo-Erfurth-Preis: Manuel Alvarex Bravo, Louise Lawler, Henk Tas." Museum Morsbroich, Leverkusen (exh. cat.).
"Whitney Biennial." Whitney Museum of American Art, New York (exh. cat.).
1993
"Kontext Kunst." Neue Galerie am Landesmuseum Joanneum, Graz (exh. cat.).
"Louise Lawler, Cindy Sherman, Laurie Simmons." Kunsternes Hus, Oslo; Museum of Contemporary Art, Helsinki (exh. cat.).
"The Language of Art." Kunsthalle Wien, Vienna.
1997
"Moving Images." Galerie für Zeitgenössische Kunst, Leipzig (exh. cat.).
1999
"The Museum as Muse." Museum of Modern Art, New York; Museum of Contemporary Art, San Diego (exh. cat.).
2003
"The Last Picture Show: Artists Using Photography 1960–1982." Walker Art Center, Minneapolis; UCLA Hammer Museum, Los Angeles (exh. cat.).

Selected Bibliography

1979
Real Life Magazine (March): 2.
1982
"A Picture Is no Substitute for Anything." *Wedge* 2 (Autumn): 58–67.
Buchloh, Benjamin. "Allegorical Procedures: Appropriation and Montage in Contemporary Art." *Artforum* (September): 48–49.
Foster, Hal. "Subversive Signs." *Art in America* (November): 88–92.
1983
Eisenman, Stephen F. "Louise Lawler." *Arts Magazine* (January): 41.
Lawler, Louise. "Arrangements of Pictures." *October* 26: 3–6.
Lichtenstein, Therese. "Louise Lawler." *Arts Magazine* (February): 5.
1985
Fraser, Andrea. "In and Out of Place." *Art in America* (June): 122–29.
1986
Art and Its Double: A New York Perspective. Text by Dan Cameron. Exh. cat. Fundació Caixa de Pensions, Barcelona.
Linker, Kate. "Rites of Exchange." *Artforum* (November): 99–100.
1987
Bankowsky, Jack. "Spotlight: Louise Lawler." *Flash Art* (April): 86.
Meinhardt, Johannes. "Louise Lawler: As Serious as a Circus." *Kunstforum* (October/November).

1988
Bankowsky, Jack. "Beige: Louise Lawler's A·C·A·D·E·M·Y." In *Louise Lawler*. Investigations, ed. Institute of Contemporary Art, University of Pennsylvania.
"Project for Flash Art." *Flash Art* (November/December): 93–94.
1989
A Forest of Signs: Art in the Crisis of Representation. Texts by Ann Goldstein and Howard Singerman. Exh. cat. The Museum of Contemporary Art, Los Angeles. Cambridge, Mass.
Storr, Robert. "Louise Lawler: Unpacking the White Cube." *Parkett* 22: 105–08.
1990
Fehlau, Fred. "Louise Lawler Doesn't Take Pictures." *Artscribe* (May) 62–65 (cover illustration).
1991
Meinhardt, Johannes. "The Places of Art: The Photography of Louise Lawler." In *Hugo-Erfurth-Preis: Internationaler Fotopreis der Stadt Leverkusen* und der Agfa Gevaert-AG Leverkusen. Exh. cat. Museum Morsbroich, Leverkusen. Heidelberg: 26–29.
1992
Meinhardt, Johannes. "Erhellung der Situation: Louise Lawlers Situierungen und Fotografien von Situierungen." *Kunstbulletin* 2.
1993
Crimp, Douglas. *On the Museum's Ruins*. With photographs by Louise Lawler. Cambridge.
1994
Buskirk, Martha. "Interviews with Sherrie Levine, Louise Lawler, and Fred Wilson." *October* 70: 104–08.
Dent, Tory. "Alreadymade 'Female' Louise Lawler." *Parachute* 76 (October–December): 20–24.
Louise Lawler: For Sale. Ed. Dietmar Elger. Texts by Dietmar Elger and Thomas Weski. Ostfildern, 1994.
1996
Krauss, Rosalind. "*Louise Lawler: Souvenir Memories*." *Aperture* 145: 36–39 (cover illustration).
1997
Baker, George. "Paint, Walls, Pictures: Something Always Follows Something Else. She Wasn't Always a Statue." *Texte zur Kunst* 26: 88–93.
Louise Lawler: Monochrome. Text by Phyllis Rosenzweig. Brochure, The Hirschorn Museum and Sculpture Garden. Washington.
1998
A Spot on the Wall. Ed. Hedwig Saxenhuber. Texts by Rosalind Krauss, Helmut Draxler, Claudia Jottes. Exh. cat. Kunstverein München, Munich; Neue Galerie am Landesmuseum Joanneum, Graz; De Appel. Amsterdam.
1999
Kroksnes, Andrea. "Louise Lawler: Specters of Modernism." *Parkett* 57: 156–61.
2000
Buchmann, Sabeth. "Auf den zweiten Blick." *Texte zur Kunst* (September): 200–07.
Louise Lawler: An Arrangement of Pictures. Text by Johannes Meinhardt. Interview with Louise Lawler by Douglas Crimp. New York.
Leguillon, Pierre. "Le début d'une histoire et la fin d'une autre." *Art Press* (*Spécial*) 21: 120–25.

Selected Publications and Printed Materials by the Artist

1972
Untitled. Publication in collaboration with Joanne Caring. New York.
1978
Untitled, Red/Blue. Publication. New York.
Untitled, Black/White. Publication. Text by Janelle Reiring. New York.
1980
The Franklin Furnace Flue. Publication and centerfold project in collaboration with Barbara Kruger and Sherrie Levine. New York.
1981
Cover, *Reallife Magazine* (Autumn).
Passage to the North. Publication in collaboration with Lawrence Weiner. Photographs by Louise Lawler. New York.
The Franklin Furnace Flue. Cover and title page. Franklin Furnace, New York.
1982
Matchbooks for the exhibition "Louise Lawler, Arrangements of Pictures." Metro Pictures, New York.
De Appel 1. Back cover. Amsterdam.
A Story. Stationery and envelopes for documenta 7, Kassel.
1983
Poster for the exhibition "A Movie Will Be Shown Without the Picture." Franklin Furnace, New York. Produced as participation in "In Other Words: Artists' Use of Language, Part 2" with support from Lawrence Weiner.
Matchbooks for the exhibition "Borrowed Time." Baskerville & Watson Gallery, New York.
Gift certificates for Leo Castelli Gallery, New York.
1984
Selection and arrangement of photos in collaboration with Brian Wallis for *Art After Modernism: Rethinking Representation*. Exh. cat. The New Museum of Contemporary Art, New York. Boston.
1986
Printed Matter. 10th Anniversary Catalog. Cover photo. New York.
1987
De Appel 2. Cover, back cover. Amsterdam: 27.
Gift certificates for Margo Leavin Gallery, Los Angeles.
Picture This. Publication design and poster for "A Movie Will Be Shown Without the Picture." Buffalo, New York: 63–69.
Brochure and flyer for the exhibition "Enough" (Projects: Louise Lawler). The Museum of Modern Art, New York.
1988
Inserts. Project by Group Material. Advertising supplement to *The New York Times* (5 May).
1990
Recognition Maybe, May Not Be Useful. Cover for *Artscribe* (May).
1991
Matchbooks for the exhibition "This Takes the Cake, Squid In Its Own Ink, The Cheese Stands Alone." Carnegie Museum of Art, Pittsburgh.
1993
Poster for the exhibition "Louise Lawler, Cindy Sherman, Laurie Simmons." Museum of Contemporary Art, Helsinki.
1993
Poster and T-shirt for the exhibition "Kontext Kunst." Neue Galerie am Landesmuseum Joanneum, Graz.
1995
Matchbooks for the exhibition "Portrait." Gramercy Park Festival, Gramercy Park Hotel, New York.
1999
Napkin for the exhibition "The Museum as Muse." The Museum of Modern Art, New York.

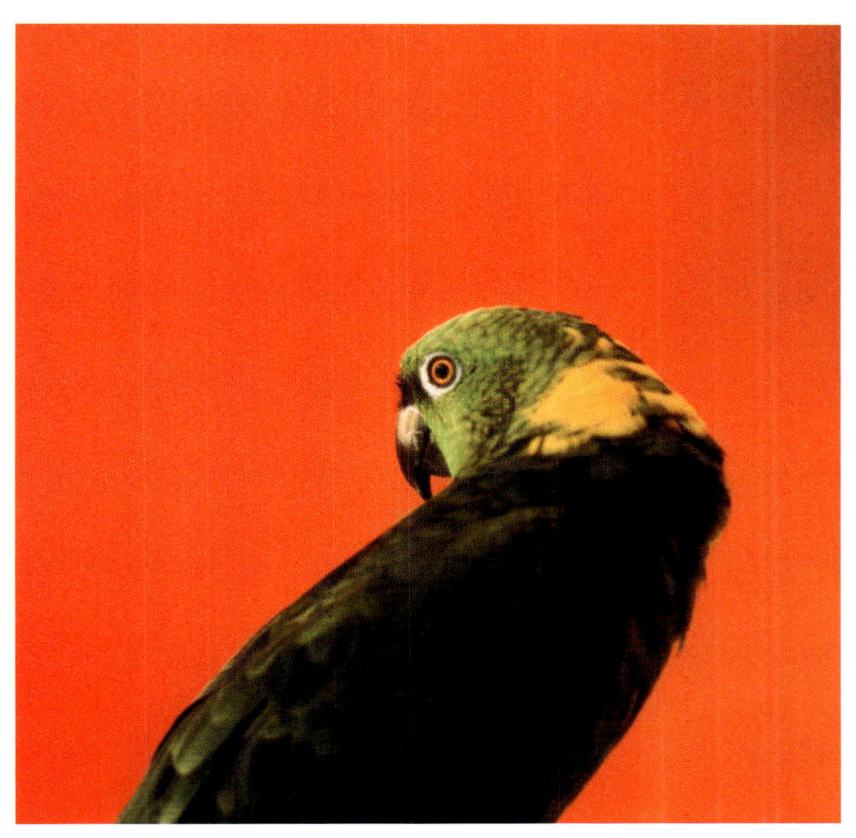

Portrait, 1982
cibachrome, 19 x 19 inches

FEBBRAIO VEMBRE STO
19 921
MARTEDI ABATO LEDI

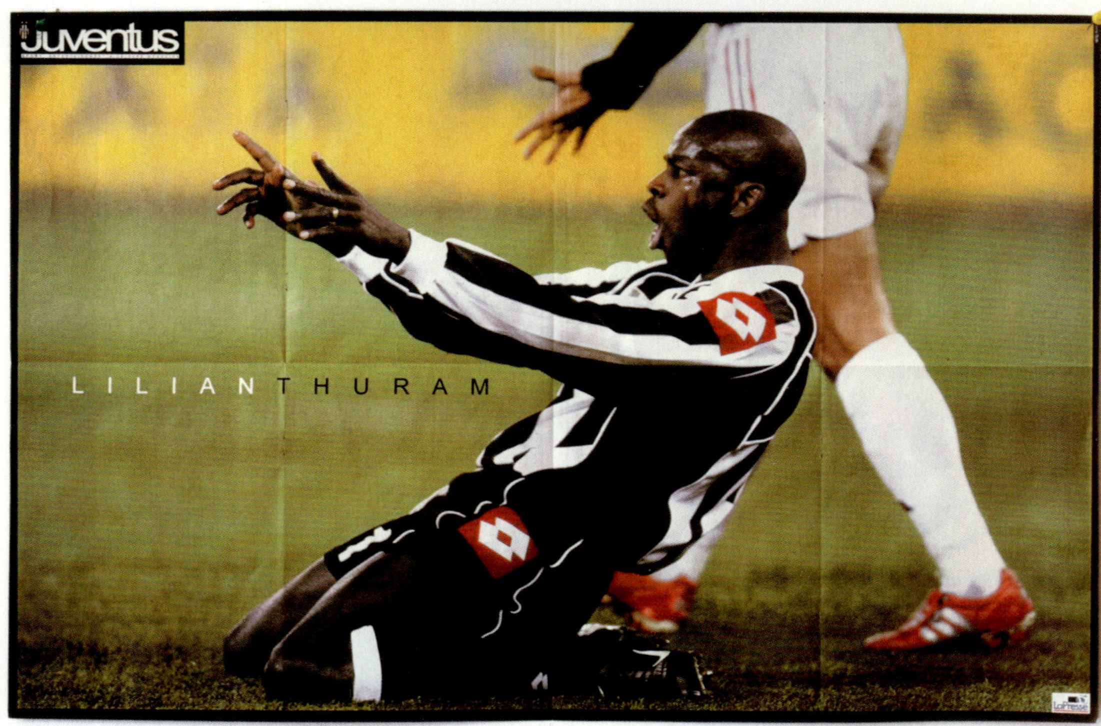
Juventus
LILIAN THURAM

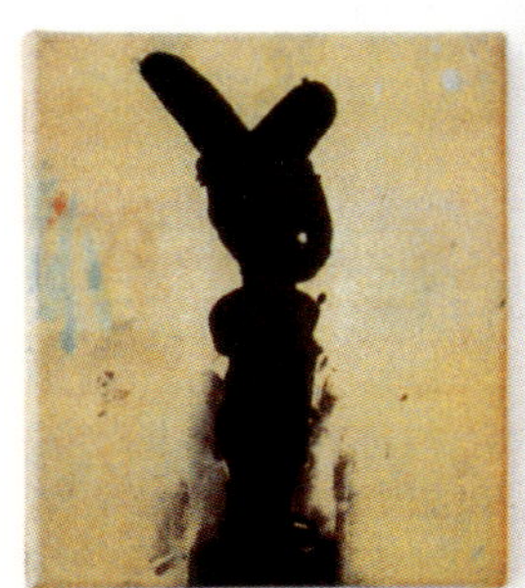

Thank You Vito, 2003/2004
cibachrome, 25 x 37 inches

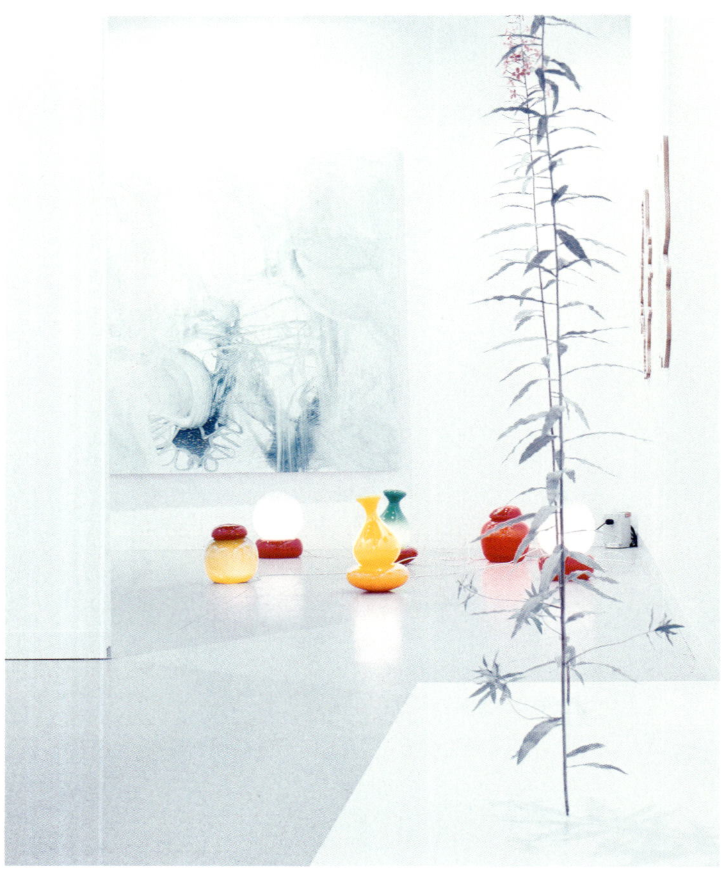

ACKNOWLEDGEMENTS

It is more than obvious that my work is indebted to others. With the production of this book, I am specifically grateful to the authors whose work and words have developed and informed the issues and efforts with such incisive, generous, interesting, and articulate lucidity. I would like to thank Mónika Sziládi, the designer of this book, for making it a pleasure. This book was produced on the occasion of an exhibition, proposed and organized by Philipp Kaiser. I am grateful to him for the attentive and open attitude in the production of both.

Louise Lawler

This catalogue is published on the occasion of the exhibition
Louise Lawler and Others
Kunstmuseum Basel, Museum für Gegenwartskunst
15 May – 29 August 2004

Exhibition

Director
Bernhard Mendes Bürgi

Curator
Philipp Kaiser

Curatorial Assistance
Katrin Steffen

Trainees
Nadja Borer
Aline Rinderer

Restorers
Marcus Jacob
Caroline Wyss

Registrar
Charlotte Gutzwiller

Press, Communication
Christian Selz
Susanne Storz

Installation
Stefano Schaller
Andreas Schweizer
Martin Werner
Klaus Sust

Kunstmuseum Basel, Museum für Gegenwartskunst
mit Emanuel Hoffmann-Stiftung
St. Alban-Rheinweg 60
4010 Basel
Switzerland
Tel. (41) 61 206 62 62
Fax. (41) 61 206 62 53
www.mgkbasel.ch

Sponsors

Fonds für künstlerische Aktivitäten im Museum für Gegenwartskunst der Emanuel Hoffmann-Stiftung und der Christoph Merian Stiftung

STANLEY THOMAS
JOHNSON STIFTUNG

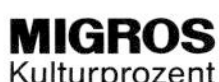

Catalogue

Editor
Philipp Kaiser

Editing
Katrin Steffen und Philipp Kaiser

Copyediting
Greg Bond

Translation from French
John Tittensor (text by Birgit Pelzer)

Translation from German
Gillian Morris (texts by Isabelle Graw, Philipp Kaiser)

Graphic Design, Layout, and Typesetting
Mónika Sziládi, www.hoopycake.com

Reproduction
Pallino Media Integration, Ostfildern-Ruit

Printed by
Dr. Cantz'sche Druckerei, Ostfildern-Ruit

Published by
Hatje Cantz Publishers
Senefelderstraße 12
73760 Ostfildern-Ruit, Germany
Tel. (49) 711 440 50, Fax (49) 711 440 52 20
www.hatjecantz.de

ISBN 3-7204-0154-5 (museum edition)
ISBN 3-7757-1464-2 (trade edition)

Printed in Germany

Cover illustration
Rainy Day in Basle 2002/2004
cibachrome, 47 1/2 x 58 5/8 inches
Illustration on page 1
Matchbooks, 1982 (published for the exhibition An Arrangement of Pictures, Metro Pictures, New York)
Illustration on page 156
No Snow, 2003
digitally produced cibachrome, 24 3/8 x 19 5/8 inches

Isabelle Graw's essay is based on a talk to be published in *Virus! Mutationen einer Metapher*, ed. Brigitte Weingart and Ruth Mayer (Bielefeld).
Birgit Pelzer's essay is a slightly revised version of a text that first appeared in the Spanish review *Exit*, no. 9, "Espacios del arte" (February–April 2003): 68–79.

Lenders of Works

This exhibition is supported generously by public and private loans. We would like to warmly thank all who have made works available, including those who wish to remain anonymous. In particular we thank Tom Heman, Helene Winer, and Janelle Reiring of Metro Pictures, New York.

Brussels
Galerie Meert Rihoux

Chester, CT
The LeWitt Collection

Geneva
Art & Public – Cabinet PH
Collection Pierre Huber
Private Collection, Courtesy BFAS Blondeau Fine Art Services

Dresden
Sammlung Schmidt-Drenhaus, Dresden/Cologne

Haigerloch
Sammlung Paul Schwenk

Hamburg
Hamburger Kunsthalle, Kupferstichkabinett

Cologne
Anna Friebe-Reininghaus

Munich
Sammlung Goetz

Montpellier
Frac Languedoc-Roussillon

New York
Benjamin Buchloh
Brooke Alexander Editions
Collection of Rachel and Jean-Pierre Lehmann
Collection of the New Museum of Contemporary Art
Collection Per Skarstedt
Fried, Frank, Harris, Shriver & Jacobson, LLP
Louise Lawler
Metro Pictures
Mr. and Mrs. Maurice A. Amon

Rotterdam
Museum Boijmans Van Beuningen

St.-Martens-Latem
Michèle Vanden Bemden

Nude, 2002/2003
cibachrome, 59 1/2 x 47 1/2 inches

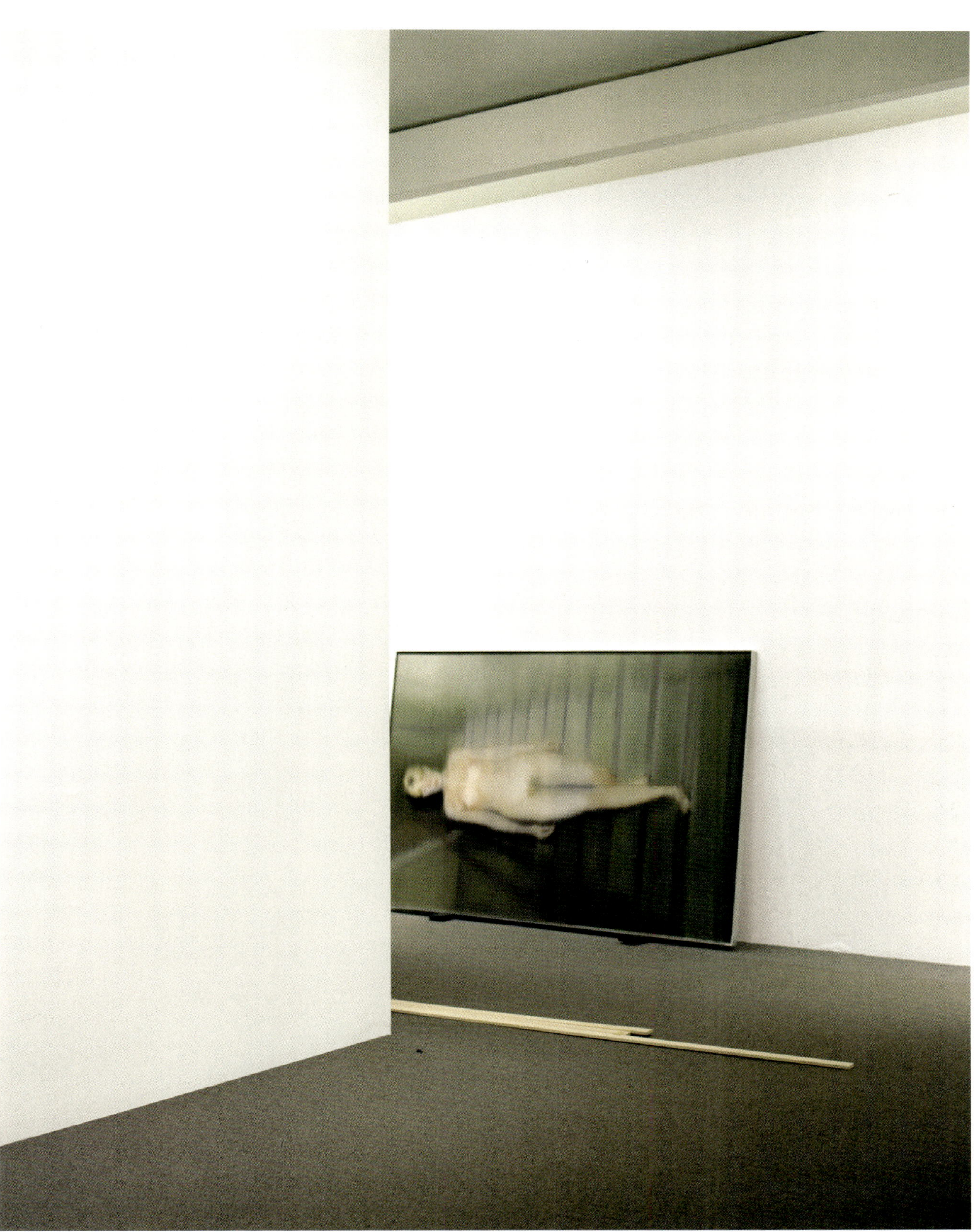

NO DRINKS FOR THOSE
WHO DO NOT SUPPORT THE
ANTI-WAR DEMONSTRATION

FOUR NUDES LOUISE LAWLER FEB 15 2003 5-7 PM
METRO PICTURES **UPSTAIRS**

519 WEST 24TH STREET NEW YORK NY 10011